1998 GOLDMINE ANNUAL

PUBLISHER: Greg Loescher

EDITOR: Irwin Soonachan

COVER DESIGN: Al West

PAGE DESIGN: Carl Babino

ADVERTISING MANAGER: Jim Felhofer

ADVERTISING SALES: Kelly Beyer and Kathy Housholder

Published by

krause
publications

700 East State Street, Iola, WI 54990-0001

Please call or write for our free catalog. Our toll-free number to place an order or
obtain a free catalog is 800-258-0929 or please use our regular business telephone
715-445-2214 for editorial comment and further information.

Library of Congress Catalog Number:
ISBN:0-87341-568-X
Printed in the United States of America

VARÈSE VINTAGE

FINELY AGED MUSIC

VSD-5788

Originally released in 1969, this album spent 30 weeks on the Billboard album chart and spawned the hit single "The Minotaur," featured on this CD. Also included are three bonus tracks. All songs are making their CD debut (12 Tracks).

VSD-5790

Features songs from several of Xavier Cugat's albums recorded in the '60s, including Bang Bang ("Bang Bang"), Adios ("Dance Party") Music To Watch Girls By ("Today") & "Chim, Chim, Cher-ee" ("Feeling Good!") Most tracks are making their CD debut (16 Tracks).

VSD-5791

Features four bonus tracks. These recordings represent the avant-garde experimental stereo sounds period of Ferrante & Teicher's career, and are quite different from the easy listening sound they were later known for. Most songs are making their CD debut (16 Tracks).

VSD-5789

Compiled by producer Irwin Chusid (of Esquivel and Raymond Scott fame), this CD collects, for the first time, the original recordings of Ernie Kovacs' TV themes & weird music from his legendary video sketches. Features The Nairobi Trio Esquivel, Edie Adams and Yma Sumac. Many of these rare tracks are making their CD debut (19 Tracks).

VSD-5792

Married to Ernie Kovacs, Edie Adams (singer-comedienne) became a star on Kovacs' TV program. This album is available for the first time on CD and features songs by Rodgers and Hart including "I Must Love You," "There's So Much More," "Why Can't I" and "He Was Too Good To Me" and others (10 Tracks).

VSD-5823

Featuring songs inspired by the Batman TV Series, including "The Batman Theme" Neal Hefti, "That Man" Peggy Lee, "Batman To The Rescue LaVerne Baker, "The Story Of Batman" Adam West, "The Joker Is Wild" Jan & Dean and more (15 tracks).

VSD-5801

VSD-5802

VSD-5803

Various Artists, **Sunshine Days, Pop Classics Of The '60s** (Three Volumes)
Companion series to the highly successful **Bubblegum Classics**, focusing on the "sun-shiny" pop hit singles of the late '60s. These compilations feature songs such as "Monday Monday" The Mamas and The Papas, "Yellow Balloon" Yellow Balloon, "Go Where You Wanna Go" The 5th Dimension, "Distant Shores" Chad & Jeremy, and "Don't Sleep In The Subway" Petula Clark (14 tracks each).

AVAILABLE AT MUSIC STORES EVERYWHERE!

If you wish to purchase any of our
titles by mail please contact:
Collectors Choice Music
1(800) 923-1122

VARÈSE SARABANDE
VARÈSE VINTAGE

For a complete catalog, Please write to:
Varèse Sarabande Records/Varèse Vintage
11846 Ventura Blvd., Suite 130
Studio City, CA 91604

Table Of Contents

STIMULATE YOUR BRAIN
With Fully-Charged Titles For Your Collectibles Library

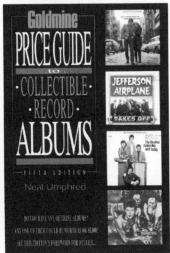

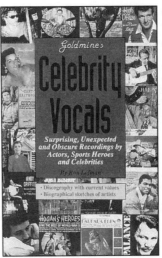

FOREWARD

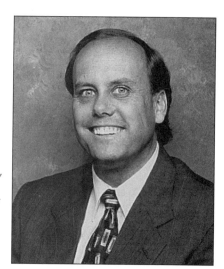

THE updated Goldmine Index to articles is now included in our expanded 1998 Annual. The Index has been by far the most requested item by Goldmine readers over the years. Here at last you will be able to instantly answer that oft-asked question, "Have you ever done an article on (name of your favorite group)?"

A word to those of you looking for back issues: we don't have them!!!! So please don't call us about back issues. Check the ads in Goldmine under "Magazines for Sale", or run an ad in our classifieds for "Magazines Wanted." Many dealers also sell back issues of Goldmine and other music-related magazines at record shows nationwide. Goldmine runs a huge listing of record conventions in every issue. One of our advertisers, C-Bub Productions, has an extensive inventory of Goldmine back issues, usually multiple copies of more recent issues. See their ads in Goldmine and this edition of the Annual. Just another of many reasons to subscribe or buy Goldmine!

We hope you will find the Goldmine Index useful, too. It's the biggest reason why we have expanded this year's Annual and last year's (1997) Annual from our normal 88 pages to 124 pages.

Don't throw out your vinyl!

Goldmine published five price guides at the tail end of 1996 — more guides than we — or any music publisher, have ever published in one year! We provide you with lists from each book of the top collectible recordings from each area covered. If you are lucky, you may have some of these gems in your collection. And from the reports our guide authors received from dealers and collectors, high-end vinyl recordings continue to increase in value. Delve deeper into each area by picking up our price guides at your favorite record store or book store, or call our offices for the books you need to stay on top of the ever-changing prices in the record collecting field.

Since its inception in 1974, Goldmine magazine has been the "bible" for record collectors, providing not only a marketplace to buy and sell recordings, but a source of information on what's happening in the hobby.

This is our seventh Goldmine Annual. We still have copies of previous editions available. The last three featured Brian Wilson of the Beach Boys (1997), the Rolling Stones (1996) and the Beatles (1995). If you need previous editions, or more copies of our 1998 edition, simply call our toll-free ordering line for more information and availability (1-800-258-0929). (Retailers: for information on selling Goldmine or Goldmine Annuals in your store, contact Regan Pourchot at 715-445-4623, ext. 318.)

Thanks for purchasing this year's edition. If you have ideas on what we can add or would like to tell us what you liked (or disliked) about this year's offering, please write us at Goldmine, Editorial Department, 700 E. State Street, Iola, WI 54990. You can also visit our website at http://www.krause.com/goldmine.

Enough chatter. Put on some Grateful Dead music and sit back and devour your copy of Goldmine's 1998 Annual!

THE OTHER ONES

JERRY GARCIA:

AN ANNOTATED SOLO Discography

by William Ruhlmann

JERRY GARCIA WAS A player. While his band, the Grateful Dead, played thousands of concerts and recorded dozens of albums over a 30-year period, Garcia also found time to play in a series of other bands and lend his voice and instrumental abilities to scores of records by other artists. On the first anniversary of Garcia's death, this article cites the guitarist's many moonlighting activities. Because it seems likely that more solo Garcia will appear on record in the future, both his known performances and actually released recordings will be included.

JEROME JOHN GARCIA WAS born at Children's Hospital in San Francisco on August 1, 1942, the son of Spanish immigrant Jose "Joe" Ramon Garcia and the former Ruth Marie Clifford. Joe Garcia had been a professional musician, playing clarinet and other reed instruments, but by the time of his second son's birth (Garcia had an older brother named Clifford), he owned and ran a bar.

The Garcias' was a musical household, and Jerry took piano lessons as a child. When he was four, he lost half of the middle finger of his right hand in a wood-chopping accident. The following year, his father drowned during a camping trip. His mother, forced to take over the family business, took him and his brother to live with his maternal grandparents. His grandmother was a country music fan who tuned in to the Grand Ole Opry every Saturday night, and that exposed him to some of the music he would play frequently in his non-Grateful Dead groups. (The title of Garcia's posthumously published memoir, *HARRINGTON STREET* [Delacorte Press, November 1995], refers to the street on which his grandparents lived.)

Garcia's mother remarried when he was 10, and he went back to live with her, as the family moved south of San Francisco to Menlo Park, on the peninsula south of the city where Palo Alto and Stanford University are located. They lived there three years, then moved back to San Francisco.

In addition to the country music he had heard at his grandmother's, Garcia became interested in R&B as a teenager; then the rock era arrived with Bill Haley and the Comets' "Rock Around The Clock" in 1955 and Elvis Presley in 1956. Garcia's mother, recogniz-ing his growing interest in music, bought him an accordion for his fifteenth birthday in 1957, then let him trade it in for what he really wanted: an electric guitar. Garcia began playing in high school bands, first in San Francisco, then in the suburbs when his family moved to Cazadero.

Garcia dropped out of high school and joined the Army in 1959. After a brief, unhappy stay, he was dishonorably discharged in 1960. He moved back down to Palo Alto and began to become involved in the music scene growing up in the coffeehouses around Stanford. There he met a former National Guardsman, Robert Hunter, and they began performing as the folk duo Bob and Jerry. Their first appearance was at the Peninsula School in Menlo Park on May 5, 1961, for which they were paid $5 each.

Garcia also played in other configurations. He appeared with singer/harmonica player Ron McKernan, who he nicknamed "Pigpen," and with banjo player Marshall Leicester (who he had known when he lived in Menlo Park) during the summer of 1961, notably at the Boar's Head Coffee

HOUSE IN SAN CARLOS. ALTHOUGH NO RECORDINGS OF GARCIA HAVE BEEN RELEASED FROM THIS PERIOD, TAPES EXIST. INFLUENCED by LEICESTER, A bluegrass fan, GARCIA BEGAN LEARN- ING TO PLAY THE banjo. DURING THIS period, HE ALSO MET AND BEFRIENDED GUITARIST DAVID NELSON AND TWO BERKELEY COLLEGE STUDENTS WHOSE PRIMARY INTEREST WAS CLASSICAL MUSIC: ROOMMATES PHIL LESH AND TOM CONSTANTEN. IN FEBRUARY 1962,

EXPERT GUIDES BY WRITERS OF NOTE

Goldmine British Invasion Record Price Guide
by Tim Neely and Dave Thompson
The British are coming! And now collectors won't have to miss even one artist or group who came ashore from 1956 through 1966. This formative decade in modern music is outlined by more than 10,000 45s, EPs and LPs from both major and minor U.K. artists. This brand new Goldmine price guide is also an industry exclusive: both U.S. and U.K. record releases are listed and valued. Includes everything from "Rock Island Line" to The Beatles Anthology. Softcover • 6 x 9 • 400 pages • 100 b&w photos • **BRIT** • **$22.95**

Goldmine Price Guide To Rock 'N' Roll Memorabilia
by Mark Allen Baker
Finally, a comprehensive guide to help you identify, authenticate and value non-recorded music collectibles. Learn to build a collection of rock 'n' roll memorabilia with tips on collecting autographs, posters and other souvenirs. The directory of more than 800 artists, from legends to cutting-edge bands, provides descriptions and values for 10,000 items, including tour books, guitar picks, magazines, instruments, jewelry and more. From the publishers of Goldmine comes the first complete guide to rock 'n' roll artifacts, an indispensable handbook for beginner and advanced collectors. Softcover • 8-1/2 x 11 • 800 pages • 300 b&w photos • 50 color photos • **RRM** • **$24.95**

Goldmine Comedy Record Price Guide
by Ronald L. Smith
Thousands of comedy snippets pack a punchline into this detailed value guide. Comedian biographer Ronald L. Smith gives prices for popular and obscure comedy records, artist trivia, biographies. Top 10 lists on the most valuable, unusual and collectible. Softcover • 6x9 • 352 pages • 300 b&w photos • **RCR01** • **$22.95**

Goldmine Christmas Record Price Guide
by Tim Neely
Celebrate the yuletide with Goldmine and this premier price guide. Revisit 50 years of Christmas 45s, EPs and LPs, each valued in three grades of condition. Hundreds of records never before listed in any price guide make Santa's list for the first time in this new release. Plus, the complete contents of Christmas LPs and EPs are examined and discussed. A must-have reference for collectors-naughty or nice. Softcover • 6 x 9 • 400 pages • 100 b&w photos • 20 color photos • **XREC** • **$19.95**

Lesh arranged for Garcia to appear on Berkeley's radio station, KPFA-FM, as part of its *Midnight Special* folk show, and Garcia became a regular guest on the show thereafter.

Garcia's bluegrass groups began to have names—in May, they were the Thunder Mountain Tub Thumpers, in June the Sleepy Hollow Hog Stompers, from June to November the Hart Valley Drifters—though they had a revolving lineup often featuring Hunter, Nelson and others. Their sets included songs like "Buck Dancer's Choice" and "Deep Elem Blues." That summer, Jorma Kaukonen moved to the area and met Garcia at a hootenanny. Soon, they were playing together, too.

By early 1963, Garcia's group was called the Wildwood Boys. It was around this time that he met Sarah Ruppenthal, and they began dating. They also began performing together; by May, when they married, they were playing as the duo of Jerry and Sarah. But with Sarah pregnant, the gigs were mostly played by the Wildwood Boys, who evolved into the Black Mountain Boys, featuring guitarist Sandy Rothman. Heather Garcia was born on December 8, 1963. Forced to settle down—as much as he ever did settle down—Garcia took a steady job, teaching music at the Dana Morgan music store in Palo Alto.

On New Year's Eve, 1963, Garcia was at the store, waiting for students who never showed up. Instead, teenage guitarist Bob Weir and a friend turned up, and as 1964 began, they decided, according to Weir, that they had the makings of a jug band.

Despite this legend, the jug band doesn't seem to have started up right away. The Black Mountain Boys were still playing dates as late as March, and Garcia and Rothman took a car trip across the country that spring with a tape recorder to make tapes of bluegrass music. On Easter weekend, they turned up at the Union Grove Fiddlers Competition in North Carolina,

where they met a young mandolin player from New Jersey named David Grisman.

When Garcia returned, the jug band got going in earnest. It was dubbed Mother McCree's Uptown Jug Champions, and in addition to Garcia and Weir, it featured Pigpen, David Parker, Bob Matthews and David Nelson. The band played in the area, notably at the Top of the Tangent in Palo Alto, and at Magoo's Pizza Parlor in Menlo Park, through the rest of 1964 and into 1965.

Though not heard until much later, Garcia was caught on tape during this period introducing the Kentucky Colonels at an October 15, 1964, show in Palo Alto for a performance released as *Livin' In The Past* (Briar BT 7202).

By the spring of 1965, the members of Mother McCree's Uptown Jug Champions had changed their style of music, their name and their personnel. Turning to electrified rock 'n' roll and R&B, they became the Warlocks with a lineup of Garcia, Weir, Pigpen, Dana Morgan, Jr., on bass and Bill Kreutzmann on drums, playing their first show in that form at Menlo College in April 1965. On June 18, Lesh replaced Morgan as the group's bassist. On December 4, they made their first appearance under a new name: the Grateful Dead.

In his memoir of his times with the Grateful Dead, Rock Scully, who was the band's manager from the mid-'60s to the mid-'80s, described the process by which the Dead were signed to Warner Bros. Records. Scully wrote that Warner was alerted to the Dead by San Francisco disc jockey/promoter/record label head Tom Donahue. "Garcia [had] done session work for [Donahue's] Autumn Records (including Bobby Freeman's single 'Do You Wanna Dance?') so Tom already [knew] him," Scully wrote.

Unfortunately, no one else seems to have confirmed these Garcia sessions, and Scully's statement seems doubtful if only because Bobby

Freeman's "Do You Want To Dance" was released on Josie Records (a subsidiary of New York-based Jubilee Records) in 1958, when Garcia was 15. Autumn would not exist until 1964, at which time Freeman did have a hit called "C'mon And Swim" on the label, however, there has never been any confirmation that Garcia may have played on that or any of Freeman's other sides for Autumn. Autumn Records expert Alec Palao confirms that there is no evidence of Garcia recording for the label, although the pre-Dead Warlocks did record some demos there that have always been known in Dead circles as the Autumn Records demos.

Of the bands that made up the psychedelic wave of San Francisco rock in the mid-'60s, the first to achieve national recognition was Jefferson Airplane, a group made up of such folkies as Kaukonen and Paul Kantner. The Airplane signed to RCA Victor Records and released their debut album, *Jefferson Airplane Takes Off*, in September 1966. In the first week of November, the Airplane assembled at RCA Studios in Hollywood (San Francisco had no major record label recording facilities at the time) to record their second album. Jerry Garcia joined them.

The process by which a guest musician sits in on a recording session is sometimes a casual one, as a musical friend who is available is asked on the spur of the moment to play. This was not the case with Garcia and the Airplane. The group would have had to fly back and forth between San Francisco and Los Angeles over the period of a month for the sessions, and Garcia seems to have flown back and forth with them. He was present on Wednesday, November 2 to play lead electric guitar on "Today," but was at the Avalon Ballroom in San Francisco with the Dead on Friday the 4th. After appearing at the Avalon on Sunday night, November 13, he was in Hollywood recording "J.P.P. McStep Blues" on Monday the 14th, but he was back in San Francisco playing the Fillmore on

Friday the 18th, Saturday the 19th and Sunday the 20th. Then, on Monday the 21st, he was at RCA Studios recording "In The Morning."

"J.P.P. McStep Blues" and "In The Morning" did not make it onto the finished album. They would be released in April 1974 on *Early Flight* (Grunt CYL 1-0437). But in addition to his work on "Today," Garcia's acoustic guitar is heard on "Comin' Back To Me," and some sources credit further acoustic playing on "Plastic Fantastic Lover" and "My Best Friend."

According to Jorma Kaukonen, who spoke to Garcia biographer

MADE IN ISRAEL? YES INDEED!

Did you know that the 60s, 70s and 80s produced hundreds of rarities in the land of milk and vinyl? Well you should! Have you ever seen the promo version of Dylan's "Desire" or Bowie's "Major Tom"?

Well, those are just samples of what awaits you when you contact the only real collectors store in Israel. Just let us know your favorite artists and we will send you an up-to-date list.

BLACK HOLE RECORDS

5 Shlomo Hamelech St.
TEL-AVIV 64377, ISRAEL
Tel/Fax 972-3-5282521

Sandy Troy, Garcia did more than just play; he actually ran the recording session in place of the official producer, Rick Jarrard. "Jerry could be credited with really being the producer in the real sense of the word, Kaukonen told Troy, "in that he was one of us and he knew what to do with the band ... He really was the producer who arranged those songs ... "

Garcia also gave the album its title by describing it as "as surrealistic as a pillow." When *Surrealistic Pillow* (RCA LPM/LSP-3766) was released in February 1967, Garcia was credited on the album jacket only as "musical and spiritual advis-

Photo Courtesy of Larry R. Hulst

er," which stood in for his actual contributions to the record, masked in part because, in the interim between the album's recording and its release, he had become an exclusive Warner Bros. Records recording artist. The previous month, in fact, the Dead had turned up in the same studio, RCA in Hollywood, and with the same engineer, Dave Hassinger, to cut their debut album, *The Grateful Dead*.

(Again, Rock Scully provided an account of Garcia's work on *Surrealistic Pillow* that is difficult to credit. Scully wrote that the Airplane was in L.A. making the album in January 1967 while the Dead were there, and mentioned contributions by Garcia only to "Somebody To Love" and "White Rabbit," saying that Garcia "[tinkered] with the guitar parts and essentially [arranged] those two

songs." While the Airplane may have been doing final overdubs in January for the February release and Garcia may well have participated, it seems unlikely that these tracks were, as Scully put it, "demos ... still in a pretty rudimentary state" at such a late date. In any case, Scully's book is so saturated with LSD that it is difficult to tell how seriously to take it, much less whether to rely on it for discographical information.)

The rigidity of the record companies with regard to sharing talent combined with the strenuous schedules of popular musicians, especially their national touring, to limit studio interaction in the late 1960s. Over the next couple of years, Jerry Garcia seems to have been too busy playing Dead concerts, recording Dead albums and flying on airplanes to do much outside playing.

Somehow, though, Garcia, along

with the rest of the Dead, found time to back up singer Jon Hendricks, of the jazz vocal group Lambert, Hendricks and Ross, on a single, probably some time in 1966. "Fire In The City"/"Sons And Daughters," used in a film called *Sons And Daughters*, was released on Verve VK-10512 in 1967. (Note: For the purposes of this article, which deals specifically with Garcia's work outside of his main gig, other recordings featuring the entire Grateful Dead are omitted. This one is being noted for its collectibility and historical interest.)

Despite his hectic schedule, there was nothing to stop Garcia from getting up onstage with other groups. This occurred on January 11, 1969, when Garcia was one of several friends, among them Dead drummer Mickey Hart, Jorma Kaukonen and Steve Miller, to join Country Joe and the Fish for what

Photo Courtesy of Larry R. Hulst

was billed as a farewell performance at the Fillmore West. Garcia, et. al., joined the band onstage for a 38-minute jam on "Donovan's Reef" that finally was released in March 1996. (*Live! Fillmore West 1969*, Vanguard 139/140-2)

Garcia's renewed interest in playing outside the Grateful Dead in the late '60s seems to have been sparked by two main factors. First, he took up a new instrument, the pedal steel guitar. Garcia bought one at a music store in Denver while the Dead were on tour, possibly in April 1969 (the group played at the University of Colorado in Boulder on April 13) or in July (there was a July 3 date in Colorado Springs). On June 11 at California Hall in San Francisco, Garcia had been part of a show billed as "Bobby Ace and His Cards from the Bottom of the Deck" with a lineup featuring Dead members Weir, Lesh, Hart and Constanten, plus his old Palo Alto friends John Dawson and David Nelson and pedal steel player Peter Grant. The group played a collection of country and country-tinged material, including a new Garcia/Hunter song called "Dire Wolf." (According to Rock Scully, Garcia had begun teaching himself to play pedal steel as early as the summer of 1967.)

On July 11, 1969, at the New York State Pavilion of the old World's Fair Grounds in Flushing Meadow Park in the New York City borough of Queens, Garcia played pedal steel onstage with the Dead for a couple of songs. On August 20, at the Aquatheatre in Seattle, Washington, one of the Dead's opening acts was a new country-rock group dubbed the New Riders of the Purple Sage, which consisted of Dawson, Nelson, Garcia (on pedal steel), Lesh and Hart. The New Riders reappeared for two dates at the end of August at the Family Dog at the Great Highway in San Francisco.

The second factor that seems to have inspired Garcia to more moonlighting was the opening of a couple of first-class recording stu-

dio in the Bay Area, Pacific High Recording (P.H.R.) in 1968 and the Wally Heider Recording Studio the following year. Jefferson Airplane recorded *Volunteers* (RCA Victor LSP-4238) at Wally Heider's during 1969, and Garcia joined them with his pedal steel on "The Farm." The album was released in November.

That same month, the New Riders held their first recording session at P.H.R., cutting the John Dawson songs "Henry," "Last Lonely Eagle" and "Cecilia," and the Garcia/Hunter/Dawson composition "All I Ever Wanted." These recordings turned up on record 17 years later when Relix Records released the New Riders/David Nelson compilation *Before Time Began* (RRLP 2024).

Garcia's most famous steel guitar work appeared on March 11 on the first album by Crosby, Stills, Nash and Young, *Deja Vu* (Atlantic SD 7200). His playing was the signature sound of Graham Nash's "Teach Your Children" (recorded at Wally Heider's on October 24, 1969), which became a Top 20 hit and a standard as the album topped the charts. In June, San Francisco group It's A Beautiful Day released *Marrying Maiden* (Columbia CS 1058), recorded at P.H.R. and Heider's, which featured Garcia on pedal steel and banjo. In late November, RCA released *Blows Against The Empire* (LSP-4448), credited to Paul Kantner and "Jefferson Starship," an extended family of San Francisco musicians including members of the Airplane, the Dead, CSNY and Quicksilver Messenger Service. Among them, of course, was Jerry Garcia, who co-wrote "XM" with Kantner, Phil Sawyer and Mickey Hart, and played banjo on "Let's Go Together" and pedal steel on "Have You Seen The Stars Tonite."

Meanwhile, the New Riders continued to make impromptu appearances with the Dead, playing a song on February 7 at the Fillmore West and again on April 17-19 at a trio of Family Dog at the Great Highway shows billed with the

Dead offshoot groups Mickey and the Hartbeats and Bobby Ace and His Cards from the Bottom. During this period, too, Dawson and Nelson were assisting in the recording of the Dead's country-oriented *Workingman's Dead* album, released in May. Starting on May 1 for an East Coast tour that kicked off at Alfred College in Alfred, New York, NRPS, now featuring bass player Dave Torbert, in addition to Dawson, Nelson, Hart and Garcia, was the Dead's regular opening act. (As if Garcia wasn't busy enough at those shows, the Dead themselves often played an acoustic set preceding the New Riders' set. Garcia would cite his exhaustion from the multi-hour workouts as his reason for leaving the New Riders.)

In late November, the Dead released *American Beauty*, another country-flavored album, which featured a cast of sidemen whose names were or would become familiar. In addition to NRPS, the album featured Garcia's old mandolin playing friend David Grisman, organist Howard Wales and pianist Ned Lagin.

CSNY had split up the previous August, with all four members preparing solo careers. In December, David Crosby began playing dates around San Francisco backed by members of the Dead, working up material for his first solo album. On December 15, 16 and 17, "Jerry Garcia & Friends," consisting of Garcia, Crosby, Lesh and Hart, played at the Matrix in San Francisco. On the 21st, the same quartet was billed as "the Acoustic Grateful Dead" at Pepperland in San Rafael, and the Acoustic Dead also played on a bill with Hot Tuna, NRPS and Lizard as a "benefit for the Montessori School and Bear" at Winterland on the 23rd.

The year 1970 also contained two cinematic appearances by Garcia that are worth noting. The Dead appeared at Woodstock in August 1969. They were not featured in the subsequent film or the three-record set released in the summer of 1970, but Garcia was,

briefly. He is seen in the film holding out a suspicious looking cigarette to the camera and saying, "Marijuana, exhibit A."

This statement also turns up on the *Woodstock* album (Cotillion SD 3-500). At the end of 1970, Italian director Michelangelo Antonioni's meditation on America in the '60s, *Zabriskie Point*, opened, and a soundtrack album was released on MGM Records (SE 4668ST). In addition to an excerpt from "Dark Star" drawn from the Dead's *Live/Dead* album, the soundtrack contained a seven-minute guitar solo by Garcia titled "Love Scene" that counts as his first "solo" recording. *Zabriskie Point* has yet to be released on CD in the United States, although a release was announced some time ago. It has been released in Europe.

Garcia and his pedal steel turned up on the first charting album by the country/folk-rock duo of Midwesterners Mike Brewer and Tom Shipley, *Tarkio* (Kama Sutra KSBS 2024) in February 1971. On February 2 and 3, Garcia appeared with jazz/R&B keyboard player Merl Saunders at the Matrix, launching a musical association that would last for decades. Garcia and Saunders played another couple of dates in May, the second of them at the Keystone Korner.

On Sunday, February 21, and again on Tuesday, February 23, the Dead played at the Capitol Theater in Port Chester, New York, with NRPS opening. By this time, the New Riders' lineup consisted of Dawson, Nelson, Torbert and former Jefferson Airplane drummer Spencer Dryden, with Garcia the only remaining Dead member in the group. The shows were culled for a 1986 live album, *Vintage NRPS*, released on Relix Records (RRLP 2025).

On the day in between, Monday, February 21, Atlantic Records released David Crosby's *If Only I Could Remember My Name* (SD 7203). The Crosby album, like Kantner's *Blows Against The Empire*, was a product of the group

of San Francisco musicians turning up for sessions at Wally Heider's who were dubbed "the Planet Earth Rock 'N' Roll Orchestra," or PERRO, by engineer Stephen Barncard. (That, anyway, is what Crosby says. Tom Constanten claims Phil Lesh coined the term.) Participating were members of CSNY, the Dead, the Airplane, Quicksilver and Santana. Garcia co-wrote the song "What Are Their Names" with Neil Young, Phil Lesh, Michael Shrieve and Crosby. He played pedal steel on "Laughing," which had been recorded during the *Deja Vu* sessions back in October 1969 on the same day as "Teach Your Children."

Graham Nash's debut solo album, *Songs For Beginners* (Atlantic SD 7204) followed on May 28. Another product of the PERRO sessions at Wally Heider's, it featured Garcia on pedal steel on the tracks "I Used To Be A King" and "Man In The Mirror."

Apparently, Garcia also appeared on Stephen Stills's *Stephen Stills 2* (Atlantic SD 7206), released June 30, though he is not credited on the album. One of the album's tracks is "Change Partners," and when it appeared on the CSN compilation album *Replay* (Atlantic SD 16026) in December 1980, Garcia was credited as playing pedal steel guitar.

On May 29 and 30, the Dead and the New Riders played at Winterland in San Francisco with R.J. Fox and James and the Good Brothers. Garcia recorded with the latter act, appearing on *James And The Good Brothers* (Columbia CS 30889), released in the fall. On July 2, the Dead and the New Riders played the last show ever at the Fillmore West, their opening act being the Rowan Brothers. Garcia would record with them, too. (The show was recorded and used to compile *Fillmore: The Last Days* [Fillmore 31390], a triple-LP box set released in June 1972 that featured a performance of "Henry," by NRPS including Garcia, as well as "Casey Jones" by the Dead.)

The exposure Garcia had received

as leader of the Dead, in the press, in the movies and as a guest artist on records made him one of the most famous musicians in rock by the early 1970s. In this era, when groups were starting to give way to solo careers, it was no surprise that Garcia began recording his own solo debut in July 1971. Another reason, as he admitted to *Rolling Stone* magazine interviewers Charles Reich and Jann Wenner, was that he needed to pay for a house he had just bought in Stinson Beach, for which he had secured a $10,000 advance from Warner Bros.

This did not mean, however, that his participation in the Dead and the New Riders was diminished. Garcia continued to tour frequently in the double-billing, and both released albums. In late August came *New Riders Of The Purple Sage* (Columbia C 30888), NRPS's formal debut album, with Garcia playing pedal steel and banjo. On September 24 came *Grateful Dead*, the Dead's second double live album.

Meanwhile, Garcia also was pursuing other musical ventures. September 1 found him back at the Keystone Korner with Saunders and Garcia (Saunders had guested on *Grateful Dead*), now featuring ex-Creedence Clearwater Revival member Tom Fogerty. And probably on Monday, November 1, Alan Douglas's Douglas Records (manufactured and distributed by Columbia) released *Hooteroll?* (KZ 30859), by Howard Wales and Jerry Garcia. This instrumental jazz-rock album is notable for a lineup that, in addition to Wales on organ and piano and Garcia on guitar, features a rhythm section of John Kahn on bass and Bill Vitt on drums, musicians who would play with Garcia frequently in the future. Douglas released a single, "Uncle Martin's"/"South Side Strut" (ZS7-6501) culled from the LP. The album was reissued in on September 21, 1987, on Rykodisc (RALP 0052/RCD/RACS 10052) with two bonus tracks.

Meanwhile, back at PERRO, the

Photo Courtesy of Larry R. Hulst

Photo Courtesy of Larry R. Hulst

Airplane had formed their own record label, Grunt, and were working hard to fill its pipeline with product. In December 1971, that meant two new albums, first *Sunfighter* (Grunt FTR 1002), credited to Paul Kantner and Grace Slick. Garcia played guitar on "When I Was A Boy I Watched The Wolves," "Million" and "Holding Together." The second release was *Papa John Creach* (Grunt FTR 1003), starring the Airplane's violin player, with Garcia playing guitar on "Soul Fever."

Finally in 1971, the San Francisco group Lamb, led by Barbara Mauritz and Bob Swanson, released *Cross Between* (Warner Bros. Records WB 1920), which contained a back cover note reading, "Special thanks to Jerry Garcia" that has been interpreted as an acknowledgement that Garcia played on the album.

On January 20, 1972, Warner Bros. Records released Jerry Garcia's first solo album, *Garcia* (BS 2582; reissued by Grateful Dead Merchandising in 1988 as GDCD 4003). It was the first studio album to come from the Dead camp since *American Beauty* more than a year earlier and, containing a set of new Garcia/Hunter compositions played by Garcia (with help on drums by Bill Kreutzmann) and sung by him, was welcomed as the followup to the group's 1970 commercial breakthrough. It hit #35 in *Billboard*, Garcia's solo career peak, and no wonder, since it contained such songs as "Deal," "Bird Song," "Sugaree," "Loser," "To Lay Me Down" and "The Wheel," all of which entered the Dead's large repertoire. Warner released two singles, "Deal"/"The Wheel" (WB 7551) and "Sugaree"/"Eep Hour" (WB 7569), with the latter getting into the Hot 100 for the week ending April 15 and peaking at #94.

Also in January 1972, the Dead began recording *Ace*, Bob Weir's debut solo album, which, unlike Garcia's, essentially was a band album with Weir songs and lead vocals. *Ace* (Warner Bros. BS

2627; reissued by Grateful Dead Merchandising in 1988 as GDCD 4004) was released in May, with a single, "One More Saturday Night"/"Cassidy" (Warner Bros. WB 7611) drawn from it.

With the Dead off the road for the first two months of the year, Garcia went back to his side projects, appearing in a quartet with Saunders, Kahn and Kreutzmann at the Keystone Korner on January 7 and doing a couple of shows with Saunders at the Lion's Share in San Anselmo the following week. On January 21, he and Howard Wales appeared at the Academy of Music in New York, and five days later they played Symphony Hall in Boston. Then Garcia made another series of appearances with Saunders back at the Keystone Korner in February and March.

If Wales/Garcia allowed the guitarist to play the most exploratory music this side of the Dead's in-concert "space" section, Saunders/Garcia, which became a regular outlet as of the start of 1972, provided far more structure. "We started doing standard songs because I loved standards," Saunders told Garcia biographer Sandy Troy in 1993. "Jerry was very interested in those songs and how to play them. As a matter of fact, one of the classic songs was 'My Funny Valentine,' which we recorded. Jerry loved standard songs. He liked the challenge."

"When I started playing with Merl, I went to a more organ-style trio," Garcia told Jon Sievert in *Guitar Player* magazine in July 1988. "I played big, fat chords and did a lot of that walking-style chord shifting on the blues numbers and things that Merl is so good at. My style is much more conventional, in a way, with him, and it's very satisfying for me to play and hear myself as a conventional player. It's a kind of playing that I don't do in the Grateful Dead."

In April, there were some familiar sessionman appearances. Atlantic released *Graham Nash/David Crosby* (SD 7220) on April 5, and Garcia played steel guitar on

"Southbound Train" and lead guitar on "The Wall Song." Garcia also appeared on the second New Riders of the Purple Sage LP, *Powerglide* (Columbia KC 31284), released later in the month. By this time, however, Buddy Cage had joined the group on pedal steel guitar, and the co-billings with the Grateful Dead were over, the last one coming on March 5 at Winterland. When the Dead launched an East Coast tour at the Academy of Music on March 21, NRPS was no longer with them. (The group did make later appearances with the Dead, however, notably on June 17 at the Hollywood Bowl, but the two bands were now separate entities.)

Simultaneous with the release of *Ace* in May came Mickey Hart's debut solo album *Rolling Thunder* (Warner Bros. BS 2635; reissued in 1986 as Relix RRLP 2026 and subsequently on CD as Grateful Dead Merchandising GDM 4011). Garcia played guitar on "The Chase (Progress)" and "Granma's Cookies," and he was credit with "insect fear" on "Pump Song." ("We have this box called the Insect Fear Device," wrote Rock Scully of the Dead's work on its 1968 second album, *Anthem Of The Sun*, "that you can plug the guitars or microphones into and play or sing through it and it makes all kinds of unearthly sounds.") Warner also released a single of "Blind John"/"Pump Song" (WB 7644).

Garcia made several other sideman appearances on 1972 albums. He was on *Rowan Brothers* (Columbia KC 31297; reissued in Italy as *Livin' The Life* [Appaloosa AP 011]). For David Bromberg's *Demon In Disguise* (Columbia KC 31753), he played electric guitar on "Sharon" and the title track. And he was on *Heavy Turbulence* (Fantasy 8421), credited to Merl Saunders, though it was in fact an album made by the Saunders-Garcia band, which was getting in about a show a month in the Bay Area during the second half of the year.

With the Dead off the road in January 1973, Garcia turned more

of his attention to the band with Saunders (filled out by Tom Fogerty, John Kahn and Bill Vitt), playing six dates in the Bay Area during the month. The group recorded two more studio albums during this period: Fogerty's *Excalibur* (Fantasy 9143) and Saunders's *Fire Up* (Fantasy 9421). (In September 1992, Fantasy released *Fire Up+* [FCD 7711], a single CD that combined some of the tracks from *Heavy Turbulence* and *Fire Up*.)

But playing in two bands wasn't enough, and on March 1 Garcia launched a third, the bluegrass outfit Old And In The Way, with a performance at the Lion's Share. The lineup was: Garcia on banjo and vocals, Richard Greene on fiddle, David Grisman on mandolin and vocals, John Kahn on acoustic bass and Peter Rowan on acoustic guitar and vocals. Old And In The Way played at least one date each month from March through November, in between Grateful Dead dates.

Garcia had been given an acknowledgement on the Jefferson Airplane album *Thirty Seconds Over Winterland*, released in March, but didn't play on the live LP. His next appearance with the Airplane conglomeration came in June with the release of *Baron Von Tollbooth & The Chrome Nun* (Grunt BFL 1-0148), credited to Paul Kantner, Grace Slick and David Freiberg. Garcia was all over the album: He played steel and lead guitar on "Ballad Of The Chrome Nun," guitar on "Fat," "Across The Board" and "Fishman," lead guitar and banjo on "Walkin'," steel guitar on "Your Mind Has Left Your Body" and lead guitar on "White Boy (Transcaucasian Airmachine Blues)" and "Sketches Of China."

On July 10 and 11, Garcia and Saunders played at the Keystone Berkeley, where they recorded the shows. The result was *Live At The Keystone* (Fantasy F 79002), released in December, a double-record set that was the definitive portrait of the band. David Grisman joined the group for a performance of Bob Dylan's

"Positively 4th Street." *Live At The Keystone* revealed the Saunders-Garcia band to be a hard-working, eclectic bar band with tastes in rock, R&B, funk, reggae and jazz, capable of playing everything from "My Funny Valentine" to "The Harder They Come." In that sense, it was a perfect vehicle for the expression of most of Garcia's musical interests. In April 1988, Fantasy returned to the shows and came up with eight overlapping CDs: *Live At The Keystone* (FCD 7701), a two-disc set; *Live At The Keystone, Volume I* (FCD 7701-1); *Live At The Keystone, Volume II* (FCD 7701-2); *Keystone Encores* (FCD 7703-2), another two-disc set; *Keystone Encores, Volume I* (MPF 4533); and *Keystone Encores, Volume II* (MPF 4534).

In September 1973, Garcia made an unusual sideman appearance, playing guitar on the song "Down In The Willow Garden" on Art Garfunkel's debut solo album, *Angel Clare* (Columbia KC 31472). A final 1973 guest shot was on rockabilly guitarist Link Wray's *Be What You Want To* (Polydor PD 5047). Garcia played pedal steel.

Having recorded one of his bands in July, Garcia recorded his other one, Old And In The Way, in October, turning on the tape recorder at a couple of Boarding House shows. The result was two albums, released 21 years apart. *Old & In The Way*, released in March 1975 on the Dead's own Round Records label (RX 103), reportedly became the best-selling bluegrass album of all time. It was reissued by Sugar Hill Records (SH-3746) and on July 1, 1986, came out on CD and cassette on Rykodisc (RCD/RACS 10009). In 1996, the same shows produced *That High Lonesome Sound*, released on David Grisman's Acoustic Disc label (ACD-19). These are the only recorded product of one of Garcia's most felicitous musical associations outside the Dead; Old And In The Way played its final show in November 1973.

Sometime during the course of the

year, Garcia participated in recording sessions conducted by singer/harmonica player/guitarist Matthew Kelly at the Record Plant in Sausalito. The sessions would not be released for 12 years, when they would appear on Relix Records under the title *A Wing And A Prayer* (RRLP 2016). Garcia played lead guitar on one track, "Dangerous Relations."

On October 15, the Dead had released *Wake Of The Flood*, the first album to appear on their own Grateful Dead Records label. Unlike the Airplane's Grunt, which was a vanity label manufactured and distributed by RCA, Grateful Dead Records was an independent company. Like the Airplane, however, the Dead needed extra recording acts to fill out a release schedule, and the prolific Garcia began to turn his attention in 1974 to filling that pipeline.

In the meantime, a couple of albums by friends were once again graced by his presence. In February, Columbia released David Bromberg's *Wanted Dead Or Alive* (KC 32717); Garcia played acoustic and electric guitar on the album. In April, the New Riders' live album, *Home, Home On The Road* (Columbia PC 32870) came out; Garcia produced it.

In January, with the Dead off the road for a couple of months, Garcia recorded his second solo album. It was released on June 6, once again with the title *Garcia* (Round RX 102). Dead Heads resolved the confusion by giving the album a de facto name based on the common practice of sending out promotional copies of albums with stickers reading, "Compliments of" with a blank space for the record company or publicist to be named. Seeing such stickers affixed to copies of *Garcia*, Dead Heads began referring to the album as *Compliments Of Garcia*. When Grateful Dead Records reissued the album in 1990 (GDCD 4009), the title was officially adopted.

Compliments Of Garcia, unlike Garcia's first solo album, was not an extension of his Grateful Dead

Goldmine 1998 Annual Page 31

persona. It was more an extension of his Saunders/Garcia persona. On this busman's holiday of a record, Garcia brought in horns and reeds to perform a series of wide-ranging covers including everything from the Rolling Stones' "Let's Spend The Night Together" to Irving Berlin's "Russian Lullaby." The idea of the record seems to have been to try things Garcia hadn't done before. "I would present him with a bunch of ideas," John Kahn, who produced the album, told Blair Jackson in *The Golden Road* magazine in 1987, "and he'd take the ones he liked and work on those. It was mainly stuff that he wouldn't ordinarily have thought of, and I think that was part of the challenge for him—to try something that was really new for him." Dead Heads were dismayed with the result, but the album was a moderate seller, reaching #49 in *Billboard*. A single, "Let It Rock"/"Midnight Town" (RX 4504) was issued.

On June 21, Round Records released Robert Hunter's debut album, *Tales Of The Great Rum Runners* (RX 101). Naturally, Garcia was involved. He played guitar solos on "Standing At Your Door" and "Keys To The Rain," and he mixed the album. Round released a single, "Rum Runners"/"It Must Have Been The Roses" (RX 4505), from the album. *Tales Of The Great Rum Runners* was reissued by Rykodisc on March 30, 1990 (RCD/RACS 10158).

On April 20, 1974, Garcia had launched the successor to Old And In The Way, the Great American String Band, with a performance at the Pilgrimage Theater in Hollywood. The lineup for the group was Garcia on banjo and vocals, Richard Greene on fiddle and David Grisman on mandolin and vocals, with two newcomers to the Dead scene: Taj Mahal on bass and vocals and David Nichtern on guitar and vocals. The group appeared through July, then folded. No recordings by them have appeared, but hope springs eternal.

Nine days after the final Great American String Band show at the Bottom Line in New York on July 3, Garcia launched a revised version of the Saunders/Garcia band, Legion of Mary. This quintet brought back John Kahn and added Martin Fierro (who had played with Saunders and Garcia off and on for some time) on reeds and percussion and Paul Humphrey on drums (replaced in February 1975 by Ron Tutt). This group, also unrecorded, played extensively during the period, playing several dates every month for a year.

The reason that Garcia was able to spend so much time with Legion of Mary was simple: after October 1974, the Dead retired from the road. They did not break up or dissolve their record labels, however, so Garcia still had lots of studio work to do. (Not released until 1980, and then in Italy, was Garcia's 1974 guest performance on Peter Rowan's *Texican Badman* [Appaloosa 010].)

In March 1975, Round Records had two new Garcia-related albums in the stores. *Keith And Donna* (RX 104), by Dead members Keith and Donna Godchaux, featured contributions from Garcia, who also provided drawings representing the thoughts of the Godchauxs' son Zion, whose picture was used for the cover. Starting in August and running through the end of the year, Garcia toured in the Keith and Donna Band, while also fronting his own Jerry Garcia Band, a quartet that featured Nicky Hopkins on piano and vocals, plus Kahn and Tutt.

Also out in March was Hunter's second album, *Tiger Rose* (RX 105). Garcia produced and arranged the album, and he performed on every track, contributing electric, acoustic and steel guitars, piano, synthesizer and background vocals. (For a reissue on Rykodisc [RCD/RACS 10115] on May 22, 1989, Hunter rerecorded all of his vocals.)

In April, Round released *Seastones* (RX 106), credited to synthesizer player Ned Lagin, who had appeared onstage with the Dead. Garcia contributed electric guitar and voice to the album, which was a collaboration between Lagin and Phil Lesh. On January 18, 1991, Rykodisc reissued the album (RCD/RACS 40193), adding to the original studio version a live version recorded in December 1975.

At this point, the Dead surrendered some of their independence, entering into a distribution deal with United Artists Records, such that the albums they released over the following year carried catalog numbers for both companies. The Dead retained the rights to the albums, however, and in the late 1980s, when they began to release albums by mail order through Grateful Dead Merchandising, the Grateful Dead and Round Records releases came back into print on CD and cassette.

In October, Garcia appeared on the New Riders album *Oh, What A Mighty Time* (Columbia PC 33688), playing guitar on "Mighty Time," "I Heard You Been Layin' My Old Lady" and "Take A Letter, Maria."

Garcia released his third solo album, *Reflections* (Round RX 107 RX-LA564-G), on February 3, 1976. *Reflections* combined covers like Hank Ballard's "Tore Up Over You," played by the Jerry Garcia Band, with Garcia/Hunter songs played by the Grateful Dead. While not, in a sense, a full-fledged solo album, it provided more songs for the Dead's repertoire, notably "They Love Each Other." It hit #42 in *Billboard*, not far from the #35 and #49 rankings of the two *Garcia* albums, and charted for 14 weeks, compared to the previous albums' 14- and 15-week runs, indicating that Garcia's solo albums were selling to a steady, limited audience of Dead Heads. *Reflections* was reissued on CD by Grateful Dead Merchandising as GDCD 4008.

In March, Round released the Good Old Boys' *Pistol Packin' Mama* (RX 109 RX-LA597-G). Garcia produced and mixed this bluegrass album. It is now available as Grateful Dead Merchandising

GDCD 4012. At the same time came *Diga* (Round RX 110 RX-LA600-G), by Diga Rhythm Band, a Mickey Hart percussion ensemble, with Garcia playing guitar on "Razooli" and "Happiness." (*Diga* was reissued by Rykodisc [RCD/RACS 10101] on November 1, 1988.)

June 1976 marked a turning point in the combined careers of Jerry Garcia and the Grateful Dead. With the band in temporary retirement, Garcia had been putting together *The Grateful Dead Movie*, drawn from a series of 1974 concerts. The completed film did not open for another year, but a new double album, *Steal Your Face*, drawn from the same shows, was released on June 26, 1976, and it was the last Dead album released by the group's record company at the time. Also, the Dead went back on the road. Hereafter, Garcia's guest appearances on the recordings of others would be less frequent, and his solo work would be restricted for the most part to the regular appearances of the successive editions of the Jerry Garcia Band.

For most of 1976 and into 1977, the lineup of that band featured the Godchauxs on vocals and piano, John Kahn on bass and Ron Tutt on drums and vocals. In the fall of 1977, Garcia toured with a slightly modified lineup in which Buzz Buchanan replaced Tutt and Maria Muldaur joined on vocals.

The Dead had signed to Arista Records with the demise of their independent record label, and in March 1978, Arista released *Cats Under The Stars* (AB 4160; reissued as AC/ARCD-85835), credited to the Jerry Garcia Band. The billing was appropriate: The album consisted of all originals, with Donna Godchaux and John Kahn compositions included among the Garcia/Hunter songs (among them "Rubin And Cherise," which later became a Dead concert favorite). *Cats Under The Stars* was the first real attempt to capture the Garcia Band sound, distinct from that of the Grateful Dead, that Garcia had

been developing in club and theater performances since at least 1975. It was a more modest, but frequently more focused sound than that of the Dead, in which Garcia's vocals and guitar playing were given more attention.

Unfortunately, by now the Dead's image was too well established for a separate Garcia musical identity to really flourish, and Arista must have considered solo records a necessary sidelight that wasn't a sales priority. *Cats Under The Stars* failed to break into the top 100 bestsellers and remains an underrated Jerry Garcia album.

The Grateful Dead were unusually active in promoting their record career in the late 1970s and into 1980, and on November 10, 1980, Earth News Radio broadcast interviews with Garcia and Weir that were pressed as a radio-only promotional album (EN 11/10/80) at a time when they were doing the live shows that would be released in 1981 as *Reckoning* and *Dead Set*.

After those albums, the Dead took a six-year sabbatical from releasing new albums. One session that went unreleased at the time was a Joan Baez date with members of the Dead backing her in 1980. Baez released a couple of tracks from the session on her *Rare, Live & Classic* boxed set in 1993, including a version of "Jackaroe" with Garcia on guitar.

In January 1979, Garcia had organized a new band called Reconstruction featuring old and new friends. The lineup was Garcia, Saunders, Kahn, Ed Neumeister on trombone, Ron Stallings on saxophone and vocals and Gaylord Birch on drums. Though Reconstruction played around the West, mostly in the Bay Area, from January through September, it never recorded. In October 1979, Garcia unveiled a streamlined Jerry Garcia Band consisting of himself, Kahn, Ozzie Allers on keyboards and vocals and Johnny de Foncesca on drums. This unit played Garcia's usual haunts in the Bay Area into February 1980, then did an East

Coast tour in February and March. Garcia replaced de Foncesca with Greg Errico for dates in July and August. Toward the end of the year, he unveiled a new unit featuring himself, Kahn, Melvin Seals on organ, Jimmy Warren on electric piano and clavinet and Daoud Shaw on drums. This version of the band toured through June 1981, at which point Garcia added singers Essra Mohawk and Liz Stires. Bill Kreutzmann began sitting in for Shaw in December, and this edition of the group stayed in place through September 1982.

Most of the musicians who made Jerry Garcia's fifth solo album, *Run For The Roses* (Arista AL 9603; reissued as ARCD 8557), which seems to have been released on November 2, 1982, were drawn from the lineups of his bands. Ron Tutt and John Kahn made up the rhythm section; Melvin Seals, Jimmy Warren and Michael O'Martian played keyboards; Julie Stafford and Liz Stires sang backup. The album was a typical mix of originals by Garcia, Hunter and Kahn with some familiar covers, among them the Beatles' "I Saw Her Standing There" (played to a reggae beat) and Bob Dylan's "Knockin' On Heaven's Door." Less ambitious than *Cats Under The Stars*, *Run For The Roses* suggested that Garcia had long-since settled into the idea that his solo career was a side trip, enjoyable for him and his subset of Dead Heads, but not in any serious competition with the Dead. Garcia toured to support the album (and just to play) with a Garcia Band lineup of himself, Kahn, Seals, Errico and singers DeeDee Dickerson and Jaclyn LaBranch. This version continued through June 1983, when David Kemper was brought in on drums.

It had been a long time since the days of PERRO when Paul Kantner released an album called *The Planet Earth Rock And Roll Orchestra* (RCA AFL1-4320) in 1983. Garcia did not appear on the album, but he was co-credited as songwriter on the track "The Mountain Song," which Kantner dedicated to "David C, Jerry G, Graham N, Grace S, David F, Billy K and Mickey H, and to one summer when all of our schedules almost didn't conflict."

The Jerry Garcia Band continued to play regularly with minor alterations in personnel. In September 1984, Gloria Jones replaced DeeDee Dickerson on vocals. In October 1985, Gaylord Birch came back on drums, though David Kemper took the drum chair back in February 1986. The band continued to play through the end of May 1987, after which Garcia disbanded it.

Jerry Garcia's diabetic coma during the summer of 1986 changed his working habits. After he recovered, the Dead began working on their first studio album since 1980. Also, for the first time in many years, Garcia began guesting on other artists' albums. He played guitar on "You're The One," a track on the Neville Brothers' album Uptown (EMI America ST 17249), released in April 1987, and he contributed "mouth sounds and chimes" to the track "Backstage Pass" on Negativland's 1987 album Escape From Noise (SST 133).

A less surprising guest appearance was Garcia's participation on Robert Hunter's Liberty (Relix RRLP 2029), released on March 1, 1988. Garcia played guitar on the whole album as part of Hunter's backup band. He made two more guest appearances in June, playing guitar on "Three Wishes," "Singing In The Shower" and "Desert Players" on Ornette Coleman's Virgin Beauty (Portrait OR 44301) and singing backup on "Silvio," a song with lyrics by Robert Hunter, on Bob Dylan's Down In The Groove (Columbia OC 40957). Also in 1988, he appeared on former Jefferson Starship bassist Pete Sears's Watchfire (Redwood RRCD 8806), playing on "Nothing Personal," "Let The Dove Fly Free" and "One More Innocent." (The album is now available as Grateful Dead Merchandising #3903.)

In August 1987, Jerry Garcia reorganized his solo band, retaining drummer David Kemper and bass player John Kahn and adding old friends David Nelson and Sandy Rothman to make up the Jerry Garcia Acoustic Band. After a couple of warmup dates in California, the group went to Broadway, opening at the Lunt-Fontanne Theatre in New York October 15-31, complete with a copy of the theater magazine Playbill for each member of the audience containing a bio of Garcia that noted he was named after Broadway composer Jerome Kern. The band then moved on to the Wiltern Theatre in Los Angeles and the Warfield in San Francisco.

These shows led to the release of Almost Acoustic (Concensus Reality/Grateful Dead Merchandising GDCD 4005), credited to the Jerry Garcia Acoustic Band, released in December 1988. The album contained many traditional country and blues songs, along with compositions by Jimmie Rodgers and Mississippi John Hurt and, at the end, the Garcia/Hunter song "Ripple."

In 1989, Garcia played guitar on "They Moved The Moon," a track on Warren Zevon's Transverse City (Virgin Records America 91068), which was released in October.

Garcia's 1990 record dates were made with familiar names. On March 2, he was credited as co-producer with Mickey Hart on Songs Of Amber (Rykodisc RCD 10130), by the Dzintars Latvian Women's Choir. In April, he was featured on four songs on Merl Saunders's Blues From The Rainforest (Sumertone S2CD-01/S2CS-16; reissued by Grateful Dead Merchandising GDCD 3901). He played guitar on "Barren Ground" and "Across The River" on A Night On The Town (RCA 2041-2-R), by Bruce Hornsby and the Range, released in June. (Hornsby would join the Grateful Dead soon.) And on Mickey Hart's At The Edge (Rykodisc RCD 10124), released on September 14, Garcia con-

tributed to three tracks, including playing "forest zone" on the opening tune, "#4 For Gaia." (A fairly esoteric recording during this period is Nicki Scully's meditation tape, The Cauldron Journey Of Healing [CAU 3], which has a musical score by Garcia and Roland Barker. Nicki Scully is Rock Scully's wife.)

In 1991, Garcia engaged in album-length musical collaborations with two old associates. Released January 22, 1991, was Country Joe McDonald's Superstitious Blues (Ragbaby/Rykodisc RCD 10201), an acoustic album on which Garcia accompanied McDonald for four songs. A fifth track from the session was released five years later on McDonald's Carry On (Ragbaby/ Shanachie 8019). Jerry Garcia/ David Grisman (Acoustic Disc ACD-2), released July 12, was, as its name suggested, a duo record by Garcia and his old mandolin-playing partner, who had set up his own independent record label. The two had been playing shows together, starting on December 17, 1990, at the Sweetwater in Mill Valley, California, and continuing with a series of shows at the Warfield Theatre in San Francisco, and their repertoire ranged from that old Garcia favorite, Irving Berlin's "Russian Lullaby," to the Dead's "Friend Of The Devil."

Of course, Garcia had continued to perform with his electric group as well, and a thorough chronicle of their 1990 performances appeared in the form of a 140-minute double album simply titled Jerry Garcia Band (Arista 18690) that was released August 27. With a steady lineup of Garcia, Kahn, Seals, Kemper, LaBranch and Jones, the group tackled a typically eclectic set list that included tunes by Bob Dylan, Smokey Robinson and Lennon and McCartney, as well as Allen Toussaint and Peter Tosh. The only Hunter/Garcia song was "Deal"; otherwise the album consisted entirely of covers, and there was no new material. At a time when the Dead were starting to release archival albums like One From The

Vault, Jerry Garcia Band seemed to serve the same historical function.

In order to promote the album, Garcia submitted to a radio interview with veteran disc jockey Scott Muni on September 13, and the result was pressed up on a promotional LP (Arista ADP 2377) that appeared in December.

In January 1992, Grateful Dead Records released Devout Catalyst (GDCD 40152), a spoken word album by Ken Nordine, the practitioner of "word jazz," on which Garcia and Grisman provided accompaniment. In July, Garcia was heard on the track "Beauty Of A Dream" on Thomas Dolby's Astronauts And Heretics (Giant 24478) album. Garcia also teamed up with Grisman for the 1992 Acoustic Disc release Bluegrass Reunion, serving as "special guest" for three cuts on bluegrass legend Red Allen's final recording, which had been made in May 1991.

Ken Kesey made a couple of interesting tapes available to mail order during this period. The first was Drive Alive (Key-Z Productions), on which the musings of Neal Cassady are accompanied by the Warlocks, with additional music by Garcia. The second was Tricker (Key-Z Productions), including spoken word and song performances by Kesey with the Thunder Machine Band, with Garcia on lead guitar.

Garcia continued to make appearances on his friends' records in 1993, playing guitar on "Passing Through" and "Pastures Of Plenty" on Bruce Hornsby's April release, Harbor Lights (RCA 66114). October saw the release of Garcia's second duo album with David Grisman, Not For Kids Only (Acoustic Disc ACD-9), an acoustic children's album.

Bassist Rob Wasserman's long-promised Trios (MCA/GRP 4021) finally appeared on February 15, 1994, featuring among its collaborations "Zillionaire," written and performed by Wasserman, Edie Brickell and Garcia. This appears to be Garcia's only record release for the year.

The year 1995, however, saw renewed activity. The first recordings in years by the Jerry Garcia Band, "Cigarettes And Coffee" and "Smoke Gets In Your Eyes," turned up on the soundtrack album for the movie Smoke (Hollywood Records 62024) on June 6. Garcia continued to tour with the band, doing a series of dates at the Warfield in January, March and April in between Dead shows, concluding with a performance on April 23.

Garcia's last guest appearance on record to come out during his lifetime was his lead guitar work on "Cruise Control," a track on Bruce Hornsby's Hot House (RCA 66584), released on July 18, 1995. But already in the pipeline was Garcia's "special guest" work on guitarist Sanjay Mishra's Blues Incantation (Rain Dog Records RDR 0098), which was released in August, shortly after his death on August 9.

Despite his relatively short life, Jerry Garcia made a lot of music in his 53 years, much of it with the Grateful Dead, but also with many other people and under his own name. While his demise means that there will be no new music from him or, given the subsequent breakup of the Grateful Dead, from his chief musical vehicle, nevertheless, his discography can only be expected to expand in the future. Grateful Dead Records' release schedule has quickened over the past year, with the Dick's Picks series now up to five volumes, and Arista, having had success with last year's Hundred Year Hall, looks forward to an album of new Dead songs that was in preparation at the time of Garcia's death. In addition, there are doubtless numerous Garcia band recordings, numerous Garcia/Grisman recordings and possibly some early material that will see release. None of it will begin to make up the loss that, a year on, Dead Heads and Garcia fans continue to suffer. But the music will live on.

*****

Sources and acknowledgements: The primary source for this article was the author's record collection. But two reference works were consulted heavily: first, the successive editions of the DeadBase books, by John W. Scott, Mike Dolgushkin and Stu Nixon (P.O. Box 499-F, Hanover, NH 03755), especially DeadBase IX; and second, The Compleat Grateful Dead Discography (The Eleventh Revision), by Ihor W. Slabicky (35 Hathaway Drive, Portsmouth, RI 02871, (401) 683-5803). Biographical material was drawn largely from the books Grateful Dead: The Music Never Stopped, by Blair Jackson (Delilah, 1983) and Captain Trips: A Biography Of Jerry Garcia, by Sandy Troy (Thunder's Mouth Press, 1994), though many other Dead publications were consulted, and special mention should be made of Grateful Dead Almanac (P.O. Box X, Novato, CA 94948). (As noted in the text, there is some discographical information in Rock Scully's book Living With The Dead, written with David Dalton [Little, Brown and Company, 1996], but it seems to be of questionable veracity.) Many of the recordings discussed here can be obtained by calling the Grateful Dead Mercantile Co. at (800) 225-3323.

The author would like to thank Steve Silberman and Jeff Tamarkin for their specific assistance, though his knowledge and appreciation of Jerry Garcia and the Grateful Dead has been increased over the last couple of decades by an army of Dead Heads and Dead family members, among whom Toni Brown, Ren Grevatt, Robert Hunter, Jim Ivers, Les Kippel, Jean Martin and Dennis McNally should be particularly noted. Thanks to all. This article is dedicated to the memory of John Kahn (1948-1996).

Expanded Goldmine Index

Title	Code	Date
Baron Records		March 1980
Barrere, Paul/Little Feat	I,D	Dec. 1983
Barrere, Paul/Little Feat		March 1, 1985
Barrere, Paul/Little Feat	I,D	Dec. 2, 1988
Barrett, Pat/Crewcuts	I,D	June 1982
Barrie, Dennis	I	March 15, 1996
Barron, Ronnie	I	June 1982
Barry And The Tamerlanes/Barry De Vorzon	I	Dec. 1, 1989
Barry, Jeff	D	April 2, 1993
Barry, Jeff's	DA	May 28, 1993
Basil, Toni		Dec. 30, 1988
Bass, Fontella		July-Aug. 1977
Bass, Fontella		Dec. 30, 1988
Batman's Greatest Hits		May 1, 1992
Bauhaus	I	April 25, 1997
Bauhaus	D	June 6, 1997
Bauman, Jon/Sha Na Na	I	Aug. 1981
Bay City Rollers		Sept. 25, 1987
Bay City Rollers		Sept. 25, 1987
Bay City Rollers	I,D	Jan. 5, 1996
Bay City Rollers		Aug. 30, 1996
Be Bop Revolution (John Bray)		March 1976
Be Bop Revolution (John Bray)		May 1976
Be Your Own Search Service (Trading With Foreign Collectors)		Dec. 15, 1989
Beach Boys, The		
Beach Boys	D	Feb. 1979
Beach Boys	D	Nov. 1980
Beach Boys	D	Aug. 1982
Beach Boys	D	July 3, 1987
Beach Boys	D	Feb. 26, 1988
Beach Boys		Nov. 18, 1988
Beach Boys Bootlegs: A Consumer's Guide		June 1, 1990
Beach Boys On CD		Dec. 15, 1989
Beach Boys On CD		June 1, 1990
Beach Boys On CD, part 2		Jan. 24, 1992
Beach Boys US discography part 2		Jan. 24, 1992
Beach Boys/Brian Wilson	D	Nov. 18, 1988
Beach Boys/Brian Wilson	I,D	Nov. 18, 1988
Beach Boys/Bruce Johnston	I	Oct. 1981
Beach Boys: Brothers, Cousins And Friends	D	June 1, 1990
Beach Boys: Brothers, Cousins And Friends	DA	June 29, 1990
Beach Boys: Brothers, Cousins And Friends	DA	Aug. 10, 1990
Beach Boys: Capitol Exec Ron Mc Carrell Discusses The Beach Boys CDs	I	June 1, 1990
Beach Boys: Collecting Solo Brian Wilson		June 1, 1990
Beach Boys: Legend Of "Smile"		April 1983
Beach Boys: the Making of the Good Vibrations boxed set		July 23, 1993
Beacon Street Union/John Lincoln	I,D	Dec. 18, 1987
Beacon Street Union/John Lincoln Wright	I,D	Dec. 18, 1987
Bear Family Records		Sept. 7, 1990
Bear Family Records/Richard Weize	I	Nov. 7, 1986
Bear Family Records		Feb. 16, 1996
Bear Family Records: Needs Help		June 21, 1996
Beastie Boys		June 5, 1987
Beastie Boys	DA	July 3, 1987
Beat, The!!!!		Feb. 5, 1993
Beatles, The		
Beatles: Anthology Collectibles		Nov. 8, 1996
Beatles: Anthology news		Nov. 10, 1995
Beatles: Anthology: A Year in the Life		Feb. 16, 1996
Beatle Beginnings: The Polydor Recordings	D	March 1982
Beatle Differences		July-Aug. 1978
Beatle Differences		July-Aug. 1978
Beatle Differences		Nov. 1978
Beatle Differences		Dec. 1978
Beatle It Or Not (Mitchell Mc Geary)		July 1976
Beatle It Or Not (Mitchell Mc Geary)		Sept.-Oct. 1976
Beatle It Or Not (Mitchell Mc Geary)		Nov.-Dec. 1976
Beatle It Or Not (Mitchell Mc Geary)		Jan.-Feb. 1977
Beatle It Or Not (Mitchell Mc Geary)		Sept. 1977
Beatle It Or Not (Mitchell Mc Geary)		Jan. 1978
Beatle It Or Not (Mitchell Mc Geary)		March 1979
Beatlemoneya		March 27, 1987
Beatles And New York Radio		March 1982
Beatles Puzzle		Aug. 16, 1985
Beatles Rarities		July 1980
Beatles Trivia Quiz		Feb. 1984
Beatles' Arrival (Mania In The Media)		Feb. 24, 1989
Beatles' Oldies But Goodies	D	Nov. 17, 1989
Beatles, Beatles, Beatles		Oct. 1982
Beatles: McCartney 93 Releases		Nov. 12, 1993
Beatles: McCartney Collectibles		Nov. 10, 1995
Beatles: The Mersey-Motown Sound		Nov. 12, 1993
Beatles: "Collector's Items" and "Casualties"		Dec. 9, 1994
Beatles: "Jukebox Only" singles		Nov. 12, 1993
Beatles: Abbey Road Revisited		March 30, 1984
Beatles: Artists who beat the Beatles out of Grammys		Nov. 12, 1993
Beatles: Beatles Book Update		Nov. 27, 1992
Beatles: Beatles Books 1994		Nov. 25, 1994
Beatles: Beatles Books in 1993		Nov. 12, 1993
Beatles: Beatles In Hamburg		Nov. 25, 1994
Beatles: Belmo's Ultimate Beatles Rarities Boxed Set		Nov. 12, 1993
Beatles: Bob Wooler	I	Nov. 8, 1996
Beatles: Bootleg As Collectible		Aug. 10, 1990
Beatles: Bootleg Dilemma (Unfounded Fingerpointing Must Stop)		Nov. 17, 1989
Beatles: Bootleg Records		March 27, 1987
Beatles: Bootleg Records		Feb. 24, 1989
Beatles: Bootleg Records		Oct. 19, 1990
Beatles: Bootlegs vs Capitol Records		Oct. 1982
Beatles: Break up of the Beatles (affadavit)		Nov. 27, 1992
Beatles: Britian Bans Beatles		April 12, 1996
Beatles: Collectibles from the Hamburg Years		Nov. 25, 1994
Beatles: Collecting Beatle Broadcasts	D	Oct. 1982
Beatles: Collecting Beatles Telecasts Part 1		Dec. 1983
Beatles: Collecting Beatles Telecasts Part 2	D	Jan. 1984
Beatles: Collecting The Memorabilia		July 29, 1988
Beatles: Colored Vinyl And The Beatles	D	Oct. 19, 1990
Beatles: Compact Discs		March 27, 1987
Beatles: Compact Discs		July 3, 1987
Beatles: Covering The Beatles' Album Covers		Feb. 24, 1989
Beatles: Eastern European Beatles Discography		July 29, 1988
Beatles: Essential Beatle Bootlegs		Nov. 17, 1989
Beatles: Ex-Beatles	D	Nov. 17, 1989
Beatles: Ex-Beatles in 1974		Nov. 25, 1994
Beatles: Fab Four Facsimiles (Beatle Related Novelty Songs)		Feb. 1981
Beatles: Fab Four Facsimiles (Beatle Related Novelty Songs)		June 1981
Beatles: Fab Three Come Together for New Recordings		Jan. 21, 1994
Beatles: Guide To Beatles Interpretation Albums		July 29, 1988
Beatles: In Person And On The Air		Aug. 16, 1985
Beatles: Inside The Beatles' Vaults (An Interview With Mark Lewisohn)	I	Nov. 17, 1989
Beatles: It Was Twenty Years Ago Today		Feb. 1984
Beatles: John Lennon Tribute Records		March 1982
Beatles: John Lennon: Passing Contacts And Indelible Memories		Dec. 7, 1984
Beatles: Klaus Voorman		Feb. 1984
Beatles: Lost Mc Cartney Album		Feb. 24, 1989
Beatles: Making Of The Beatles Anthology		Nov. 8, 1996
Beatles: McCartney Solo Releases [esp. CDs]		Nov. 12, 1993
Beatles: Memorabilia		Nov. 17, 1989
Beatles: Missing Compact Beatles		Nov. 27, 1992
Beatles: Misunderstanding All You See: CD, LSD And The Act You've Known All These Years		Feb. 24, 1989
Beatles: More Beatle News		Sept. 1981
Beatles: on Bootlegs, in their own words		Nov. 10, 1995

Entry	Code	Date
Beatles: On Stage Aug. 12, 1963		Aug. 16, 1985
Beatles: Pete Best	I, D	Oct. 1982
Beatles: Pete Best		Aug. 1983
Beatles: Pete Best	DA	Dec. 1983
Beatles: A Proposal		Nov. 8, 1996
Beatles: Promoter Of Toronto Lennon Concert (John Brower)		Feb. 24, 1989
Beatles: Putting Together A Palatable 'Let It Be'		July 29, 1988
Beatles: Quick Look At Latest Beatles' Boots		Aug. 16, 1985
Beatles: Real American TV Debut Of The Beatles		March 1982
Beatles: Release Their First CD-ROM		April 12, 1996
Beatles: Remastered McCartney CDs		Nov. 12, 1993
Beatles: Roots Of The Beatles		Dec. 16, 1988
Beatles: See Heading (Collecting Beatles)		
Beatles: See Heading (Sgt. Pepper's Lonely Hearts Club Fans) and also		
Beatles: see Martin, George		
Beatles: Sgt. Pepper's Lonely Hearts Club Band		July 17, 1987
Beatles: Solo Beatles Picture Disc Discography		Oct. 19, 1990
Beatles: Stongs the Beatles Gave Away		Nov. 10, 1995
Beatles: Sue To Stop Stamp Sales		Nov. 22, 1996
Beatles: The Coolest Beatle Collectibles		Nov. 25, 1994
Beatles: Their Solo Years		Aug. 16, 1985
Beatles: Turn Down Megabucks for Tour		March 29, 1996
Beatles: Two Of Us: A List Of Beatles Songs w/Multiple Versions & Mixes	D	July 29, 1988
Beatles: Two Of Us: A List Of Beatles Songs w/Multiple Versions & Mixes		Feb. 24, 1989
Beatles: Who Was The Real Fifth Beatle?		Nov. 17, 1989
Beatles: Without Words	D	Oct. 19, 1990
Beatlesongs LP Cover		June 1982
Beau Brummels	I,	March 14, 1997
Beau Brummels/Dec Mulligan/Sal Valentino	I,D	March 14, 1986
Beau Brummels/Dec Mulligan/Sal Valentino	DA	April 25, 1986
Beau-Marks	D	Aug. 1983
Beaumont, Jimmy/Skyliners	I,D	Sept. 1981
Beausoleil/Michael Doucet	I	Jan. 31, 1997
Beck, Jeff	D	Nov. 20, 1987
Beck, Jeff	DA	March 11, 1988
Bee Gees, The	D	Feb. 1984
Bee Gees, The	DA	April 13, 1984
Bee Gees: Japan	D	March 1, 1985
Bee Gees: Japan	DA	April 12, 1985
Bee Gees: Their Early Compositions As Recorded By Australian Artists	D	April 20, 1990
Belairs	I,D	Dec. 1982
Belairs	DA	Sept. 1983
Belkin, Herb/Mobile Fidelity Sound Lab	I	Nov. 4, 1988
Bell, Freddie & The Bellboys	D	July 3, 1987
Bell, Napier/John's Children	I,D	Aug. 10, 1990
Bell, William	I,D	Feb. 13, 1987
Bell, William	I,D	Feb. 13, 1987
Belland, Bruce/Four Preps	I,D	Oct. 5, 1990
Belvin, Jesse		Dec. 7, 1984
Belvin, Jesse	D	Dec. 5, 1986
Belvin, Jesse	DA	Jan. 2, 1987
Bennett, Joe & The Sparkletones	D	Aug. 1981
Bennett, Tony	I, D	Jan. 10, 1992
Benson, Ray/Asleep At The Wheel	I,D	Oct. 1979
Benson, Ray/Asleep At The Wheel	I,D	March 1981
Benson, Ray/Asleep At The Wheel	D,DO	May 10, 1985
Benson, Ray/Asleep At The Wheel	I,D	April 21, 1989
Berberich, Bob/Hangmen	I,D	Dec. 6, 1985
Berlin		Dec. 1, 1989
Berman, Shelley	D	March 1980
Bernard, Rod	D	July 6, 1984
Bernard, Rod	DA	Aug. 17, 1984
Bernard, Rod	D	July 6, 1984
Bernard, Rod	I, D	March 31, 1995
Bernholm, Jonas/Route 66 Records	I	June 2, 1989
Bernstein, Leonard	D	March 31, 1995
Berry, Chuck	I,D	Nov. 1979
Berry, Chuck	I,D	Sept. 1982
Berry, Chuck	I,D	Nov. 1983
Berry, Chuck	DA	Sept.-Oct. 1976
Berry, Chuck	DA	Jan. 29, 1988
Berry, Chuck	DA	Feb. 26, 1988
Berry, Chuck		Feb. 24, 1989
Berry, Chuck	DA	Apr. 3, 1992
Berry, Richard	I,D	June 1983
Berry, Richard	I	April 25, 1986
Berry, Richard/Flairs	I	Dec. 6, 1985
Berserkley Records		June 2, 1989
Berton's Corner (Ralph Berton)		May 25, 1984
Berton's Corner (Ralph Berton)		Aug. 3, 1984
Bertram, Bob/International Records	D	Feb. 1983
Bertron's Corner		May 25, 1984
Best In Texas: A Guide To Independent And Collector Shops		March 13, 1987
Best Of '84		Jan. 4, 1985
Best, Pete	I,D	Oct. 1982
Best, Pete		Aug. 1983
Best, Pete	DA	Dec. 1983
Biafra, Jello/Dead Kennedys	I,D	March 24, 1989
Big Bopper		Nov.-Dec. 1976
Big Bopper	D	March 13, 1987
Big Bopper	D	Feb. 10, 1989
Big Broadcast Of 1932/Bing Crosby		Aug. 1979
Big Broadcast Of 1932/Bing Crosby		Aug. 1979
Big Brother And The Holding Company/David Getz	I,D	July 19, 1985
Big Maybelle (Maybelle Louis Smith)	D	Dec. 4, 1987
Big Ten Inch Record		July-Aug. 1977
Big Twist And The Mellow Fellows	I,D	Aug. 1982
Big Youth	I,D	March 1981
Big Youth		March 1981
Bihari Brothers		May 1979
Billingslea, Joe/Contours	I,D	Nov. 21, 1986
Bingenheimer, Rodney		May 8, 1987
Bingenheimer, Rodney	I	June 17, 1988
Biograph Records/Arnold Caplin	I	Sept. 7, 1990
Black Crowes, the	I	July 24, 1992
Black Crowes, The	I	Oct. 11, 1996
Black Gospel Quartets	D	March 2, 1984
Black Sabbath	D	May 19, 1989
Black Top Records		March 18, 1994
Black Uhuru		Sept. 1981
Black, Bill	D	Aug. 26, 1988
Black, Bill Combo/Bob Tucker	I,D	March 1981
Black, Bill Combo/Bob Tucker	D,DO	May 10, 1985
Black, Cilla	D	Nov. 10, 1995
Black, Jimmy Carl/Mothers Of Invention	I,D	Jan. 16, 1987
Black, Jimmy Carl/Mothers Of Invention		Nov. 20, 1987
Black, Jimmy Carl/Mothers Of Invention	DA	March 25, 1988
Black Vinyl	I	May 10, 1996
Blackwell, Otis	I,D	June 1983
Blackwell, Otis	I	July 31, 1987
Blaine, Hal	I,D	Oct. 5, 1990
Blaine, Hal	DA	Nov. 2, 1990
Blake, Cicero	D	Oct. 1981
Blake, Tommy	D	July 10, 1992
Bland, Billy		Dec. 30, 1988
Bland, Bobby	I,D	Jan. 16, 1987
Bland, Bobby	I,D	Jan. 16, 1987
Bland, Bobby "Blue"	D	July 21, 1995
Blane, Marcie	I	Dec. 30, 1988

Entry	Code	Date
Blasters/Dave Alvin	I	May 1982
Blind Faith		March 27, 1987
Blind Faith		March 27, 1987
Blind Melon	I	April 1, 1994
Blind Pig Records		Aug. 1980
Bloomfield, Mike		April 1981
Bloomfield, Mike	D	Jan. 4, 1985
Bloomfield, Mike	DA	Aug. 16, 1985
Bloomfield, Mike	DA	Jan. 17, 1986
Blossom, Dave/50 Foot Hose	I	Sept. 1980
Blotto	I	March 29, 1985
Blotto	I	March 29, 1985
Blue Cheer/Dick Peterson	I,D	May 23, 1986
Blue Note Records		Aug. 21, 1992
Blue Oyster Cult	I,D	June 7, 1996
Blue Suede Shoes (Nightclub)		May 24, 1985
Blue Suede Shoes (Nightclub)		May 24, 1985
Blue Suede Shoes (Song)		May 8, 1987
Blue Thumb	I,	May 10, 1996
Blue Wave Records		May 12, 1995
Bluegrass: Collector's Guide To Some Rare Vinyl		March 14, 1986
Blues In Poland		Feb. 23, 1990
Blues Magoos/Peppy Castro	I,D	May 1983
Blues Magoos/Peppy Castro	DA	Dec. 7, 1984
Blues Project	I,D	July 1981
Blues Traveler	I, D	March 17, 1995
Blues, New Faces in the		May 13, 1994
Bluestown Record Label	D	Aug. 1980
Blur		Feb. 16, 1996
Blythe, Arthur	I,D	July 20, 1984
Bob Dylan: Various Artists Sing Bob Dylan	D	Dec. 1983
Bobbettes	I, D	Feb. 21, 1992
Bobbettes, The	I,D	Sept. 1981
Bobbettes, The		Dec. 30, 1988
Boberg, Jay/I.R.S. Records	I,D	Feb. 1982
Boettcher, Curt/Sagittarius/Millennium	I,D	Nov. 2, 1990
Bolan, Marc	D	April 1983
Bolan, Marc	DA	May 1983
Bolan, Marc	DA	Aug. 1983
Bolan, Marc	DA	Dec. 7, 1984
Bolan, Marc and T. Rex	I,D	Dec. 20, 1996
Bomp Records/Greg Shaw	I	Sept. 7, 1990
Bomp! Records		May 12, 1995
Bon Jovi, Jon	I	June 11, 1993
Bon Jovi/Jon Bon Jovi	I	Oct. 23, 1987
Bond, Eddie	D	Nov. 1978
Bond, Eddie	I,D	Aug. 1, 1986
Bond, James: Double Naught Music	D	Dec. 21, 1984
Bond, James: Double Naught Music	DA	Feb. 14, 1986
Bonds, Gary U.S.	I,D	Jan. 1979
Bonds, Gary U.S.	DA	April 1979
Bonds, Gary U.S.	I,DA	Aug. 1981
Bonds, Gary U.S.	DA	Oct. 1981
Bongos	I	Feb. 1984
Bongos	I	Feb. 1984
Bonniwell, Sean	I	Sept. 29, 1995
Bonniwell, Sean/Music Machine	I,D	Aug. 29, 1986
Bookbinder, Roy	I,D	March 29, 1985
Bookbinder, Roy	DA	Jan. 17, 1986
Booker T & The MG's/Booker T Jones	I,D	July 1981
Booker, James		Dec. 30, 1988
Boo Radleys		
Boone, Debby		Dec. 1, 1989
Boone, Pat	I,D	July-Aug. 1978
Boone, Pat	I,D	Feb. 22, 1991
Boone, Pat	I	May 23, 1997
Booting The Blues		Nov. 21, 1986
Bootlegging, Pirating: Taping Pirates Not Guilty Of Theft		Nov. 9, 1984
Bootlegs: Supreme Court Rules On Bootleg Shipments		Aug. 16,1985
Boots (Marianne Biskup)		Jan. 16, 1987
Boston Sound, the	D	June 26, 1992
Boswell Sisters		June 22, 1984
Boswell Sisters	D	July 6, 1984
Boswell Sisters	DA	Sept. 28, 1984
Boswell Sisters	DA	Jan. 17, 1986
Both Sides Now (Bud Buschardt)		
Both Sides Now (Callahan,Buschardt,Goddard)		Aug. 1980
Both Sides Now (Mike Callahan)		Sept., 1980
Both Sides Now (Mike Callahan)		Oct. 1980
Both Sides Now (Mike Callahan)		April 1981
Both Sides Now (Mike Callahan)		March 1982
Both Sides Now (Mike Callahan)		Sept. 28, 1984
Both Sides Now: "Lost" Rolling Stones Stereo Hits		May 1983
Both Sides Now: Additions & Corrections		March 1980
Both Sides Now: Beach Boys	D	Nov. 1980
Both Sides Now: Beatles Rarities		July 1980
Both Sides Now: British Invasion	D	Jan. 1980
Both Sides Now: British Invasion	DA	April 1980
Both Sides Now: British Invasion	DA	April 1980
Both Sides Now: Cadence Records Story	D	Nov. 1981
Both Sides Now: Cadence Records Story	DA	March 1982
Both Sides Now: Chicago's Rock Groups	D	Oct. 1982
Both Sides Now: Del Shannon	I,D	Oct. 1983
Both Sides Now: First Years (1957-58)	D	Oct. 1979
Both Sides Now: First Years (1957-58)	DA	March 1980
Both Sides Now: Larry Levine,		
One Hit Wonders And Yellow Balloons	D	June 1980
Both Sides Now: Laurie Records	D	Jan. 1981
Both Sides Now: Mono's Last Stand		
(Stereo Disappointments 1969-1975)	D	May 1980
Both Sides Now: New Orleans Rock & Roll	D	Feb. 1981
Both Sides Now: Phil Spector	D	March 1980
Both Sides Now: Phil Spector	D	April 1980
Both Sides Now: Phil Spector		Dec. 1980
Both Sides Now: Reprocessed Stereo Blues		Dec. 1979
Both Sides Now: Rick Nelson	D	Aug. 1980
Both Sides Now: Stereo 45 Reissues		March 1981
Both Sides Now: Stereo Quiz #2		Nov. 1981
Both Sides Now: Stereo Quiz #2		March 1982
Both Sides Now: Stereo Singles (1959 - 1961)		Nov. 1979
Both Sides Now: Stereo Singles (1959 - 1961)		March 1980
Both Sides Now: Stereo Singles (1959 - 1961)		Aug. 1983
Both Sides Now: Vee Jay Records		May 1981
Bowie, David		
Bowie, David	D	March 1980
Bowie, David		Dec. 1983
Bowie, David: In The 80's	I,D	June 6, 1997
Bowie, David: Mick Ronson	I,D	Dec. 14, 1990
Bowie, David: Rare International Albums 1967 - 1971		Dec. 14, 1990
Bowie, David:		Dec. 14, 1990
Rykodisc Responds To The Preceding Article (Sound And Vison)		
Bowie, David: Sound And Vision		Dec. 14, 1990
(The World Of David Bowie Collectibles)		
Bowie, David: The Berlin Years And The Eno Trilogy		Dec. 14, 1990
Bowie, David: U.S. Discography And Price Guide		Dec. 14, 1990
Bowie, David: U.S. Discography And Price Guide		Jan. 11, 1991
Bowie, David: Unreleased Bowie (Is Rykodisc Holding		
Back The Good Stuff)/Tony Visconti	I	Dec. 14, 1990
Boxcar Willie	I	Nov. 1983
Boy George and the Culture Club	I, D	Dec. 8, 1995
Boydcarthage, Joe Records	I	Nov. 21, 1986
Bradley, Jan	I	Dec. 30, 1988
Bradley, Jan	I,D	Nov. 22, 1996

Entry	Code	Date	Entry	Code	Date
Byrds, The/Roger McGuinn	I	Nov. 22, 1996	Carter, Clarence		Dec. 1983
			Carter, Clarence		May 11, 1984
C			Carter, Clarence		July 20, 1984
C.J. Records	D	March+April 1977	Carter, Clarence	DA	Feb. 15, 1985
C.J. Records/Carl Jones	I,D	March 1982	Carter, Mel	I,D	March 15, 1985
C.O.D.'s	D	Dec. 1977	Carter, Mel	DA	Feb. 13, 1987
C/Z Records		March 18, 1994	Carthage Records/Joe Boyd	I	Nov. 21, 1986
C/Z Records discography		Apr. 17, 1992	Caruso, Enrico		June 1980
Cadence Records	D	Nov. 1981	Casa Grande Records/Frank Paul	I,D	Jan. 1980
Cadets, the/Jacks	I,D	April 26, 1996	Cash, Alvin	D	Feb. 1978
Cadillacs	D	April 6, 1990	Cash, Alvin	D	Aug. 1980
Cadillacs	DA	Aug. 24, 1990	Cash, Johnny		Dec. 20, 1985
Cahan, Andy/Grandmothers	I	June 1981	Cash, Johnny	I	July 19, 1996
Cale, John	I, D	Dec. 23, 1994	Cashman and West	I, D	April 30, 1993
Cale, John and Moe Tucker/Velvets	I	May 24, 1996	Cashman, Pistilli & West	D	Dec. 1981
California, Randy/Spirit	I,D	May 23, 1986	Cashman, Terry	D	Dec. 1981
Cameo	D	Aug. 14, 1987	Cassidy, Ed/Spirit	I	May 9, 1986
Cameo Parkway Records		Nov. 4, 1988	Castaways		July-Aug. 1977
Cameo Parkway Records		May 5, 1989	Castaways/Dennis Craswell/Roy Hensley	I	Dec. 1, 1989
Cameron, George/Left Banke	I,D	May 20, 1988	Castillo, Emilio/Tower Of Power	I,D	March 24, 1989
Cameron, George/Left Banke	DA	Dec. 2, 1988	Castle Communications Records/Terry Shand	I	Sept. 7, 1990
Camp, Jon/Renaissance	I	Aug. 1979	Caston, Leonard/Five Breezes	I,D	Jan. 4, 1985
Campbell, Little Milton	I, D	Oct. 28, 1994	Castro, Peppy/Blues Magoos	I,D	May 1983
Camper Van Beethoven/David Lowery	I,D	Nov. 4, 1988	Castro, Peppy/Blues Magoos	DA	Dec. 7, 1984
Campi, Ray	I,D	March+April 1977	Cat Record Label	D	May 25, 1984
Campi, Ray	I	July 1982	Cataloging Your Record Collection		Oct. 1980
Can/Holger Czukay	I,D	Oct. 19, 1990	Cavaliere, Felix/Rascals	I,D	Jan. 1981
Canadian Music		May 24, 1996	Cavaliere, Felix/Rascals	I,D	May 6, 1988
Canadian Music		Sept. 27, 1996	Cavaliere, Felix/Rascals		July 1, 1988
Canned Heat/Fito De La Parra	I,D	Sept. 12, 1986	Cavaliere, Felix/Rascals	DA	Aug. 26, 1988
Cannibal And The Headhunters/Frankie			Cavaliere, Felix/Rascals	DA	Aug. 26, 1988
"Cannibal" Garcia,	I,D	Nov. 1983	Cavaliere, Felix/Rascals	DA	Sept. 9, 1988
Cannon, Ace		June 17, 1988	Cave, Nick	I,D	March 14, 1997
Cannon, Freddie	I,D	Nov. 1979	Cavern's/Bob Wooler	I	Nov. 8, 1996
Cannon, Freddie		May 1980	CBS's One-Sided Singles	D	Sept. 9, 1988
Cannon, Freddie	D,DO	Oct. 1983	CD Longevity		Sept. 18, 1992
Capaldi, Jim/Traffic	I,D	April 13, 1984	Celebrating Ten Years Of The "Vinyl Junkie"/Cub Koda,	I,D	Oct. 20, 1989
Capitols (Not The Karen Recording Group)		April 1979	Censored! An Overview Of The History Of Banned And		
Capitols/Ollie Mc Laughlin (Record Label Owner),	I,D	June 3, 1988	Censored Records In America	D	Feb. 22, 1991
Capitols/Ollie Mc Laughlin (Record Label Owner),	I,D	June 3, 1988	Censorship: Dave Marsh	I	Feb. 22, 1991
Caplin, Arnold/Biograph Records	I	Sept. 7, 1990	Censorship: Frank Zappa	I	Feb. 22, 1991
Capris		Dec. 1, 1989	Censorship: Jennifer Norwood	I	Feb. 22, 1991
Captain Beefheart	D	Oct. 24, 1986	Censorship: Parent Group (PMRC) Seeks Warning		
Cara, Irene	D	June 5, 1987	Labels On Music		Sept. 13, 1985
Cara, Irene	DA	Dec. 4, 1987	Censorship: Pat Boone	I	Feb. 22, 1991
Caravan	D	Oct. 6, 1989	Cervenka, Exene/X	I	Oct. 1982
Carbo, Chuck/Spiders	I,D	Jan. 29, 1988	Chad And Jeremy	I,D	April 13, 1984
Carbo, Chuck/Spiders	DA	July 1, 1988	Chadwick, Porky	I	Feb. 1980
Cardinals	D	April 6, 1990	Chairmen Of The Board/Norman Johnson	I,D	Nov. 16, 1990
Cardona, Pepe/Alive 'N Kickin'	I	Dec. 1, 1989	Chambers Brothers	D	March 25, 1988
Carella, Vinny/Randy And The Rainbows	I,D	Feb. 8, 1991	Chambers Brothers	D	March 25, 1988
Caribbean Christmas Music	D	Dec. 25, 1992	Chambers Brothers, the	I, D	May 13, 1994
Carman, Brian/Chantays	I,D	Dec. 16, 1988	Champaign	D	April 10, 1987
Carmen, Eric	I	Feb. 13, 1987	Champlin, Bill		June 20, 1997
Carmen, Eric	D	Feb. 24, 1989	Champs	I,D	Aug. 1982
Carmen, Eric	I	Feb. 13, 1987	Champs	DA	Oct. 1983
Carnival Rock (The Movie)		Dec. 1980	Champs/Danny Flores	I,D	Aug. 12, 1988
Carr, Phyllis/Quin-Tones	I,D	Dec. 28, 1990	Chance Records		Sept. 17, 1993
Carr, Vikki	D	Feb. 1982	Chance, Larry/Earls	I,D	Sept. 27, 1985
Carrasco, Joe "King"	I	Oct. 16, 1992	Chance, Larry/Earls	DA	Feb. 13, 1987
Carroll, Jim	I	Aug. 1982	Chance, Nolan	D	July-Aug. 1978
Carroll, Jimmy		Aug. 1982	Chandler, Bryan 'Chas'		Aug. 16, 1996
Carroll, Johnny	D	July 1980	Chandler, Gene	I,D	Jan. 1980
Cars, The	I,D	Aug. 1, 1997	Channel 3	D	Feb. 1979
Carson, Martha	D	May 25, 1984	Channel, Bruce	I,D	May 1982
Carson, Martha	DA	May 24, 1985	Chantays	D	Sept. 1980
Carter, Clarence	I,D	Oct. 1983	Chantays/Brian Carman/Bob Spickard	I,D	Dec. 16, 1988

Entry	Code	Date
Collins, Tommy	DA	Aug. 1982
Collins, William "Bootsy"	I,D	Jan. 25, 1991
Colorado Record Stores		Sept. 25, 1987
Colorado Record Stores		Nov. 17, 1989
Coltrane, John	D	June 23, 1995
Columbia Historic Editions		June 1982
Columbia/Epic Playback Series	D	April 8, 1988
Columbia/Epic Playback Series	DA	July 1, 1988
Columbia/Epic Playback Series	DA	Dec. 2, 1988
Communications Files: A Chronology Of Useful Trivia		March 15, 1985
Compact Disc Guide (Highlights Of 1988)		Feb. 10, 1989
Compact Disc Guide (Highlights Of 1988)		April 7, 1989
Compact Disc Holiday Shopping Guide (1990)		Nov. 2, 1990
Compact Disc Holiday Shopping Guide (1990)		Nov. 16, 1990
Compact Disc Holiday Shopping Guide (1990)		Jan. 11, 1991
Compact Disc Reissue Boom		July 27, 1990
Compact Disc Wants And Desires Of Goldmine Readers Poll		March 11, 1988
Compact Discs (Bruce Eder)		Jan. 1, 1988
Compact Discs (Bruce Eder)		Feb. 12, 1988
Compact Discs (Bruce Eder)		March 25, 1988
Compact Discs (Bruce Eder)		June 3, 1988
Compact Discs (Bruce Eder)		July 15, 1988
Compact Discs (Bruce Eder)		Sept. 9, 1988
Compact Discs (Bruce Eder)		Oct. 21, 1988
Compact Discs (Bruce Eder)		Dec. 2, 1988
Compact Discs (Bruce Eder)		Jan. 13, 1989
Compact Discs (Bruce Eder)		April 7, 1989
Compact Discs (Bruce Eder)		June 2, 1989
Compact Discs (Bruce Eder)		July 28, 1989
Compact Discs (Bruce Eder)		Oct. 6, 1989
Compact Discs (Bruce Eder)		Nov. 17, 1989
Compact Discs (Bruce Eder)		April 6, 1990
Compact Discs (Bruce Eder)		Aug. 10, 1990
Compact Discs (Bruce Eder)		Oct. 5, 1990
Compact Discs (Bruce Eder)		Nov. 30, 1990
Compact Discs (Bruce Eder)		Feb. 22, 1991
Compact Discs British Invasion		Dec. 4, 1987
Compact Discs Explaining CD + G And Oversampling		June 29, 1990
Compact Discs: A Guide To Recent Reissues		July 27, 1990
Compact Discs: A Guide To Recent Reissues		Aug. 10, 1990
Complete Control (Philip Grabash))		
Complete Control: Cramps		Jan. 1979
Complete Control:Slits		May 1980
Computer Assisted Record Collecting		March 29, 1985
Computerized Record Files		Dec. 1981
Comstock, Bobby	I,D	July-Aug. 1977
Conley, Arthur	D	June 15, 1990
Connor, Charles	I,D	April 10, 1987
Constellation Records	I	May 9, 1997
Continental Cowboys: Country Music In Sweden		June 8, 1984
Contours/Joe Billingslea	I,D	Nov. 21, 1986
Cooder, Ry	D	Jan. 1, 1988
Cook, Little Joe	D	Oct. 23, 1987
Cooke, Sam		Sept.-Oct. 1976
Cooke, Sam		Nov. 1977
Cooke, Sam	D	Jan. 2, 1987
Cooke, Sam	DA	Feb. 13, 1987
Cooke, Sam		Feb. 26, 1988
Cooper, Alice	I,D	March 9, 1990
Cooper, Michael (Photographer)		March 9, 1990
Cooper, Neil/Roir Records	I,D	March 1, 1985
Copas, Cowboy		July-Aug. 1977
Cope, Julian		May 8, 1987
Copeland, Johnny	D	April 22, 1988
Copyright Basics for Record Collectors		June 29, 1990
Corea, Chick	I, D	March 5, 1993
Corntry & Worstern		Dec. 1977

Entry	Code	Date
Correro, Joe/Paul Revere & The Raiders	I	April 20, 1990
Corsairs, The		Dec. 1, 1989
Cosby, Hank	I	Oct. 1980
Costabile, Toni/Poni-Tails	I	Dec. 1, 1989
Costello, Elvis	D	Jan. 1983
Costello, Elvis	I	Dec. 1983
Costello, Elvis	DA	Nov. 23, 1984
Costello, Elvis	DA	Dec. 7, 1984
Cotton, James	I,D	Aug. 26, 1988
Cotton, James	I,D	Aug. 26, 1988
Count Five		Dec. 30, 1988
Counterfeits, Bootlegs, The Law And You		June 1, 1990
Country Joe & The Fish/Country Joe		
Country Joe & The Fish/Country Joe		
Country Music And The Hall Of Fame		Nov.-Dec. 1976
Country Music, Early Days Of		Feb. 1978
Courtney, Ron/Nine Nobles	I	May 9, 1986
Cousin Brucie (Morrow) (Dj)	I	Jan. 1983
Cover Records Of The Fifties	D	Sept.-Oct. 1976
Cowboy Carl Records	D	June 1980
Cowboy Jazz/Barry Sless	I	Aug. 1982
Cowboy Junkies/Margo Timmins	I	June 30, 1989
Cox, Herbie/Cleftones	I,D	May 1980
Cramps		Jan. 1979
Cramps		June 19, 1987
Cramps, the	D	July 7, 1995
Craswell, Roy/Castaways	I	Dec. 1, 1989
Crawford, Kent/Vanguard Records	I	Sept. 7, 1990
Cray, Robert	I,D	April 24, 1987
Creach, Papa John		Oct. 30, 1992
Cream/Ginger Baker/Jack Bruce/Felix Pappalardi	I	Oct. 11, 1985
Creedence Clearwater Revival/John Fogerty	I,D	June 8, 1984
Creedence Clearwater Revival/John Fogerty		July 20, 1984
Creedence Clearwater Revival/John Fogerty	DA	Feb. 1, 1985
Creedence Clearwater Revival/Tom Fogerty	I	May 24, 1985
Crenshaw, Marshall		Feb. 1982
Crenshaw, Marshall	I	Aug. 1983
Crenshaw, Marshall	I	Aug. 1983
Crests/Johnny Maestro	I	March+April 1977
Crewcuts, The	I,D	Sept. 9, 1988
Crewcuts, The/Pat Barrett	I,D	June 1982
Crewe, Bob	D	Oct. 1983
Crewe, Bob	I	July 1, 1988
Crickets, The/Jerry Allison	I	May-June 1978
Crickets, The/Joe Mauldin	I	May-June 1978
Crickets, The/Joe Mauldin	D	Feb. 10, 1989
Crickets, The/Niki Sullivan	I,D	Sept. 1978
Crickets, The/Niki Sullivan	D	Sept. 14, 1984
Criss, Peter/Kiss	I	June 29, 1990
Critters, The/Don Ciccone	I,D	Oct. 24, 1986
Critters, The/Don Ciccone	DA	Dec. 5, 1986
Croce, Jim	D	June 30, 1989
Crockett, G.L.	D	April 8, 1988
Crockett, G.L.	D	April 8, 1988
Cropper, Steve	I	June 15, 1990
Crosby, Bing	D	Dec. 1977
Crosby, Bing	D	Dec. 24, 1993
Crosby, Bing/Big Broadcast Of 1932		Aug. 1979
Crosby, David	I	Oct. 1982
Crosby, David	I,D	Nov. 1982
Crosby, David	I, D	July 7, 1995
Crosby, Still and Nash	I,D	Jan. 24, 1992
Crossfires, The	I,D	Dec. 1981
Crossroads (See "On Making Crossroads)		
Crow, Sheryl	I	May 24, 1996
Crowded House	I, D	Mar. 6, 1992
Crowell, Rodney	I,D	Feb. 9, 1990

Crows, The		April 8, 1988	Davies, Dave/Kinks	I,D	April 1981
Crystals, The/Dee Dee Kennibrew	I,D	Dec. 1980	Davies, Ray	I	March 1, 1996
Crystals, The/Dee Dee Kennibrew	I	Oct. 1983	Davis, Dale	D	Dec. 1978
Crystals, The/Lala Brooks	I	June 17, 1988	Davis, Danny/Philles Records	I	June 17, 1988
Cultivating The Motown Catalog		June 20, 1986	Davis, Gregory/Dirty Dozen Brass Band	I,D	Dec. 15, 1989
Culture Club and Boy George	I, D	Dec. 8, 1995	Davis, Hank	I,D	Sept. 8, 1989
Cumberland Three, The	D	March 1980	Davis, James	I,D	April 22, 1988
Cummings, Burton/Guess Who	I,D	June 30, 1989	Davis, James	I,D	April 22, 1988
Cummings, Burton/Guess Who		Aug.11, 1989	Davis, Larry	D	July 1, 1988
Cummings, Burton/Guess Who		Sept. 8, 1989	Davis, Miles	I,D	July 13, 1990
Cummings, Burton/Guess Who	DA	Oct. 6, 1989	Davis, Skeeter	I,D	Jan. 31, 1986
Cuneiform Records		June 2, 1989	Davis, Skeeter		April 11, 1986
Cunningham, B.B./Hombres	I	Dec. 1, 1989	Davis, Skeeter		April 11, 1986
Cure, the	D	July 9, 1993	Davis, Skeeter		April 25, 1986
Curtis, Mac (Wesley Erwin Curtis)		Nov. 1977	Davis, Skeeter		May 9, 1986
Curtis, Mac (Wesley Erwin Curtis)	D	Oct. 1983	Davis, Skeeter	DA	May 9, 1986
Curtis, Mac (Wesley Erwin Curtis)	DA	Feb. 15, 1985	Davis, Spencer/The Spencer Davis Group	I,D	Oct. 1983
Curtis, Sonny	I	July 18, 1986	Davis, Spencer/The Spencer Davis Group		Dec. 1983
Curtola, Boby (Bobby)	I,D	April 8, 1988	Davis, Spencer/The Spencer Davis Group	DA	May 11, 1984
Curtola, Boby (Bobby)	I,D	April 8, 1988	Davis, Tyrone	D	Dec. 1980
Curved Air		March 25, 1988	Day The Music Died, The		May-June 1978
Curved Air		March 25, 1988	Day, Bobby	I,D	May 23, 1986
Cylinder Discs		Oct. 23, 1987	Day, Bobby		July 4, 1986
Cylinder Discs: Those Old CD's (Cylinder Discs)		Oct. 23, 1987	Day, Bobby	DA	Oct. 24, 1986
Cymbal, Johnny/Derek	I	Dec. 1, 1989	Day, Bobby	DA	Dec. 5, 1986
Cyrkle/Don Dannemann	I,D	July 1982	Day, Bobby	DA	Jan. 2, 1987
Cyrus, Billy Ray	I	Dec. 25, 1992	Daye, Cory/Dr. Buzzard's Original Savannah Band		Feb. 12, 1988
Czukay, Holger/Can	I,D	Oct. 19, 1990	Daylighters, The	D	Dec. 1978
			Daylighters, The	D	Feb. 1981
D			DCC Compact Classics		Sept. 17, 1993
D'Arby, Terence Trent		June 17, 1988	De Barge		July 17, 1987
Dab Record Label	D	Aug. 1979	De La Parra, Fito/Canned Heat	I,D	Sept. 12, 1986
Daddy G (Gene Barge)	I,D	March 1982	De Lauro, Tony		Sept. 1981
Dale, Dick & The Del-Tones	I,D	July 1983	DeMent, Iris	I	Jan. 17, 1997
Daltrey, Roger	I	July 8, 1994	De Santo, Sugar Pie	D	July 3, 1987
Damned	D	Feb. 7, 1992	De Santo, Sugar Pie	D	July 3, 1987
Damned	DA	Mar. 20, 1992	De Shannon, Jackie	D	Feb. 1982
Dana, Vic	D	Jan. 1978	De Shannon, Jackie	DA	May 1982
Dando, Evan	I	Dec. 20, 1996	De Shannon, Jackie	DA	June 1982
Daniel, Howard/Charioteers	I,D	June 1980	De Shannon, Jackie	DA	Jan. 1983
Danko, Rick and Levon Helm of The Band	I	Aug. 16, 1996	DeFever, Warren	I	March 14, 1997
Dannemann, Don/Cyrkle	I,D	July 1982	De Vorzon, Barry/Barry & The Tamerlanes	I	Dec. 1, 1989
Danny & The Juniors/Joe Terranova	I	Nov.-Dec. 1976	Dead Kennedys/Jello Biafra	I,D	March 24, 1989
Danny & The Juniors/Joe Terry	I,D	May 9, 1986	Dean, James (The Actor)	D	Jan. 1981
Danny & The Juniors/Terranova, Joe	I	Nov.-Dec. 1976	Deary, Joan	I	Jan. 1983
Danny & The Juniors/Terry, Joe	I,D	May 9, 1986	Decca 'Sepia' Series	D	Nov. 9, 1984
Dante and the Evergreens	I, D	Sept. 29, 1995	Decca Records		Aug. 19, 1994
Dante, Ron	D	Sept. 8, 1989	Dedicated Follower In Fandom		Aug. 1982
Darin, Bobby	D	March 1981	Dee, Dave, Dozy, Beaky, Mick & Tich/Dave Harmon	I,D	Oct. 21, 1988
Darin, Bobby	DA	June 1981	Dee, Joey & The Starlighters	I,D	Nov. 1977
Darin, Bobby	DA	Nov. 21, 1986	Dee, Joey & The Starlighters	I,D	Aug. 17, 1984
Darin, Bobby	DA	Dec. 4, 1987	Dee, Joey & The Starlighters	DA	Feb. 1, 1985
Darin, Bobby	DA	April 7, 1989	Deep Purple	D	May 19, 1989
Darin, Bobby	D	April 7, 1989	Deep River Boys/Harry Douglass	I,D	July 1979
Darin, Bobby	D	Oct. 27, 1995	Deep River Boys/Harry Douglass		Oct. 1979
Dark Horse Records	D	July 29, 1988	Deep River Boys/Harry Douglass		March 1980
Darnell, Larry	I,D	July 1980	Deep River Boys/Harry Douglass	DA	April 1980
Darnell, Larry	DA	Dec. 1980	Def Leppard	I, D	June 11, 1993
Darren, James	I,D	Dec. 1982	Defense Of The Compact Disc		July 27, 1990
Darren, James		Feb. 1983	Del Ray, Teisco	I	July 8, 1994
Darren, James	DA	Sept. 1983	Del Santo, Dan	I	April 21, 1989
Dateline: Charly & Ace Records		Dec. 7, 1984	Del Vikings	D	Feb. 21, 1992
Dateline: Demon Records		Oct. 12, 1984	Del-Lords	I	Aug. 16, 1985
Dateline: London (Mark Pugash)			Del-Lords, The	I	Aug. 16, 1985
Dateline: Rock Auction		Jan. 18, 1985	Delaney & Bonnie		June 5, 1987
Dave Clark Five	I, D	Sept. 3, 1993	Delaney & Bonnie		June 5, 1987
Davies, Bob/The Rhythm Jesters	D	April 12, 1996	Delivery	D	Oct. 6, 1989

Entry	Code	Date	Entry	Code	Date
Dells/Chuck Barksdale/Marvin Junior/Mickey Mc Gill	I,D	May 25, 1984	Diggin' Up Discographies: Motown Records	D	Dec. 1977
Dells/Chuck Barksdale/Marvin Junior/Mickey Mc Gill	I,D	July 20, 1984	Diggin' Up Discographies: Motown Records	D	Feb. 1978
Dells/Chuck Barksdale/Marvin Junior/Mickey Mc Gill	I,D	Aug. 3, 1984	Diggin' Up Discographies: Soul Records	D	Sept. 1977
Dells/Chuck Barksdale/Marvin Junior/Mickey Mc Gill	DA	Feb. 15, 1985	Diggin' Up Discographies: Soul Records	D	Oct. 1977
Delmark Records/Bob Koester	I	June 2, 1989	Diggin' Up Discographies: Starla Records	D	March 1976
Delmore Brothers, The	D	Oct. 1981	Diggin' Up Discographies: Tamla Records	D	May-June 1977
Delta Rhythm Boys/Lee Gaines	D	March 1979	Diggin' Up Discographies: Tamla Records	D	July-Aug. 1977
Delta Rhythm Boys/Lee Gaines	DA	May 1979	Diggin' Up Discographies: Tri-Phi	D	Nov. 1978
Demon Records		Oct. 12, 1984	Digging In The Dust (Pete Grendysa)		May 1976
Demon Records/Andy Childs	I	June 2, 1989	Digging In The Dust (Pete Grendysa)		March+April 1977
Densmore, John/Doors		June 21, 1985	Digging In The Dust (Pete Grendysa)		May-June 1977
Densmore, John/Doors		July 5, 1985	Digging In The Dust (Pete Grendysa)		July-Aug. 1977
Depeche Mode	D	May 27, 1994	Digging In The Dust (Pete Grendysa)		Sept. 1977
Derek/Johnny Cymbal	I	Dec. 1, 1989	Digging In The Dust (Pete Grendysa)		March 1978
Derringer, Rick	I,D	Feb. 1983	Digging In The Dust (Pete Grendysa)		July-Aug. 1978
Derringer, Rick		April 1983	Digging In The Dust (Pete Grendysa)		Sept. 1978
Derringer, Rick	DA	Dec. 7, 1984	Digging In The Dust (Pete Grendysa)		Nov. 1978
Design, Diplomat & Other Budget Record Labels, D		Sept. 9, 1988	Digging In The Dust (Pete Grendysa)		Dec. 1978
Detroit Discographies	D	March+April 1977	Digging In The Dust (Pete Grendysa)		Jan. 1980
Detroit Gospel Quartets		Nov. 20, 1987	Digging In The Dust: Atlantic Records 78 RPM Albums	D	Nov.-Dec. 1976
Detroit's '60s Rock Scene		Dec. 4, 1987	Digging In The Dust: Atlantic Records Colorography		Dec. 1978
Detroit's '60s Rock Scene		Dec. 4, 1987	Digging In The Dust: Atlantic's Minor Series		Jan.-Feb. 1977
Deutekom, Cristina	D	May 25, 1984	Digging In The Dust: Bihari Brothers		May 1979
Devo	D	March 9, 1990	Digging In The Dust: Films Featuring Rock & Roll		Sept.-Oct. 1976
Devo	DA	April 6, 1990	Digging In The Dust: Glory Of Love		July 1976
Devo	DA	April 20, 1990	Digging In The Dust: Hits Of 1951		Feb. 1976
Devo	DA	June 29, 1990	Digging In The Dust: Hits Of 1952		March 1976
Devotions, The		Dec. 1, 1989	Digging In The Dust: Honkers & Shouters (The Book)		Sept. 1979
Dexys Midnight Runners	I	April 1983	Digging In The Dust: Honkers & Shouters (The Book)		Dec. 1979
Dexys Midnight Runners		Dec. 30, 1988	Digging In The Dust: Ivory Joe Hunter	D	Oct. 1978
Dexys Midnight Runners	D	Feb. 14, 1997	Digging In The Dust: J. Caleb Ginyard		Nov. 1977
Diablos, The		July-Aug. 1977	Digging In The Dust: J. Caleb Ginyard		Dec. 1977
Diablos, The		Jan. 3, 1986	Digging In The Dust: Kansas City (The Song)		June 1979
Diablos, The/Nolan Strong		July-Aug. 1977	Digging In The Dust: R&B Collector		May-June 1978
Diablos, The/Nolan Strong	D	Jan. 3, 1986	Digging In The Dust: Story Of Music Licensing Societies		Jan. 1979
Diablos, The/Nolan Strong		June 20, 1986	Digging In The Dust: Story Of Music Licensing Societies		Feb. 1979
Diamond Head	D	June 11, 1993	Digging In The Dust: Story Of Music Licensing Societies		March 1979
Diamond, Lee (DJ)	I	April 1983	Digging In The Dust: Treniers	D	Feb. 1978
Diamond, Neil		Sept. 1983	Digging In The Dust: Wilbert Harrison	D	June 1979
Diamond, Neil	D	Sept. 1983	Digital Technology And The Compact Disc		March 2, 1984
Diamond, Neil	DA	May 11, 1984	Dillard, Varetta	D	May 20, 1988
Diamond, Neil	DA	July 20, 1984	Diltz, Henry/MFG	I,D	Nov. 30, 1990
Diamond, Neil	DA	Nov. 23, 1984	Dino, Desi & Billy/Billy Hinsche	I,D	Dec. 6, 1985
Diamond, Neil		Sept. 11, 1987	Dino, Kenny	I, D	May 15, 1992
Diamonds, The	I,D	June 5, 1987	Dinosaurs/Barry Melton	I	Aug. 1983
Diamonds/David Somerville	I	March 2, 1984	Dinwiddie Colored Quartet	D	June 1979
Dickinson, Jim	I, D	Sept. 16, 1994	Dion	I	Aug. 29, 1986
Diddley's, Bo Top Ten		Feb. 1980	Dion	I,D	Aug. 28, 1987
Diddley, Bo	I	Sept.-Oct. 1976	Dion		Dec. 4, 1987
Diddley, Bo	I	June 21, 1985	Dion		Jan. 1, 1988
Diddley, Bo	I	Feb. 26, 1988	Dion		May 6, 1988
Diddley, Bo	I,D	July 27, 1990	Dion	I	Feb. 10, 1989
Diddley, Bo [Doo Wop Career]	D	April 16, 1993	Dipsyland Jazz		Jan. 1978
Diddley, Bo		March 1, 1996	Dirty Dozen Brass Band/Gregory Davis	I,D	Dec. 15, 1989
Diddley, Bo		April, 26, 1996	Dischord Records		March 18, 1994
Diddley, Bo	I	Feb. 28, 1997	Dixie Cups, The	I, D	May 27, 1994
DiFranco, Ani		May 9, 1997	Dixie Cups/Barbara Hawkins/Rosa Hawkins	I,D	Dec. 5, 1986
Dig Records	D	May 1976	Dixon, Clarence/Four Knights	I,D	Sept. 1979
Diggin' Up Discographies (Gary Calta)			Dixon, Clarence/Four Knights		May 1980
Diggin' Up Discographies: Anna Records	D	Sept.-Oct. 1976	Dixon, Clarence/Four Knights	I,D	March 1981
Diggin' Up Discographies: Cobra Records	D	July 1976	Dixon, Floyd	I,D	Feb. 23, 1990
Diggin' Up Discographies: Dig Records	D	May 1976	Dixon, Willie	I,D	Jan. 1982
Diggin' Up Discographies: Early Motown LPs	D	May-June 1978	Dixon, Willie		March 1982
Diggin' Up Discographies: Gordy Records	D	Nov.-Dec. 1976	Dixon, Willie		Feb. 24, 1989
Diggin' Up Discographies: Gordy Records	D	Jan.-Feb. 1977	Dixon, Willie	D	Feb. 23, 1990
Diggin' Up Discographies: Mel-O-Dy Records	D	March+April 1977	Dixon, Willie—tribute		Mar. 20, 1992
Diggin' Up Discographies: Motown LPs	D	May-June 1978	Do, Dicky & The Don'ts/Gerry Granahan	I,D	Dec. 28, 1990

Entry	Code	Date	Entry	Code	Date
Dobkins, Carl Jr.	I,D	Aug. 1980	Duran Duran	D	June 12, 1992
Doggett, Bill	I,D	Aug. 1979	Durden, Tommy	D	March 1, 1985
Doggett, Bill		Nov. 1979	Dyke and the Blazers	I, D	May 14, 1993
Doggett, Bill		Jan. 1980	Dylan, Bob	D	May 1980
Doggett, Bill		May 1980	Dylan, Bob	DA	July 1980
Doggett, Bill	I,D	May 10, 1985	Dylan, Bob	DA	Aug. 1980
Doggett, Bill	DA	July 19, 1985	Dylan, Bob	DA	Nov. 7, 1986
Doggett, Bill	DA	Feb. 13, 1987	Dylan, Bob	DA	Feb. 26, 1988
Dohanyi, Christoph Von: The Cleveland Orchestra		June 8, 1984	Dylan, Bob	DA	July 1, 1988
Dojo Records		March 18, 1994	Dylan, Bob		July 1, 1988
Domino, Fats	I	Feb. 1981	Dylan, Bob An Annotated Discography Of Albums		
Domino, Fats		Feb. 26, 1988	Featuring Dylan Songs	D	Dec. 1983
Domino, Fats	DA	Apr. 3, 1992	Dylan, Bob As A Student		Aug. 25, 1989
Don And Den	D	May 1976	Dylan, Bob Goes Digital (A Guide To Bad Recordings On CD)	D	Aug. 25
Don And Den	D	May 1976	1989		
Don And Juan	I	Dec. 30, 1988	Dylan, Bob In Print	D	Aug. 25, 1989
Don And The Goodtimes		July 1976	Dylan, Bob in the mid-'70s	D	Sept. 30, 1994
Donnegan, Lonnie		March 27, 1987	Dylan, Bob: An Annotated Discography Of Foreign		
Donner, Ral	I,D	Nov. 1979	Bob Dylan Albums	D	Aug. 25, 1989
Donner, Ral	D	Aug. 14, 1987	Dylan, Bob: Discography And Price Guide	D	Aug. 25, 1989
Donovan	I,D	Dec. 5, 1986			
Donovan	D	Nov. 13, 1992	E		
Doors, The	D	July 19, 1985	E (Escovedo), Sheila	I,D	Sept. 23, 1988
Doors, The On Compact Disc		Feb. 10, 1989	E Street Band, The	I	March 23, 1990
Doors, The/John Densmore/Ray Manzarek		June 21, 1985	Eagles, the	D	July 9, 1993
Doors, The/John Densmore/Ray Manzarek		July 5, 1985	Earle, Steve	I,D	Feb. 9, 1990
Dore Records	D	Dec. 1978	Earle, Steve	DA	July 13, 1990
Dore Records	DA	March 1979	Earle, Steve	I	Dec. 6, 1996
Dorman, Harold	D	Sept. 23, 1988	Earls, Jack		July 1976
Dorsey, Lee		Jan. 30, 1987	Earls/Larry Chance	I,D	Sept. 27, 1985
Dorsey, Tommy	D	June 10, 1994	Earls/Larry Chance	DA	Feb. 13, 1987
Double Puzzle (Charles Reinhart)			Early Rock Cinema		Sept. 1979
Double Puzzle: Groups/Lead Singers		Dec. 19, 1986	Earwig	I	May 10, 1996
Double Puzzle: One Word Song Titles		Nov. 21, 1986	East-West Record Label	D	Dec. 21, 1984
Douglas, Chip/MFG	I,D	Nov. 30, 1990	Easton, Lynn/Kingsmen	D	Aug. 1983
Douglass, Harry/Deep River Boys	I,D	July 1979	Eddie & The Cruisers/Kenny Vance	I	Aug. 1, 1986
Douglass, Harry/Deep River Boys		Oct. 1979	Eddie & The Showmen	D	Oct. 1981
Douglass, Harry/Deep River Boys		March 1980	Eddy, Duane	I,D	Oct. 9, 1987
Douglass, Harry/Deep River Boys	DA	April 1980	Eddy, Duane	DA	April 22, 1988
Dovells/Jerry Gross	I,D	Jan. 1982	Edit Records: Schwartz, Bernard/Time/Edit Records	I,D	Sept. 7, 1990
Dowd, Tom	I	Dec. 6, 1996	Edmunds, Dave		Oct. 1977
Downing, Al		Aug. 1981	Edmunds, Dave		May 8, 1987
Dozier, Lamont	I	June 20, 1986	Edmunds, Dave	I, D	May 13, 1994
Dr. Buzzard's Original Savannah Band/Cory Daye	I	Feb. 12, 1988	Edwards, Tommy (The Dj, Not The Singer)	I	Jan. 1981
Dr. Buzzard's Original Savannah Band/Cory Daye	I	Feb. 12, 1988	Egan, Walter/Malibooz	I,D	March 2, 1984
Dr. Demento	I	Feb. 14, 1986	Egg	D	Oct. 6, 1989
Dr. Hook/Dennis Locorriere/Ray Sawyer	I,D	April 1981	Eight Days A Week (Not The Song)		Jan. 1978
Dr. John	I,D	April 24, 1987	Eight Tracks		April 13, 1984
Dragon, Paul		March 1978	Eighties R&B		
Drake, Nick		Jan. 16, 1987	Eighties R&B: A.C. Reed	D	Nov. 4, 1988
Drake, Nick		Jan. 16, 1987	Eighties R&B: Anita Baker	I,D	May 22, 1987
Drake, Nick	D	Sept. 3, 1993	Eighties R&B: Artie White	D	Dec. 16, 1988
Draper, Terry/Klaatu	I,D	Sept. 11, 1987	Eighties R&B: Buckwheat Zydeco	I,D	Aug. 12, 1988
Draper, Terry/Klaatu	DA	Nov. 20, 1987	Eighties R&B: Cameo	D	Aug. 14, 1987
Dreamlovers/James Ray Dunn	I,D	Dec. 28, 1990	Eighties R&B: Chaka Khan	D	July 31, 1987
Dreamlovers/James Ray Dunn	DA	Jan. 11, 1991	Eighties R&B: Champaign	D	April 10, 1987
Drifters		Feb. 26, 1988	Eighties R&B: De Barge		July 17, 1987
Drifters/Bill Pinckney	I	May-June 1978	Eighties R&B: Eddy Clearwater	D	Dec. 4, 1987
Drive-In Movie: Things Got Groovy At The Drive-In Movie		Sept. 8, 1989	Eighties R&B: Fat Boys	D	Dec. 18, 1987
Duke, Patty		Dec. 1, 1989	Eighties R&B: Freddie Jackson	I	March 27, 1987
Duke/Peacock Records		Sept. 7, 1990	Eighties R&B: Gloria Estefan & Miami Sound Machine	I	Oct. 21, 1988
Dunbar, Mickey/Renaissance	I	Aug. 1979	Eighties R&B: Irene Cara	D	June 5, 1987
Dunbar, Richard/Knight Brothers	I,D	Dec. 1983	Eighties R&B: Janet Jackson	D	Jan. 1, 1988
Duncan, Cleve/Penguins	I	Dec. 1, 1989	Eighties R&B: Jeffrey Osborne	D	Sept. 11, 1987
Duncan, High Pockets	I	Sept. 1979	Eighties R&B: Jets	D	April 8, 1988
Dunn, James Ray/Dreamlovers	I,D	Dec. 28, 1990	Eighties R&B: Jimmy Johnson	D	Feb. 12, 1988
Duprees/Joey Vann	D	March 1, 1985	Eighties R&B: Jody Watley	I	Oct. 9, 1987

Eighties R&B: John Lee Hooker	D	Jan. 16, 1987
Eighties R&B: Johnny Copeland	D	April 22, 1988
Eighties R&B: Johnny Littlejohn	D	March 25, 1988
Eighties R&B: Koko Taylor	D	May 20, 1988
Eighties R&B: Kool And The Gang	D	Feb. 13, 1987
Eighties R&B: Larry Davis	D	July 1, 1988
Eighties R&B: Lionel Richie	D	Nov. 6, 1987
Eighties R&B: Lisa Lisa And The Cult Jam		June 3, 1988
Eighties R&B: Magic Slim & The Teardrops	D	Sept. 9, 1988
Eighties R&B: Michael Jackson		March 11, 1988
Eighties R&B: New Edition	D	Feb. 27, 1987
Eighties R&B: Nile Rodgers/Chic	I,D	June 19, 1987
Eighties R&B: Prince	D	Jan. 29, 1988
Eighties R&B: Prince		Aug. 26, 1988
Eighties R&B: Richard "Dimples" Fields	D	Jan. 30, 1987
Eighties R&B: Rick James	D	May 8, 1987
Eighties R&B: Run D.M.C.	D	April 24, 1987
Eighties R&B: Sade		Nov. 20, 1987
Eighties R&B: Shalamar		Jan. 2, 1987
Eighties R&B: Shiela E	I,D	Sept. 23, 1988
Eighties R&B: Shiela E (Escovedo)	I,D	Sept. 23, 1988
Eighties R&B: Son Seals	D	Jan. 15, 1988
Eighties R&B: Teena Marie	D	July 3, 1987
Eighties R&B: Terence Trent D'Arby		June 17, 1988
Eighties R&B: Time	D	Sept. 25, 1987
Eighties R&B: Tina Turner	D	Oct. 23, 1987
Eighties R&B: Whitney Houston	D	Aug. 28, 1987
Eighties R&B: Womack And Womack/Cecil & Linda Womack	I	Dec. 2, 198
Eighties R&B: Z Z Hill	I,D	March 13, 1987
Eighties Rock		
Eighties Rock: Bangles	D	Sept. 11, 1987
Eighties Rock: Beach Boys		July 3, 1987
Eighties Rock: Beastie Boys		June 5, 1987
Eighties Rock: Billy Bragg	I	Dec. 4, 1987
Eighties Rock: Bon Jovi/Jon Bon Jovi	I	Oct. 23, 1987
Eighties Rock: Bruce Hornsby		July 17, 1987
Eighties Rock: Bruce Springsteen		Jan. 30, 1987
Eighties Rock: Camper Van Beethoven/David Lowery	I,D	Nov. 4, 1988
Eighties Rock: Church	D	Aug. 26, 1988
Eighties Rock: Cramps		June 19, 1987
Eighties Rock: Cyndi Lauper		March 25, 1988
Eighties Rock: David Lee Roth	D	Feb. 13, 1987
Eighties Rock: David Lee Roth		Jan. 13, 1989
Eighties Rock: English Beat	D	Feb. 12, 1988
Eighties Rock: Fabulous Thunderbirds		March 13, 1987
Eighties Rock: Frank Zappa		April 24, 1987
Eighties Rock: Huey Lewis & The News	D	Sept. 25, 1987
Eighties Rock: Husker Du/Bob Mould	I,D	Feb. 27, 1987
Eighties Rock: Iron Maiden	D	Oct. 21, 1988
Eighties Rock: Jason And The Scorchers	D	May 20, 1988
Eighties Rock: Joan Jett	I,D	Jan. 2, 1987
Eighties Rock: John Waite	D	Jan. 15, 1988
Eighties Rock: Julian Cope		May 8, 1987
Eighties Rock: Kate Bush	D	March 11, 1988
Eighties Rock: Long Ryders/Sid Griffin	I	Aug. 14, 1987
Eighties Rock: Los Lobos	I,D	May 22, 1987
Eighties Rock: Lyres	I,D	Sept. 9, 1988
Eighties Rock: Metallica	D	July 1, 1988
Eighties Rock: Monkees		Dec. 18, 1987
Eighties Rock: Neil Young & The Bluenotes	I	Sept. 23, 1988
Eighties Rock: Psychedelic Furs		April 10, 1987
Eighties Rock: Radiators	I,D	Jan. 29, 1988
Eighties Rock: Rank And File/Chip Kinman	I	Oct. 9, 1987
Eighties Rock: Redd Kross/Steve Mc Donald	I,D	Dec. 2, 1988
Eighties Rock: Robert Palmer		Jan. 16, 1987
Eighties Rock: Robyn Hitchcock	D	March 27, 1987
Eighties Rock: Ry Cooder	D	Jan. 1, 1988
Eighties Rock: Simply Red/Mick Hucknall	I	June 3, 1988
Eighties Rock: Sonic Youth	D	Aug. 28, 1987
Eighties Rock: Squeeze		Nov. 20, 1987
Eighties Rock: Squire	D	April 8, 1988
Eighties Rock: Suzanne Vega	I	Aug. 12, 1988
Eighties Rock: Twin/Tone Records	D	Nov. 6, 1987
Eighties Rock: U2		July 31, 1987
Eighties Rock: Van Halen	D	Feb. 13, 1987
Eighties Rock: Was (Not Was)/David Weiss	I,D	Dec. 16, 1988
Eighties Rock: Wild Seeds/Michael Hall	I,D	April 22, 1988
Eighties Rock: Wire	D	June 17, 1988
Eitzel, Mark	I	June 6, 1997
El Dorados	D	April 1979
El Dorados	D	July 1980
El Dorados		Dec. 1, 1989
El Dorados, The	I, D	June 25, 1993
Elastica		Feb. 16, 1996
Electric Light Orchestra	D	Oct. 21, 1988
Elegants, The		Dec. 30, 1988
Ellington, Duke	D	Oct. 29, 1993
Elliott, Ramblin' Jack	I	July 4, 1997
Ellipsis Arts	I, D	May 9, 1997
Ellis, Jimmy/Orion	I,D	June 7, 1985
Ellis, Jimmy/Orion	D,DO	July 5, 1985
Ellison, Andy/Chiswick Records	I	Sept. 7, 1990
Ellison, Lorraine	D	Jan. 26, 1990
Ellison, Lorraine	DA	May 4, 1990
Ely, Joe		Aug. 1981
Ely, Joe	I,D	April 21, 1989
Ely, Joe	I	Jan. 19, 1996
Emerson, Keith: From The Nice To ELP	D	Aug. 24, 1990
Emerson, Keith: From The Nice To ELP	DA	Oct. 19, 1990
Emerson Lake & Palmer	I,D	Dec. 6, 1996
Emotions High During Hearing On 'Porn Rock'		Nov. 8, 1985
Empty Stocking Blues (Fiction)		Dec. 1978
Endsley, Melvin	I	Aug. 26, 1988
England's Music Club		Dec. 20, 1996
Engler, Jerry	I.,D	July 10, 1992
English Beat	D	Feb. 12, 1988
Eno, Brian	I,D	March 1983
Entwistle, John/Who	I	Dec. 1981
Entwistle, John/Who	D	Jan. 1982
Entwistle, John/Who	I	July 5, 1996
Epps, Earl		Sept. 1980
Era/Dore	I	May 10, 1996
Erickson, Roky	D	March 13, 1987
Erman Record Company	I	May 9, 1997
Ertegun, Ahmet		Feb. 26, 1988
ESP-Disk' Records		Sept. 17, 1993
Esquivel	I, D	Sept. 29, 1995
Essay On Record Collecting		April 1978
Essex		Dec. 1, 1989
Establishing Rock Standards		May 1979
Estefan, Gloria & Miami Sound Machine	I	Oct. 21, 1988
Eugene Record/Chi-Lites	I	Nov. 8, 1985
Eugene Record/Chi-Lites	I,D	Nov. 22,1985
Eurovision song contest		July 8, 1994
Eurythmics/Annie Lennox	I	Dec. 15, 1989
Evans, Bill	I,D	Oct. 12, 1984
Evans, Bill	I	Oct. 26, 1984
Everett, Betty	I,D	April 10, 1987
Everly Brothers	I,D	March 2, 1984
Everly Brothers		July 5, 1985
Everly Brothers		Feb. 26, 1988
Everly Brothers	D	June 25, 1993
Everly Brothers: Their Solo Careers/Don/Phil	I,D	Aug. 11, 1989

Title	Code	Date
Fifties Rock: Lonnie Donegan		March 27, 1987
Fifties Rock: Melvin Endsley	I	Aug. 26, 1988
Fifties Rock: Otis Blackwell	I	July 31, 1987
Fifty Foot Hose/Dave Blossum	I,D	Sept. 1980
Fillmore Posters		March 24, 1989
Finn Brothers	I	Sept. 13, 1996
Finn, Tom/Left Banke	I	May 6, 1988
Fire-Fury Records		Aug. 21, 1992
Fireballs, The	D	Dec. 16, 1988
Fireflies/Gerry Granahan	I,D	Dec. 28, 1990
Fisher, Little Reuben	I,D	Dec. 1983
Five Breezes/Leonard Caston	I,D	Jan. 4, 1985
Five By Five		July 1976
Five Chances, The	D	April 6, 1990
Five Discs, The/Marge Hunt/Paul Albano	I,D	Feb. 8, 1991
Five Dutones, The/Leroy Joyce	I,D	Jan. 1982
Five Echoes, The	D	April 1979
Five Keys, The		Aug. 26, 1988
Five Keys, The	DA	Nov. 18, 1988
Five Royales, the	I, D	Feb. 19, 1993
Five Satins, The	I	Feb. 1982
Five Satins, The	D	Jan. 1, 1988
Five Satins, The	DA	April 8, 1988
Five Satins, The	DA	Aug. 26, 1988
Five Satins, The/Fred Parris	I,D	May 1979
Five Sharps, The	D	Dec. 2, 1988
Five Thrills, The/Levi Jenkins	I,D	Feb. 8, 1991
Flairs/The Richard Berry	I	Jan. 31, 1986
Flamin' Groovies	I, D	Jan. 8, 1993
Flamingos, The		May-June 1978
Flamingos, The	D	April 6, 1990
Flamingos, The/Earl Lewis	I	May 1979
Flamingos, The/Jake & Zeke Carey	I	Sept. 1981
Flamingos, The/Nate Nelson	I,D	March 1978
Flash Cadillac	I,D	Jan. 31, 1997
Flashcubes, The	D	Jan. 5, 1996
Flat Town Music Group/Floyd Soileau	I	Nov. 4, 1988
Flatlanders/Jimmie Dale Gilmore	I,D	Oct. 5, 1990
Fleetwood Mac	D	Sept. 18, 1992
Fleetwood, Mick	I	Sept 18, 1992
Fleetwoods, The	D	April 1979
Fleetwoods, The	DA	Aug. 1979
Fleshtones, The/Pete Zaremba	I	June 1982
Fletcher, Darrow	D	April 1980
Fletcher, Darrow	D	Aug. 1981
Flip Records	D	July 1976
Flipper	D	Dec. 15, 1989
Flo And Eddie/Mark Volman	I	April 1980
Flo And Eddie/Mark Volman/Howard Kaylan	I,D	Dec. 1982
Flo And Eddie/Mark Volman/Howard Kaylan		Feb. 1983
Flo And Eddie/Mark Volman/Howard Kaylan		Sept. 1983
Flo And Eddie/Mark Volman/Howard Kaylan	I	May 18, 1990
Flo And Eddie/Mark Volman/Howard Kaylan vs. De La Soul	I	May 18, 1990
Flores, Danny/Champs	I,D	Aug. 12, 1988
Flores, Rosie	I	April 25, 1997
Flying Fish Records		Sept. 1980
Flying Saucer Rock N Roll	D	Feb. 12, 1988
Flying Saucer Rock N Roll	D	Feb. 12, 1988
Flyright Records	D	July 1981
Fogerty, John/Creedence Clearwater Revival	I,D	June 8, 1984
Fogerty, John/Creedence Clearwater Revival		July 20, 1984
Fogerty, John/Creedence Clearwater Revival	DA	Feb. 1, 1985
Fogerty, John/Creedence Clearwater Revival	I,D	July 18, 1997
Fogerty, Tom/Creedence Clearwater Revival	I	May 24, 1985
Foghat	I, D	Aug. 4, 1995
Foley, Kim	I, D	Nov. 26, 1993

Title	Code	Date
Folk Era Profile		
Folk Era Profile: Brothers Four	D	Dec. 1979
Folk Era Profile: Journeymen	D	Sept. 1979
Folk Era Profile: Rooftop Singers		Oct. 1979
Folk Era Profile: Tom Rush	D	Jan. 1980
Folk Era Profile: Whiskey Hill Singers		Nov. 1979
Folk Profiles		
Folk Profiles: Bob Gibson	D	Oct. 1981
Folk Profiles: Bud & Travis	D	March 1981
Folk Profiles: Chad Mitchell Trio	D	July 1980
Folk Profiles: Cumberland Three	D	March 1980
Folk Profiles: Gateway Singers	D	Feb. 1980
Folk Profiles: Gateway Trio	D	Feb. 1980
Folk Profiles: Gordon Lightfoot	D	Aug. 1980
Folk Profiles: Highwaymen	D	June 1980
Folk Profiles: Hoyt Axton	D	Aug. 1981
Folk Profiles: Ian & Sylvia	D	Oct. 1980
Folk Profiles: Joni Mitchell	D	Nov. 1980
Folk Profiles: Judy Collins	D	July 1981
Folk Profiles: Knob Lick Upper 10,000	D	Oct. 1980
Folk Profiles: Limeliters	D	Dec. 1981
Folk Profiles: Modern Folk Quartet	D	Feb. 1981
Folk Profiles: Tom Paxton	D	Sept. 1980
Folk Profiles: Weavers	D	Feb. 1982
Folk Scene (Allan Shaw)		March 30, 1984
Folk Scene (Allan Shaw)		May 25, 1984
Folk Scene: Knob Lick Upper 10,000	D	April 1982
Folk Scene: Steve Goodman		Dec. 7, 1984
Folk Scene: Tom Russell		Jan. 18, 1985
Fontaine, Eddie	I,D	March 1981
Fontana, D J	I	Jan. 1981
Fontana, D J	I	Aug. 14, 1987
Fontana, Wayne & The Mindbenders/Eric Stewart/ Graham Gouldman	D	Jan. 16, 1987
Fontana, Wayne & The Mindbenders/Eric Stewart/ Graham Gouldman	DA	Feb. 27, 1987
Fonville, Bobby	D	July 1981
For Elvis Fans Only (Jim Van Hollebeke)		Jan. 1976
For Elvis Fans Only (Jim Van Hollebeke)		Feb. 1976
For Elvis Fans Only (Jim Van Hollebeke)		March 1976
For Elvis Fans Only (Jim Van Hollebeke)		May 1976
For Elvis Fans Only (Jim Van Hollebeke)		July 1976
For Elvis Fans Only (Jim Van Hollebeke)		Sept.-Oct. 1976
For Elvis Fans Only (Jim Van Hollebeke)		Nov.-Dec. 1976
For Elvis Fans Only (Jim Van Hollebeke)		March-April 1977
For Elvis Fans Only (Jim Van Hollebeke)		May-June 1977
For Elvis Fans Only (Jim Van Hollebeke)		Sept. 1977
For Elvis Fans Only (Jim Van Hollebeke)		Nov. 1977
For Elvis Fans Only (Jim Van Hollebeke)		Jan. 1978
For Elvis Fans Only (Jim Van Hollebeke)		March 1978
For Elvis Fans Only (Jim Van Hollebeke)		May-June 1978
For Elvis Fans Only (Jim Van Hollebeke)		July-Aug. 1978
For Elvis Fans Only (Jim Van Hollebeke)		Sept. 1978
For Elvis Fans Only (Jim Van Hollebeke)		Nov. 1978
For Elvis Fans Only (Jim Van Hollebeke)		Jan. 1979
For Elvis Fans Only (Jim Van Hollebeke)		April 1979
For Elvis Fans Only (Jim Van Hollebeke)		June 1979
For Elvis Fans Only (Jim Van Hollebeke)		Aug. 1979
For Elvis Fans Only (Jim Van Hollebeke)		Oct. 1979
For Elvis Fans Only (Jim Van Hollebeke)		April 1980
For Elvis Fans Only (Jim Van Hollebeke)		Dec. 1979
For Elvis Fans Only (Jim Van Hollebeke)		Feb. 1980
For Elvis Fans Only (Jim Van Hollebeke)		June 1980
For Elvis Fans Only (Jim Van Hollebeke)		Aug. 1980
For Elvis Fans Only (Jim Van Hollebeke)		Oct. 1980
For Elvis Fans Only (Jim Van Hollebeke)		Dec. 1980
For Elvis Fans Only (Jim Van Hollebeke)		April 1981

Name	Code	Date
For Elvis Fans Only (Jim Van Hollebeke)		July 1981
For Elvis Fans Only (Jim Van Hollebeke)		Sept. 1981
For Elvis Fans Only (Jim Van Hollebeke)		March 1982
For Elvis Fans Only (Jim Van Hollebeke)		May 1982
For Elvis Fans Only (Jim Van Hollebeke)		July 1982
For Elvis Fans Only (Jim Van Hollebeke)		Sept. 1982
For Elvis Fans Only (Jim Van Hollebeke)		Nov. 1982
For Elvis Fans Only (Jim Van Hollebeke)		Jan. 1983
For Elvis Fans Only (Jim Van Hollebeke)		March 1983
For Elvis Fans Only (Jim Van Hollebeke)		June 1983
For Elvis Fans Only (Jim Van Hollebeke)		Aug. 1983
For Elvis Fans Only (Jim Van Hollebeke)		Oct. 1983
For Elvis Fans Only (Jim Van Hollebeke)		Dec. 1983
For Elvis Fans Only (Jim Van Hollebeke)		Feb. 1984
For Elvis Fans Only (Jim Van Hollebeke)		March 16, 1984
For Elvis Fans Only (Jim Van Hollebeke)		May 25, 1984
For Elvis Fans Only (Jim Van Hollebeke)		July 20, 1984
For Elvis Fans Only (Jim Van Hollebeke)		Nov. 9, 1984
For Elvis Fans Only (Jim Van Hollebeke)		Jan. 18, 1985
For Ladies Only		Dec. 20, 1985
Ford, Frankie	D	Nov.-Dec. 1976
Ford, Frankie	I,D	June 1982
Ford, Frankie		Jan. 1983
Ford, Frankie		Aug. 1983
Ford, Frankie	D	June 19, 1987
Ford, Frankie	I, D	Mar. 6, 1992
Ford, Lita	I	June 11, 1993
Fortune Records/Devora Brown	I,D	Sept. 1983
Fortune Records/Devora Brown		Nov. 23, 1984
Fortune Records/Devora Brown		Jan. 3, 1986
Fortune Records/Devora Brown	I	June 20, 1986
Fortune, Johnny	I,D	Dec. 1980
45s: Stars On 45		
Four (4) Buddies, The	D	April 1979
Four Aces, The		Dec. 1977
Four Blazes, The	D	March 30, 1984
Four Blue Jackets, The	D	Jan. 4, 1985
Four Clefs, The	D	Jan. 4, 1985
Four Coins, The	D	May 22, 1987
Four Coins, The		June 5, 1987
Four Deep Tones, The	D	May 8, 1987
Four Freshmen	D	Jan. 1, 1988
Four Freshmen, The	D	Jan. 1, 1988
Four Freshmen, The	DA	June 3, 1988
Four Freshmen, The	DA	June 17, 1988
Four Imperials, The	D	Sept.-Oct. 1976
Four Knights, The/Clarence Dixon	I,D	Sept. 1979
Four Knights, The/Clarence Dixon		May 1980
Four Knights, The/Clarence Dixon	I,D	March 1981
Four Lads, The/Frank Busseri	I,D	June 3, 1988
Four Lads/Frank Busseri	I,D	June 3, 1988
Four Lovers, The	I,D	June 1982
Four Preps, The/Bruce Belland/Ed Cobb	I,D	Oct. 5, 1990
Four Seasons, The		Jan. 1976
Four Seasons, The	D	Aug. 1981
Four Seasons, The		March 9, 1990
Four Seasons, The/Frankie Valli	I	Aug. 1983
Four Tops, the	I, D	March 3, 1995
Four Tops, The/Duke Fakir	I,D	Aug. 1981
Four Tops, The/Duke Fakir	DA	Nov. 1981
Four Tunes, The	D	Jan. 27, 1989
Fourteen (14) Karat Soul/Glenny Wright	I	Sept. 1981
Fowler, Lummie/Lummtone Records	I,D	July 4, 1986
Foxx, Charlie and Inez	I,D	Aug. 1, 1997
Francis, Connie	I,D	May 1982
Francis, Connie	I, D	May 14, 1993
Frankhauser, Merrell	I,D	April 26, 1996
Franklin, Aretha		Feb. 26, 1988
Franklin, Aretha	D	March 10, 1989
Franklin, Aretha	D	July 8, 1994
Fraternity Records		Sept. 7, 1990
Frayne, George/Commander Cody	I,D	Jan. 16, 1987
Frazier, Al/Rivingtons	I	Sept. 22, 1989
Frazier, Joe/Impalas	I	Aug. 1982
Fred, John	I,D	March 1982
Fred, John	I	March 25, 1988
Fred, John	I	March 25, 1988
Fred, John	I	March 29, 1996
Freddie and the Dreamers	I, D	March 19, 1993
Freed, Alan		Oct. 1979
Freed, Alan		Feb. 1, 1985
Freed, Alan		Feb. 26, 1988
Freeman, Ernie	D	Nov. 1982
Freeman, Ernie	DA	Aug. 1983
Freeman, Ernie	DA	Sept. 1983
Frehley, Ace	I	June 29, 1990
Friend And Lover/Jim Post	I	Dec. 1, 1989
Fripp, Robert/King Crimson	I,D	Sept. 1980
Fripp, Robert/King Crimson	I	April 1982
Frost, Frank	I,D	Feb. 23, 1990
Frost, Max And The Troopers		Dec. 1, 1989
Furtwängler, Wilhelm	I,	March 15, 1996
Fuller, Bobby Four		Jan.-Feb. 1977
Fuller, Bobby Four	D	May 25, 1984
Fuller, Bobby Four/Jim Reese	I,D	Feb. 1, 1985
Fulson, Lowell	I,D	Jan. 1982
Fulson, Lowell		Jan. 1983
Fulson, Lowell	I,D	Feb. 23, 1990
Funicello, Annette	D	July-Aug. 1977
Funicello, Annette	D	Sept. 1978
Funicello, Annette	D	July 1983
Fuqua, Harvey	I	March 15, 1985
Fuqua, Harvey/Moonglows	I,D	Feb. 8, 1991
Furtwaengler, Wilhelm	D	Oct. 25, 1985
Fury, Billy	D	May 24, 1985
Future Of Satanic Music		Jan. 27, 1989

G

Name	Code	Date
Gabriel, Peter	D	Sept. 12, 1986
Gaines, Grady and the Texas Upsetters		Oct. 16, 1992
Gaines, Lee/Delta Rhythm Boys	D	March 1979
Gans, David/Grateful Dead Hour	I	March 24, 1989
Garcia, Frankie "Cannibal"/Cannibal And The HeadHunters	I,D	Nov. 1983
Garcia, Jerry Acoustic Band		March 24, 1989
Garcia, Jerry/Grateful Dead	I	July 17, 1987
Garcia, Jerry/Grateful Dead	I	Nov. 2, 1990
Garcia, Jerry		Aug. 16, 1996
Gardner, Hy	I	Aug. 10, 1990
Garland, Judy	D	May 20, 1988
Garrett, Jo Ann	D	March 1978
Garrett, Jo Ann	D	Jan. 1981
Gas Huffer discography		Apr. 17, 1992
Gates, David		June 17, 1988
Gates, David	D,DO	July 15, 1988
Gateway Singers		Feb. 1980
Gateway Trio		Feb. 1980
Gatton, Danny	DA	Jan. 10, 1992
Gaye, Marvin		Feb. 26, 1988
Gaye, Marvin	D	June 16, 1989
Gee (The Song)		Oct. 21, 1988
Geils, J Band/Peter Wolf	I,D	Oct. 1983
Geils, J Band/Peter Wolf	DA	July 20, 1984
Geller, Gregg: Reshaping The Elvis Catalog	I	Aug. 30, 1985

Name	Code	Date
Grassroots, The/Rob Grill		Sept. 1983
Grassroots, The/Rob Grill		Oct. 1983
Grassroots, The/Rob Grill	DA	May 11, 1984
Grassroots, The/Rob Grill	DA	July 6, 1984
Grateful Dead, The		July 17, 1987
Grateful Dead, The	D	Sept. 11, 1987
Grateful Dead, The	D	March 24, 1989
Grateful Dead, The, Hour/David Gans	I	March 24, 1989
Grateful Dead, The/Jerry Garcia	I	July 17, 1987
Grateful Dead, The/Jerry Garcia/Bob Weir	I	Nov. 2, 1990
Grateful Dead, Jerry Garcia		Jan. 5, 1996
Grateful Dead, Bob Weir & Phil Lesh	I	Feb. 2, 1996
Great Balls Of Fire (Movie)/Adam Fields	I	July 14, 1989
Great Green Paint Rim Job Controversy		July 27, 1990
Greaves, R.B.	I	May 29, 1992
Green Day	I, D	Sept. 15, 1995
Green Linnet Records		March 18, 1994
Green, Al	D	Aug. 14, 1987
Green, Al	D	Aug. 14, 1987
Green, Garland	D	July 1979
Green, Ray	I	Jan. 21, 1994
Greenwich, Ellie		April 12, 1985
Greenwich, Ellie	I, D	May 27, 1994
Griffin	I	May 10, 1996
Griffin, Buck	D	Sept. 8, 1989
Griffin, Paul and the Musicians of Brill Building Pop		Sept. 3, 1993
Griffin, Sid/Long Ryders	I	Aug. 14, 1987
Grill, Rob/Grassroots	D	Dec. 1982
Grill, Rob/Grassroots	D	Oct. 1983
Grisman, David	D	Jan. 1979
Grisman, David	I,D	Feb. 15, 1985
Grisman, David	I, D	Aug. 6, 1993
Grisman, David	I	June 7, 1996
Gross, Jerry/Dovells	I,D	Jan. 1982
Grove, George/Kingston Trio	I	Feb. 1979
GRP Records		March 18, 1994
GTO's, The	I	Jan. 26, 1990
Guess Who, The		April 1983
Guess Who, The/Burton Cummings	I,D	June 30, 1989
Guess Who, The/Burton Cummings		Aug. 11, 1989
Guess Who, The/Burton Cummings		Sept. 8, 1989
Guess Who, The/Burton Cummings	DA	Oct. 6, 1989
Guess Who, The/Jim Kale	I,D	April 1983
Guide To 'Frisco's '60s Albums		July 17, 1987
Guide To 'Frisco's '60s Albums		Oct. 23, 1987
Guide To Canterbury Rock	D	Oct. 6, 1989
Guide To Memphis Record Stores		June 15, 1990
Guide To Rolling Stone Collectibles		May 1983
Guide To San Francisco Bay Area Record Stores		March 24, 1989
Guide To The Basics Of Fan Clubbing		Dec. 19, 1986
Guns N' Roses	D	May 19, 1989
Guns N' Roses/Slash	I,D	May 19, 1989
Guns N' Roses/Slash	I,D	May 19, 1989
Gunter, Arthur	D	Dec. 1979
Gunter, Shirley	D	Jan. 16, 1987
Guralnick, Peter	I	Feb. 22, 1991
Gusick, Michael/Accord/Townhouse Records	I,D	Sept. 1982
Gusick, Michael/Accord/Townhouse Records	D	May 1983
Guthrie, Woody		Feb. 26, 1988
Guthrie, Woody		Dec. 6, 1996
Guy, Buddy	D	Feb. 23, 1990
Guy, Buddy	I, D	April 16, 1993

H

Name	Code	Date
Haley, Bill	D	April 1980
Haley, Bill	D	April 1981
Haley, Bill	D	May 1982

Name	Code	Date
Haley, Bill	DA	Jan. 1983
Haley, Bill	DA	Nov. 9, 1984
Haley, Bill		Feb. 26, 1988
Hall, Loyd		Nov. 1981
Hall, Michael/Wild Seeds	I,D	April 22, 1988
Hall Of Fame Inductions		Nov. 22, 1996
Hall, Roy	D	March 30, 1984
Hambone Kids, The	D	Sept. 1980
Hamilton 4-Speed Record Players		Feb. 27, 1987
Hamilton, Roy	D	April 1979
Hamlin, Rosie/Rosie And The Originals	I	Dec. 1, 1989
Hammill, Peter	D	March 9, 1990
Hammond, John	I,D	Feb. 23, 1990
Hammond, John	I	Sept. 7, 1990
Hammond, John	I	April 25, 1997
Hang Ten (Robert Dalley)		May 1981
Hang Ten (Robert Dalley)		March 1982
Hang Ten (Robert Dalley)		Aug. 1982
Hang Ten (Robert Dalley)		Oct. 1982
Hang Ten (Robert Dalley)		Dec. 1982
Hang Ten (Robert Dalley)		Oct. 1983
Hang Ten (Robert Dalley)		Dec. 1983
Hang Ten (Robert Dalley)		Feb. 1984
Hang Ten (Robert Dalley)		April 13, 1984
Hang Ten, see also Surf		
Hang Ten: All Star Surf Band		Oct. 1981
Hang Ten: Battle Of The Surfing Bands:		
Hang Ten: Crossword Puzzle		May 1982
Hang Ten: Crossword Puzzle		June 1982
Hang Ten: Del-Fi 1235		May 11, 1984
Hang Ten: Live Instrumental Surf Music	D	May 1983
Hang Ten: Look At Surfin' 45 Rarities		Feb. 1983
Hang Ten: Looking At Surf Rarities		April 1981
Hang Ten: Picture Sleeves & Colored Wax	D	July 1981
Hang Ten: Surfer's Quiz		Sept. 1981
Hangmen/Bob Berberich	I,D	Dec. 6, 1985
Hansen Brothers/Paul Hansen	I,D	Feb. 1980
Happy Goodman Family	D	May 11, 1984
Hardesty, Herb	D	June 1980
Hardin, Tim	D	April 10, 1987
Hardin, Tim	D	April 10, 1987
Hardin, Tim	D	June 24, 1994
Harmon, David/Dave Dee, Dozy, Beaky, Mick And Tich	I,D	Oct. 21, 1988
Harmonizing Four, The	D	July 8, 1994
Harpo, Slim	D	March 11, 1988
Harpo, Slim	D	March 11, 1988
Harptones, The	I	March 1983
Harptones, The	D,DO	April 1983
Harris, Emmylou		Jan. 2, 1987
Harris, Emmylou	I,D	Jan. 1, 1988
Harris, Emmylou		April 8, 1988
Harris, Emmylou		April 22, 1988
Harris, Emmylou	DA	Sept. 9, 1988
Harris, Emmylou		Jan. 2, 1987
Harris, Emmylou	DA	April 8, 1988
Harris, Emmylou	DA	April 22, 1988
Harris, Emmylou	I,D	Aug. 2, 1996
Harris, Emmylou		March 28, 1997
Harris, Mickey/Shirelles	I	Sept. 1980
Harris, Peppermint	I	Feb. 23, 1990
Harris, R.H. & The Soul Stirrers		March 25, 1988
Harris, Ray (Engineer For Hi Records)	I	June 15, 1990
Harris, Richard	D	Sept. 21, 1990
Harris, Rolf		Dec. 30, 1988
Harris, Thurston	I,D	June 17, 1988
Harris, Wynonie	D	Oct. 1979
Harris, Wynonie	DA	Dec. 1979

Name	Code	Date	Name	Code	Date
Harris, Wynonie	DA	March 1980	Hi Records		June 2, 1989
Harris, Wynonie	DA	May 1980	Hi Records		May 12, 1995
Harris, Wynonie	DA	May 1980	Hickey, Ersel	D	Sept.-Oct. 1976
Harrison, George		Aug. 16, 1985	Hicks, Dan/Dan Hicks & His Hot Licks	I,D	March 24, 1989
Harrison, George	D	July 29, 1988	Higgins, Chuck	I, D	July 10, 1992
Harrison, George	I	Nov. 27, 1992	High Inergy	D	Nov. 16, 1990
Harrison, Wilbert	D	June 1979	Highwaymen	D	June 1980
Harrison, Wilbert	DA	Sept. 1979	Highwaymen	DA	Sept. 1980
Harrison, Wilbert	DA	Dec. 1979	Hill, Jessie	I,D	Oct. 21, 1988
Harrison, Wilbert	I,D	July 3, 1987	Hill, Jessie	I,D	Oct. 21, 1988
Hartford, John	D	Dec. 25, 1992	Hill, Z Z	I,D	March 13, 1987
Haslam, Annie	I, D	Dec. 22, 1995	Hillage, Steve	D	Oct. 6, 1989
Hatfield, Bobby/Righteous Brothers	D	Oct. 6, 1989	Hillman, Chris	I	Jan. 11, 1991
Hatfield, Bobby/Righteous Brothers	I,D	May 11, 1984	Hillman, Chris	I	April 11, 1997
Hatfield, Bobby/Righteous Brothers		June 21, 1985	Hillman, Chris/Byrds	I	Feb. 1979
Hatfield, Bobby/Righteous Brothers	DA	Feb. 14, 1986	Hillman, Chris/Byrds	I	Jan. 11, 1991
Haunted, The	I,D	June 30, 1989	Hillman, Chris/Byrds	DA	Feb. 8, 1991
Hauser, Tim/Manhattan Transfer	I,D	July 6, 1984	Hilltoppers	D	Nov. 6, 1987
Havens, Richie	I,D	Nov. 1982	Hinsche, Billy/Dino, Desi & Billy	I,D	Dec. 6, 1985
Havens, Richie	I	Sept. 25, 1987	Hinton, Joe	D	Oct. 5, 1990
Havens, Richie	I	Sept. 25, 1987	Hip Hop	I	May 24, 1996
Havens, Richie	I, D	June 10, 1994	History Of Radio Music Surveys		March 2, 1984
Hawkins, Barbara/Dixie Cups	I,D	Dec. 5, 1986	Hitchcock	I, D	Oct. 30, 1992
Hawkins, Dale	I, D	Nov. 27, 1992	Hitchcock, Robyn	D	March 27, 1987
Hawkins, Hawkshaw		July-Aug. 1977	Hitchcock, Robyn	I,D	Oct. 11, 1996
Hawkins, Jennell	I	Nov. 20, 1987	Hite, Bob		July 1981
Hawkins, Jennell	I	Nov. 20, 1987	Hits And Their Original Labels	D	April 1978
Hawkins, Ronnie	D	June 15, 1990	Hobbs, Becky	D	Sept. 1982
Hawkins, Rosa/Dixie Cups	I,D	Dec. 5, 1986	Hobbs, Becky	DA	Sept. 1983
Hawkins, Screaming Jay	I,D	Nov. 1978	Hodge, Gaynel/Turks	I,D	Feb. 8, 1991
Hawkwind	D	July 9, 1993	Hoffman, Steve	I	Nov. 1983
Hayes, Isaac	D	Feb. 13, 1987	Holden, Ron	I,D	Sept. 11, 1987
Hayes, Isaac	D	Feb. 13, 1987	Holden, Ron	I,D	Sept. 11, 1987
Haynes, Tiger/Three Flames	I,D	April 1980	Holiday CD Shopping Guide (1990)		Nov. 2, 1990
Hayward, Justin	D	Oct. 6, 1989	Holiday CD Shopping Guide (1990)		Nov. 16, 1990
Head, Roy	I,D	Oct. 5, 1990	Holland, Eddie	D	Nov. 16, 1990
Heartbeats/Wally Roker	I,D	Dec. 1980	Holley, Larry	I	July 18, 1986
Heatwave	I, D	March 17, 1995	Hollies, The		July 1976
Heaven & Earth	D	March 27, 1987	Hollies, The	I	Dec. 1981
Heaven And Earth	D	March 27, 1987	Hollies, The	D	Jan. 1982
Heavy Metal		June 21, 1996	Hollies, The	DA	Feb. 1982
Helms, Bobby	I,D	Sept. 1978	Hollies, The	DA	May 1982
Help On Laserdisc: How It Was Done		June 3, 1988	Hollies, The	DA	May 25, 1984
Hendricks, Bobby	I,D	April 24, 1987	Hollies, The	I	July 5, 1996
Hendrix, Jimi			Hollies, The: A Critical Guide To Their Albums 1964-1980	D	May 4, 1990
Hendrix, Jimi: About The Band Of Gypsys		Sept. 21, 1990			
Hendrix, Jimi: Buddy Miles On Jimi Hendrix	I	Sept. 21, 1990	Hollies, The: A Critical Guide To Their Albums 1964-1980	DA	July 27, 1990
Hendrix, Jimi: Complete Jimi Hendrix Discography	D	Sept. 21, 1990			
Hendrix, Jimi: Eric Burdon Remembers Jimi Hendrix	I	Sept. 21, 1990	Hollies, The: A Critical Guide To Their Albums 1964-1980	DA	Aug. 24, 1990
Hendrix, Jimi: Hendris In London	I	June 20, 1997	Holloway, Brenda	I,D	Nov. 16, 1990
Hendrix, Jimi: Hendrix Lives (Slight Return)	I	May 10, 1996	Holly, Buddy		Nov.-Dec. 1976
Hendrix, Jimi: His Legacy, and the City of Seattle		June 20, 1997	Holly, Buddy		Feb. 26, 1988
Hendrix, Jimi: Sorting Out The Jimi Hendrix Discography		Sept. 21, 1990	Holly, Buddy & The Crickets/Joe Mauldin	I,D	Feb. 10, 1989
Henry, Clarence Frogman	I,D	Sept. 1980	Holly, Buddy & The Crickets/Niki Sullivan	I,D	Sept. 1978
Henry, Clarence Frogman		Nov. 1980	Holly, Buddy & The Crickets/Niki Sullivan	I,D	Sept. 14, 1984
Henry, Clarence Frogman	I,D	May 22, 1987	Holly, Buddy Discography	D	Oct. 1977
Henry, Clarence Frogman	I,D	May 22, 1987	Holly, Buddy Discography	DA	Dec. 1977
Hensley, Roy/Castaways	I	Dec. 1, 1989	Holly, Buddy Week 1984		Sept. 14, 1984
Herman's Hermits	I,D	Jan. 1980	Holly, Buddy: A Collector's Price Guide		Sept. 14, 1984
Herman's Hermits	DA	June 1980	Holly, Buddy: As Fate Would Have It		Oct. 1977
Herman's Hermits/Peter Noone	I	March 1981	Holly, Buddy: Beyond The Buddy Holly Box Set	D	April 22, 1988
Hernandez, Ralph	D	July 1981	Holly, Buddy: Bobby Vee, Dion & Tommy Allsup/The Days After The Crash	I	Feb. 10, 1989
Hester, Carolyn	I,D	Jan. 26, 1990			
Hewitt, Ben	I,D	Oct. 25, 1985	Holly, Buddy: Holly's Legend Lives On: Lubbock 1984		Oct. 26, 1984
Hewitt, Ben	DA	Feb. 13, 1987	Holly, Buddy: John Pickering & The Picks		
Hey Joe (The Song)		Jan. 15, 1988	(Behind The Crickets Sounds)	D	Sept. 14, 1984
Hey Joe (The Song)		Jan. 15, 1988			

Holly, Buddy: John Pickering & The Picks			
(Behind The Crickets Sounds)		Sept. 14, 1984	
Holly, Buddy: Lubbock '85		Oct. 11, 1985	
Holly, Buddy: Lubbock '86		July 18, 1986	
Holly, Buddy: Lubbock '86		Oct. 24, 1986	
Holly, Buddy: Lubbock 1986		July 18, 1986	
Holly, Buddy: Memorial Concert (1980)		May 1980	
Holly, Buddy: New Facts About Buddy Holly's Last Tour		Feb. 10, 1989	
Holly, Buddy: Norman Petty (In The Studio With			
Buddy Holly)	I	Sept. 14, 1984	
Holly, Buddy: Reminiscing With Hi Pockets Duncan			
(Business Mgr For Buddy & Bob)	I	Sept. 1979	
Holly, Buddy: Report From Clear Lake (25 And Still Alive)		June 8, 1984	
Holly, Buddy: Select Price Guide		Sept. 14, 1984	
Holly, Buddy: Those Who Knew Him		July 18, 1986	
Holly, Buddy: Those Who Knew Him		Aug. 29, 1986	
Holly, Maria Elena	I	Aug. 29, 1986	
Hollywood Argyles		Dec. 30, 1988	
Hollywood Flames		Dec. 1, 1989	
Holman, Eddie	I	Dec. 1, 1989	
Holy Modal Rounders	D	Oct. 23, 1987	
Holy Modal Rounders	D	Oct. 23, 1987	
Holy Modal Rounders/Peter Stampfel	I,D	May 1982	
Holzman, Keith/Rom Records	I	Sept. 7, 1990	
Hombres/B.B. Cunningham	I	Dec. 1, 1989	
Honey Cone	D	Sept. 9, 1988	
Honey Cone	D	Sept. 9, 1988	
Honeycombs, The		Dec. 30, 1988	
Honeys, The		May-June 1978	
Honeys, The	I,D	July 1983	
Honeys, The	D,DO	Dec. 2, 1988	
Honeys, The [see Wilson, Mary]			
Hot Rod Music		Sept. 17, 1993	
Hoodoo Gurus/Dave Faulkner	I	Dec. 15, 1989	
Hooker, John Lee	D	Jan. 16, 1987	
Hooker, John Lee	D	Mar. 20, 1992	
Hopkin, Mary	I, D	April 14, 1995	
Hopkins, Lightnin'	D	Oct. 5, 1990	
Horne, Elliot	I	Aug. 17, 1984	
Hornets, The	D	April 6, 1990	
Hornsby, Bruce		July 17, 1987	
Horton, Johnny	D	March 1981	
Hot Chocolate	D	May 8, 1987	
Hot Chocolate	D	May 8, 1987	
Hot Record Society Records	D	Sept. 26, 1986	
Hot Tuna		Nov. 1983	
Hotlegs/Graham Gouldman/Eric Stewart	I,D	Jan. 16, 1987	
Hotlegs/Graham Gouldman/Eric Stewart	DA	Feb. 27, 1987	
House Passes Anti-Record Rental Bill		Oct. 12, 1984	
House, Vince/Rhythm Aces	I,D	Feb. 8, 1991	
Houston, Whitney	D	Aug. 28, 1987	
How To Buy From Goldmine Advertisements		Aug. 15, 1986	
How To Buy From Goldmine Advertisements		Aug. 14, 1987	
How To Buy Records		Sept.-Oct. 1976	
How To Sell At Record Shows		Jan. 27, 1989	
How To Start A Successful Fan Club		Dec. 15, 1989	
Hucknall, Mick/Simply Red	I	June 3, 1988	
Hues Corporation		Dec. 30, 1988	
Hugg, Dick "Huggy Boy"	I	Oct. 21, 1988	
Hughes, Jimmy		Dec. 1, 1989	
Hula Love		March 2, 1984	
Hula Love: Strange Case Of "Hula Love"		March 2, 1984	
Human Switchboard		Nov. 1979	
Humble Pie	D	Aug. 14, 1987	
Humble Pie	D	Aug. 14, 1987	
Humes, Helen	D	March 11, 1988	
Hunt, Marge/Five Discs	I,D	Feb. 8, 1991	

Hunter, Ian/Mott The Hoople	D	Oct. 26, 1984	
Hunter, Ian/Mott The Hoople	DA	March 14, 1986	
Hunter, Ian/Mott The Hoople	DA	Dec. 5, 1986	
Hunter, Ivory Joe	D	Oct. 1978	
Hunter, Ivory Joe	DA	Feb. 1979	
Hurley, Robin/Rough Trade Records	I	Nov. 4, 1988	
Husker Du/Bob Mould	I,D	Feb. 27, 1987	
Hutson, Leroy		Oct. 23, 1987	
Hutson, Leroy		Oct. 23, 1987	
Hutton, Danny/Three Dog Night	I,D	April 27, 1984	
Huxley, Rick/Dave Clark Five		Nov. 1982	
Hyde, Bob/Murray Hill Records	I	June 2, 1989	
Hyland, Brian	I, D	April 15, 1994	
I			
I Almost Gave Up Collecting		May-June 1978	
I.R.S. Records/Jay Boberg	I,D	Feb. 1982	
Ian & Sylvia	D	Oct. 1980	
Ian and Sylvia	I, D	July 8, 1994	
Ian, Janis	I,D	Jan. 26, 1990	
Ibbotson, Jimmie/Nitty Gritty Dirt Band	I,D	Feb. 9, 1990	
Ibbotson, Jimmie/Nitty Gritty Dirt Band	DA	March 23, 1990	
Ideals	D	Feb. 1979	
Ides Of March		Sept. 1981	
Idle Race	D	June 1981	
Idle Race	D	Oct. 25, 1985	
Idle Race	DA	Feb. 13, 1987	
Iglauer, Bruce/Alligator Records	I,D	Jan. 1982	
Iglauer, Bruce/Alligator Records		Nov. 4, 1988	
Immediate Records		Aug. 21, 1992	
Impalas, The		Feb. 24, 1989	
Impalas, The/Joe Frazier	I	Aug. 1982	
Import Albums (Federal Court Ruling Imperals)		July 17, 1987	
Import Albums (Federal Court Ruling Imperals)		Aug. 14, 1987	
Import Albums (Federal Court Ruling Imperals)		Aug. 28, 1987	
Impressions	D	Oct. 9, 1987	
Impressions, The	D	Oct. 9, 1987	
Impressions, The/Curtis Mayfield	I	Jan. 25, 1991	
Impressions, The/Jerry Butler/Curtis Mayfield	I,D	June 1983	
Impressions, The/Jerry Butler/Curtis Mayfield	DA	Dec. 7, 1984	
Independent Record Labels	D	Nov. 4, 1988	
Independents	D	Jan. 15, 1988	
Independents	D	Jan. 15, 1988	
Ingmann, Jorgen	D,DO	July 5, 1985	
Ingmann, Jorgen	I	March 28, 1986	
Ink Spots	I,D	Sept. 14, 1984	
Innes, Neil	D	June 1980	
Innocence	D	Aug. 14, 1987	
Innocents	I,D	Sept. 1980	
Inspirational Ballads		Oct. 9, 1987	
Instrumentals: Where Have All The Instrumentals Gone		July 1983	
Insuring Your Record Collection		June 1980	
International Records/Bob Bertram	D	Feb. 1983	
Intro Records	D	Aug. 1979	
Intro Records	DA	Nov. 1979	
Intro Records	DA	March 1980	
Introduction To Pre-War Collecting		Jan.-Feb. 1977	
Invictas	D	Feb. 1979	
Invincibles		July 1981	
Iron Butterfly	D	April 10, 1987	
Iron Butterfly	DA	Sept. 25, 1987	
Iron Butterfly	I,D	Sept. 13, 1996	
Iron Maiden	D	Oct. 21, 1988	
Irwin, Bobby/Sundazed Records	I	Sept. 7, 1990	
Is It A First Or Second Pressing?		July 1981	
Is Saturday Night Fever An Incurable Disease?		Feb. 1979	
Isley Brothers/Ernie Isley	I,D	Aug. 1981	

Artist	Code	Date
Isley, Ernie/Isley Brothers	I,D	Aug. 1981
It's A Beautiful Day	I, D	April 30, 1993
Izatso (Larry Stidom) (See Also "Records:Trivia")		July-Aug. 1978
Izatso (Larry Stidom) (See Also "Records:Trivia")		Sept. 1978
Izatso (Larry Stidom) (See Also "Records:Trivia")		Nov. 1978
Izatso (Larry Stidom) (See Also "Records:Trivia")		Dec. 1978
Izatso (Larry Stidom) (See Also "Records:Trivia")		Jan. 1979
Izatso (Larry Stidom) (See Also "Records:Trivia")		April 1979
Izatso (Larry Stidom) (See Also "Records:Trivia")		Aug. 1979
Izatso (Larry Stidom) (See Also "Records:Trivia")		March 1980
Izatso (Larry Stidom) (See Also "Records:Trivia")		July 1980
Izatso (Larry Stidom) (See Also "Records:Trivia")		Sept. 1980
Izatso (Larry Stidom) (See Also "Records:Trivia")		Oct. 1980
Izatso (Larry Stidom) (See Also "Records:Trivia")		Feb. 1981
Izatso (Larry Stidom) (See Also "Records:Trivia")		June 1981
Izatso (Larry Stidom) (See Also "Records:Trivia")		Sept. 1981
Izatso (Larry Stidom) (See Also "Records:Trivia")		Oct. 1981
Izatso (Larry Stidom) (See Also "Records:Trivia")		June 1982
Izatso (Larry Stidom) (See Also "Records:Trivia")		Aug. 1982
Izatso (Larry Stidom) (See Also "Records:Trivia")		Nov. 1982

J

Artist	Code	Date
Jackie Cochran	D	Sept.-Oct. 1976
Jacks, Terry/Poppy Family	I,D	June 30, 1989
Jackson Five, the	D	Sept. 29, 1995
Jackson, Bullmoose	I,D	Nov. 1979
Jackson, Bullmoose	D	Nov. 23, 1984
Jackson, Chuck	I,D	July 4, 1997
Jackson, Deon	I,D	Sept. 23, 1988
Jackson, Deon	I,D	Sept. 23, 1988
Jackson, Freddie	I	March 27, 1987
Jackson, Janet	D	Jan. 1, 1988
Jackson, Joe	I,D	July 3, 1987
Jackson, Joe	DA	Sept. 25, 1987
Jackson, Michael		March 11, 1988
Jackson, Walter	I,D	Aug. 1979
Jackson, Wanda	I	May 22, 1987
Jackson, Wanda	D	June 5, 1987
Jackson, Wanda	DA	March 25, 1988
Jackson, Wanda	I,	March 1,1996
Jagger, Mick	I	July 29, 1988
Jam, The		Sept. 25, 1987
Jam/Paul Weller	I	June 1981
Jamerson, James		Nov. 1983
James, Elmore	D	July 17, 1987
James, Elmore	D	July 17, 1987
James, Elmore	DA	Oct. 23, 1987
James, Elmore	D	Mar. 20, 1992
James, Joni	D	Dec. 1982
James, Joni	DA	Sept. 1983
James, Leon		Oct. 1983
James, Rick	D	May 8, 1987
James, Rick		June 6, 1997
James, Tommy and the Shondells	I, D	Mar. 6, 1992
James, Tommy/Tommy James & The Shondells	I,D	July 1980
James, Tommy/Tommy James & The Shondells	DA	Dec. 1980
James, Tommy/Tommy James & The Shondells	D	Sept. 1977
Jan And Arnie	D	July 17, 1987
Jan And Dean	D	Dec. 1978
Jan And Dean	DA	Feb. 1979
Jan And Dean	I,DA	April 1982
Jan And Dean	DA	June 1, 1990
Jan And Dean	I,DA	June 1, 1990
Jan And Dean	DA	July 13, 1990
Jan And Dean	DA	Aug. 24, 1990
Japan	D	Oct. 28, 1994
Jason And The Scorchers	D	May 20, 1988

Artist	Code	Date
Jay & The Americans		Feb. 1976
Jay & The Americans/Kenny Vance	I	Aug. 1, 1986
Jay, Bobby/Laddins	I,D	April 6, 1990
Jay And The Techniques	I,D	March 15, 1996
Jaynettes		Dec. 30, 1988
Jazz at RCA Victor		May 28, 1993
Jazz News & Views (Dennis Ashley)		Sept. 1978
Jefferson Airplane	D	April 1982
Jefferson Airplane	D	Oct. 30, 1992
Jeffreys, Garland	I,D	Feb. 1981
Jeffreys, Garland		June 1981
Jeffreys, Garland	I	Aug. 12, 1988
Jeffreys, Garland	I	Aug. 12, 1988
Jenkins, Gordon/Weavers	I,D	March 15, 1985
Jenkins, Gus		July-Aug. 1978
Jenkins, Levi/Five Thrills	I,D	Feb. 8, 1991
Jennings, Waylon	D	Dec. 1979
Jennings, Waylon	DA	March 1980
Jennings, Waylon	DA	April 1980
Jennings, Waylon	I, D	Dec. 23, 1994
Jensen, Kris	I,D	Dec. 1982
Jensen, Kris		Feb. 1983
Jensen, Kris		Sept. 1983
Jensen, Kris	DA	Sept. 1983
Jethro Tull/Ian Anderson	I,D	Feb. 12, 1988
Jethro Tull/Ian Anderson		May 20, 1988
Jethro Tull/Ian Anderson	DA	Aug. 12, 1988
Jets, The		April 8, 1988
Jett, Joan	I,D	Jan. 2, 1987
Jett, Jody	I, D	Aug. 19, 1994
Jewels	D	Jan. 2, 1987
Jewels, The	D	Jan. 2, 1987
Jewel/Paula/Ronn	I	May 10, 1996
Jimmie Lee Maslon		May 1979
Jive Five/Eugene Pitt	I,D	March 1982
Jive Five/Eugene Pitt	I,D	Aug. 12, 1988
Jocque, Beau	I	Aug. 1, 1997
Jody songs	D	April 15, 1994
Joe and Eddie	D	Feb. 5, 1993
Joe, Billy and Eddy Shaver	I	Nov. 22, 1996
Joel, Billy	D	Jan. 7, 1994
John Fred	D	March 1982
John's Children/Napier Bell	I,D	Aug. 10,1990
John's Children/Napier Bell	DA	Oct. 5, 1990
John, Elton	D	Sept. 23, 1988
John, Little Willie		May 1982
John, Little Willie	D	Feb. 13, 1987
John, Mable	ID	Aug. 7, 1992
Johnnie & Joe/Johnnie Richardson	I,D	Feb. 1983
Johnnie & Joe/Johnnie Richardson	DA	Nov. 23, 1984
Johnny & The Hurricanes	D	Nov.-Dec. 1976
Johnny & The Hurricanes	D,DO	May 10, 1985
Johnny & The Hurricanes (Member Eddie Waganfeald Replies)		Oct. 1981
Johnny & The Hurricanes/Johnny Paris	D	Feb. 1981
Johnny & The Hurricanes/Johnny Paris	DA	April 1981
Johnny & The Hurricanes/Johnny Paris	DA	June 1981
Johnson, David Ceasar/Little Ceasar & The Romans	I,D,	Aug. 12, 1988
Johnson, Eric	I,D	April 21, 1989
Johnson, Gary/Elvis Sun Promo (The Second Rarest Disc)	I	Sept. 22, 1989
Johnson, Jimmy	D	Feb. 12, 1988
Johnson, Johnnie	I	Sept. 21, 1990
Johnson, Johnnie	I,D	July 19, 1996
Johnson, Luther	I,D	March 29, 1985
Johnson, Plas	D	Oct. 1983
Johnson, Robert		Feb. 26, 1988

Name	Code	Date	Name	Code	Date
Johnson, Robert		Feb. 22, 1991	Kendalls/Royce Kendall/Jeannie Kendall	I,D	Sept. 28, 1984
Johnson, Syl	I,D	Oct. 1983	Kendalls/Royce Kendall/Jeannie Kendall	DA	Aug. 2, 1985
Johnson, "General" Norman	I,D	Nov. 16, 1990	Kendrick(s), Eddie	D	June 16, 1989
Johnston, Bruce/Beach Boys	I	Oct. 1981	Kenickie	I	July 18, 1997
Jones, Booker T/Booker T & The MG's	D	July 1981	Kennebrew, Dee Dee/Crystals	I,D	Dec. 1980
Jones, Brian	D	Nov. 23, 1984	Kennebrew, Dee Dee/Crystals	I	Oct. 1983
Jones, Brian	DA	March 14, 1986	Kenner, Chris	D	Feb. 12, 1988
Jones, Carl/C.J. Records	I,D	March 1982	Kenner, Chris	D	Feb. 12, 1988
Jones Country Opens		Sept. 28, 1984	Kenny And The Kasuals	D	Oct. 1981
Jones, Davy/Monkees	I	Dec. 18, 1987	Kershaw, Doug/ & Rusty	DA	May 24, 1985
Jones, George	D	Feb. 1984	Kershaw, Doug/& Rusty	D	Oct. 1983
Jones, George	DA	Nov. 23, 1984	Keyes, Jimmy and the Chords	D	Aug. 6, 1993
Jones, Jeff/Ocean	I	Dec. 30, 1988	Keyes, Jimmy/Chords	I,D	June 19, 1987
Jones, Joe		Dec. 30, 1988	Keyes, Johnny	D	April 1979
Jones, Orville "Hoppy"		Oct. 1978	Keystone Rhythm Band/Billy Price	I,D	Aug. 1982
Jones, Rickie Lee	D	Dec. 18, 1987	Khan	D	Oct. 6, 1989
Jones, Rickie Lee	D	Dec. 18, 1987	Khan, Chaka	D	July 31, 1987
Jones, Spike	D	May 1980	Khan, Chaka	I,D	Jan. 31, 1997
Jones, Terry/Monty Python	I,D	Dec. 4, 1987	Kiderian Records/Ray Peck	I	July-Aug. 1977
Jones, Tom	D	June 3, 1988	Kihn, Greg	I,D	Dec. 1979
Joplin, Janis		March 13, 1987	Kihn, Greg	I,D	Jan. 5, 1996
Jordan, Louis	D	June 1983	King Crimson	I, D	Jan. 10, 1992
Jordan, Louis	DA	Sept. 1983	King Crimson trivia contest		Jan. 10, 1992
Jordan, Louis	DA	Dec. 7, 1984	King Crimson/Robert Fripp	I,D	Sept. 1980
Jordan, Louis		Feb. 26, 1988	King Crimson/Robert Fripp	I	April 1982
Jordan, Sheila	I	Jan. 3, 1986	King Floyd	I,D	Aug. 1983
Jordanaires/Gordon Stoker	I	Jan. 1979	King Floyd	DA	March 1, 1985
Jordanaires/Gordon Stoker	I	March 1981	King Records/Ray Pennington	I	Feb. 9,1990
Jordanaires/Gordon Stoker	I	Aug. 11, 1989	King Records/Ray Pennington		April 6, 1990
Josie And The Pussy Cats	D	Jan. 1, 1988	King Sisters, The	I, D	July 21, 1995
Josie Records	D	March 1979	King Solomon		March 1978
Journeymen	D	Sept. 1979	King Sunny Ade	I	June 1983
Joy Division/New Order	D	Feb. 7, 1992	King Toppers		April 1979
Joy Division/New Order	DA	Mar. 20, 1992	King, Albert	D	Feb. 27, 1987
Joyce, Leroy/Five Dutones	I,D	Jan. 1982	King, Albert	D	Feb. 27, 1987
Jubilee Records		June 2, 1989	King, Albert	I, D	Mar. 20, 1992
Julian, Don/Larks	I,D	Aug. 26, 1988	King, B. B.	D	April 29, 1994
Junior, Marvin/Dells	I,D	May 25, 1984	King, B.B.	I	June 1983
Junior, Marvin/Dells	I,D	July 20, 1984	King, B.B.		Feb. 26, 1988
Junior, Marvin/Dells	DA	Feb. 15, 1985	King, Ben E.		Sept. 1977
Jury	I,D	Dec. 19, 1986	King, Ben E.	I	Aug. 1981
Justis, Bill	D	June 15, 1990	King Biscuit	I	Jnuary 31, 1997
K			King, Claude	D	Dec. 1983
K-Doe, Ernie	I	Dec. 1981	King, Freddie	I,D	June 22, 1984
K Records	I	May 10, 1996	King, Freddie	D	March 13, 1987
Kaiser, Henry	I,D	March 24, 1989	King, Freddie	D	March 13, 1987
			King, Freddy	I,D	Sept. 27, 1996
Kale, Jim/Guess Who	I,D	April 1983	King, Jonathan	I, D	March 19, 1993
Kasem, Casey	I	May 11, 1984	King/Federal Records		Sept. 7, 1990
Kasem, Casey	I	March 28, 1997	Kingsmen, The	D	Feb. 1981
Katz, Matthew	I	April 30, 1993	Kingsmen, The	DA	June 1981
Kay, John/Steppenwolf	I,D	Dec. 21, 1984	Kingsmen, The	DA	Dec. 1983
Kay, John/Steppenwolf		Jan. 17, 1986	Kingsmen, The	D,DO	May 10, 1985
Kay, John/Steppenwolf	DA	Jan. 17, 1986	Kingsmen, The/Dick Peterson	I,D	Aug. 1983
Kaye, Lenny/Patti Smith Group	I	May 1980	Kingsmen, The/Dick Peterson	DA	Dec. 1983
Kaylan, Howard/Turtles	I,D	Dec. 1982	Kingsmen, The/Lynn Easton	I,D	Aug. 1983
Kaylan, Howard/Turtles		Feb. 1983	Kingsmen, The/Lynn Easton	DA	Dec. 1983
Kaylan, Howard/Turtles	DA	Sept. 1983	Kingsmen, The/Mike Mitchell	I,D	Aug. 1983
KC & The Sunshine Band	D	Nov. 4, 1988	Kingsmen, The/Mike Mitchell	DA	Dec. 1983
KC & The Sunshine Band	DA	Feb. 24,1989	Kingston Korner (Jack Rubeck & Benjamin Blake)		Nov. 1978
KC & The Sunshine Band	D	Nov. 4, 1988	Kingston Korner (Jack Rubeck & Benjamin Blake)		Dec. 1978
Keep 'Em Coming...An Appreciation Of Second Pressings		July-Aug. 1978	Kingston Korner (Jack Rubeck & Benjamin Blake)		Jan. 1979
Keisker, Marion		Feb. 9,1990	Kingston Korner (Jack Rubeck & Benjamin Blake)		Feb. 1979
Keith (James Barry Keefer)	I,D	July 4, 1986	Kingston Korner (Jack Rubeck & Benjamin Blake)		March 1979
Keith (James Barry Keefer)		June 2, 1989	Kingston Korner (Jack Rubeck & Benjamin Blake)		May 1979
Kelly, Paul	I	Jan. 5, 1996	Kingston Korner (Jack Rubeck & Benjamin Blake)		June 1979
Keltner, Jim	I	March 15, 1996	Kingston Korner (Jack Rubeck & Benjamin Blake)		July 1979

Name	Code	Date
Little Eva	DA	March 9, 1990
Little Eva	I,D	May 20, 1988
Little Eva	DA	Aug. 12, 1988
Little Feat On CD		Aug. 12, 1988
Little Feat/Paul Barrere	I,D	Dec. 1983
Little Feat/Paul Barrere	DA	March 1, 1985
Little Feat/Paul Barrere & Bill Payne	I,D	Dec. 2, 1988
Little Johnny Taylor	I,D	Aug. 28, 1987
Little Johnny Taylor	DA	Oct. 23, 1987
Little Milton	I	May 1981
Little Reuben Fisher	D	Dec. 1983
Little Richard	I	April 10, 1987
Little Richard		Feb. 26, 1988
Little Steven	I,D	Feb. 1983
Little Steven	I	Nov. 9, 1984
Little Steven (Van Zandt)	I	Nov. 9, 1984
Little Willie John		May 1982
Little Willie John	D	Feb. 13, 1987
Littlejohn, Johnny	D	March 25, 1988
Lively Ones	I,D	Oct. 1980
Livsey, Barbara	D	Sept. 1981
Locorriere, Dennis/Dr. Hook	I,D	April 1981
Lofgren, Nils	I,D	July 19, 1985
Lofgren, Nils	DA	Feb. 13, 1987
Logsdon, Jimmie	I,D	Feb. 1980
Loizzo, Gary/American Breed	I,D	Sept. 1980
London's Record Shops		Aug. 28, 1987
London's Reggae Record Stores, Guide To		Oct. 26, 1984
London, Julie	D	Jan. 1984
Long Ryders/Sid Griffin	I	Aug. 14, 1987
Looking At Surf Rarities		April 1981
Looking Back At Goldmine's Founding		May 25, 1984
Lopez, Gil/Tuneweavers	I,D	Feb. 8, 1991
Loren, Donna	D	March 1980
Los Angeles' Rarest Labels		Feb. 1983
Los Lobos	I,D	May 22, 1987
Los Lobos	I, D	Sept 4, 1992
Lothar & The Hand People	D	Feb. 13, 1987
Louie Louie		Jan. 2, 1987
Louie Louie Anniversary Tour, interviews with Len Barry, Sonny Geraci, and Jack Ely		May 1, 1992
Lounge Music	D	April 26, 1996
Louvin Brothers	D	March 1981
Louvin Brothers	DA	June 1981
Love	D	Feb. 13, 1987
Love		Feb. 13, 1987
Love, Darlene	I	April 12, 1985
Love, Darlene	I	June 17, 1988
Love, Darlene	I	March 4, 1994
Love, Mike	I	July 1983
Love, Mike	I	Sept. 18, 1992
Lovett, Lyle		Oct. 16, 1992
Lovin Spoonful/John Sebastian	I,D	July 1982
Lovin Spoonful/John Sebastian	DA	Jan. 1983
Lowe, Nick	I,D	June 1982
Lowe, Nick		Aug. 1982
Lowe, Nick	DA	Aug. 1982
Lower Court Must Rehear Richard Minor Case		Jan. 3, 1986
Lowery, David/Camper Van Beethoven	I,D	Nov. 4, 1988
Lucky 13 (Richard Haggett)		July-Aug. 1978
Luke, Robin	D	July 10, 1992
Lulu	I,D	Feb. 1982
Lulu		May 1982
Lulu		June 1982
Lulu		Nov. 6, 1987
Lulu	DA	March 11, 1988
Lulu	I, D	April 1, 1994
Luman, Bob	D	Jan. 1980
Luman, Bob	DA	April 1980
Luman, Bob	DA	Aug. 1980
Luman, Bob	I	Sept. 8, 1989
Lummtone Records/Lummie Fowler	I,D	July 4, 1986
Lynch, Stan	I	Dec. 6, 1996
Lymon, Frankie & The Teenagers		Sept. 1977
Lymon, Frankie & The Teenagers/Jimmy Merchant	I,D	March 1982
Lymon, Lewis & The Teenchords	I,D	Jan. 1983
Lynn, Barbara	D	March 13, 1987
Lynn, Barbara	D	March 13, 1987
Lynyrd Skynyrd	I, D	May 29, 1992
Lyon, Johnny/Southside Johnny	I,D	May 25, 1984
Lyons, Leo/Ten Years After	I,D	Oct. 6, 1989
Lyons, Leo/Ten Years After	DA	Dec. 29, 1989
Lyres, The	I,D	Sept. 9, 1988

M

Name	Code	Date
Mabon, Willie	D	July 5, 1985
Mac Curtis (Wesley Erwin Curtis)		Nov. 1977
MacCall, Kirsty	I,D	Sept. 13, 1996
Mack, Lonnie	I,D	Nov. 8, 1985
Mack, Lonnie	DA	Jan. 3, 1986
Maddox Brothers And Rose		Feb. 9,1990
Madison, Stewart/Malaco Records	I	June 2, 1989
Madness/Daniel Woodgate	I	Nov. 1983
Madness/Daniel Woodgate	I	Nov. 1983
Madonna	ID	July 24, 1992
Mael, Ron/Sparks	I,D	April 1983
Mael, Ron/Sparks	DA	Dec. 7, 1984
Maestro, Johnny/Crests	I	March+April 1977
Maghett, Sam	D	Jan. 15, 1988
Maghett, Sam	DA	June 3, 1988
Maghett, Sam	D	Jan. 15, 1988
Magic Slim & The Teardrops	D	Sept. 9, 1988
Magicians	D	Nov. 6, 1987
Magicians, The	D	Nov. 6, 1987
Magnificents, The	D	April 1979
Magnum	I	May 19, 1989
Mahal, Taj	I,D	Feb. 28, 1986
Mahal, Taj	DA	May 9, 1986
Mailing Tips: Shipping 78s The Right Way		Nov. 21, 1986
Mainman	I	June 6, 1997
Majors, The	I,D	Dec. 28, 1990
Makem, Tommy/Liam Clancy/Clancy Brothers & Tommy Makem	I,D	Aug. 17, 1984
Making Tracks Chicago Style	D	Jan.4, 1985
Malaco		May 10, 1996
Malaco Records/Stewart Madison	I	June 2, 1989
Malibooz/John Zambetti/Walter Egan	I,D	March 2, 1984
Mama's & Papa's	I,D	April 1982
Mama's & Papa's		Aug. 1982
Mama's & Papa's	DA	Jan. 1983
Mama's & Papa's/Michelle Phillips	I,D	Sept. 1980
Man		June 19, 1987
Man		June 19, 1987
Mandel, Harvey	I, D	Aug. 19, 1994
Mandrake Memorial/Craig Anderton	I,D	Feb. 27, 1987
Manfred Mann	I, D	June 12, 1992
Manhattan Transfer/Tim Hauser	I,D	July 6, 1984
Manhattans	D	March 25, 1988
Manhattans	D	March 25, 1988
Manilow, Barry		Sept. 27, 1996
Mann, Barry		Dec. 30, 1988
Mann, Barry/Cynthia Weil	I,D	Aug. 1982
Mann, Barry/Cynthia Weil		Feb. 1983
Mann, Barry/Cynthia Weil	DA	Sept. 1983

Name	Code	Date	Name	Code	Date
Mann, Carl		April 24, 1987	Mc Call, Cash	D	Aug. 14, 1987
Mann, Manfred	D	Feb. 1983	Mc Coy, Van		Dec. 1, 1989
Mann, Manfred	DA	April 1983	Mc Donald	I,D	Dec. 7, 1984
Mann, Manfred	DA	Sept. 1983	Mc Donald	DA	Jan. 17, 1986
Mann, Manfred	DA	Oct. 1983	Mc Donald, Country Joe/Country Joe & The Fish	D	Dec. 7, 1984
Mann, Manfred	DA	Dec. 7, 1984	Mc Donald, Steve/Redd Kross	I,D	Dec. 2, 1988
Manzarek, Ray	I	April 14, 1995	Mc Elrath, John/Swingin' Medallions	I	Dec. 1, 1989
Manzarek, Ray/Doors		June 21, 1985	Mc Garrigle, Kate & Anna	D	Jan. 26, 1990
Manzarek, Ray/Doors		July 5, 1985	Mc Gill, Mickey/Dells	I,D	May 25, 1984
Mar Vel Records/Harry Glenn/Cowboy Carl Schneider	I	Nov. 1981	Mc Gill, Mickey/Dells	I,D	July 20, 1984
Marathons/Walter Ward/Olympics	I	Dec. 1, 1989	Mc Gill, Mickey/Dells	I,D	Aug. 3, 1984
March, Peggy	I,D	Sept. 23, 1988	Mc Gill, Mickey/Dells	DA	Feb. 15, 1985
March, Peggy	I,D	Sept. 23, 1988	Mc Guinn, Clark & Hillman		Feb. 1979
Marchan, Bobby	I,D	Sept. 25, 1987	Mc Guinn, Roger	I	Jan. 11, 1991
Marchan, Bobby	I,D	Sept. 25, 1987	Mc Guinn, Roger/Byrds	I	Feb. 1979
Maresca, Ernie	I	Nov. 1980	Mc Guinn, Roger/Byrds	I,D	Nov. 1983
Maresca, Ernie/Laurie Records	I	Oct. 1982	Mc Guinn, Roger/Byrds		May 25, 1984
Maria, Tania	I	April 26, 1985	Mc Guinn, Roger/Byrds		July 1, 1988
Marie, Teena	D	July 3, 1987	Mc Guinn, Roger/Byrds	I	Jan. 11, 1991
Marillion	D	Dec. 15, 1989	Mc Guinn, Roger/Byrds	DA	Feb. 8, 1991
Marley, Bob	D	July 1981	Mc Guire, Barry		Dec. 30, 1988
Marley, Bob	D	Jan. 12, 1990	Mc Kenzie, Scott	D	March 11, 1988
Mars, Chris	I	Jan. 31, 1997	Mc Kenzie, Scott	D	March 11, 1988
Marsalis, Wynton	I,D	May 25, 1984	Mc Lain, Tommy	D	Sept. 21, 1990
Marsden, Gerry/Gerry And The Pacemakers	D	March 29, 1985	Mc Lain, Tommy	DA	Oct. 19, 1990
Marshall Crenshaw	I, D	Aug. 4, 1995	Mc Laughlin, Ollie	I	June 3, 1988
Marshall, Percy	I	Oct. 1978	Mc Lean, Don	D	Oct. 1977
Martha & The Vandellas/Martha Reeves	I,D	June 1981	Mc Lean, Don	D	Oct. 11, 1985
Martha & The Vandellas/Martha Reeves	I,D	June 16, 1989	Mc Lean, Don	I	Aug. 29, 1986
Martha Reeves and the Vandellas	I, D	March 3, 1995	Mc Murry, Lillian/Trumpet Records	D	Jan. 1980
Martignon, J.D./Midnight Records	I	June 2, 1989	Mc Murry, Lillian/Trumpet Records	DA	April 1980
Martin, Janis		Jan.-Feb. 1977	Mc Murry, Lillian/Trumpet Records	DA	July 6, 1984
Martinez, Rudy/? And The Mysterians	I,D	April 1982	Mc Murry, Lillian/Trumpet Records	DA	Feb. 1, 1985
Marvelettes, The	I,D	June 8, 1984	Mc Nally, John/Searchers	I,D	June 1981
Marvelows, The		Dec. 1, 1989	Mc Neely, Big Jay	I,D	Dec. 6, 1985
Marx Brothers, the	D	June 24, 1994	Mc Neely, Big Jay	I	Nov. 2, 1990
Mask Man, the, and his agents	I, D	May 13, 1994	Mc Phatter, Clyde	D	June 1983
Maslon, Jimmie Lee		May 1979	Mc Phatter, Clyde	DA	Dec. 7, 1984
Mason, Dave	I,D	Feb. 16, 1996	Mc Phatter, Clyde		Feb. 26, 1988
Mason Proffit	D	March 9, 1990	Mc Rae, Teddy	D	Aug. 14, 1987
Matador Records		March 18, 1994	Mc5	D	Sept. 9, 1988
Match The Doo Wops Contest		June 30, 1989	Mc5	DA	Nov. 18, 1988
Match The Doo Wops Contest		Nov. 3, 1989	Mc5	D	Sept. 9, 1988
Matchbox (The Group)		Feb. 1981	Mc5/Dennis Thompson	I,D	May 1979
Mathis, "Country" Johnny	I, D	May 28, 1993	MCA Records' Steve Hoffman		Nov. 1983
Mathis, Johnny	I, D	May 28, 1993	MCA's Berry And Dixon Box Sets		Feb. 24, 1989
Mathis, Johnny		Jan. 5, 1996	McCartney's, Paul Choba B Cccp Album		Nov. 17, 1989
Mauldin, Joe/Crickets	I	May-June 1978	McCartney's, Paul Lost Album		Feb. 24, 1989
Mauldin, Joe/Crickets	I,D	Feb. 10, 1989	McCartney, Mike	D	Oct. 19, 1990
Mauriat, Paul		Dec. 1, 1989	McCartney, Paul		Aug. 16, 1985
Maxwell, Holly	D	Sept. 1978	McCartney, Paul: Melodiya Mystery		Oct. 19, 1990
Maxwell, Holly	I,D	Jan. 1, 1988	McClain, Charly	D	Sept. 1982
May, Phil/Pretty Things	I,D	Oct. 6, 1989	McClain, Charly	DA	Sept. 1983
May, Phil/Pretty Things	I,D	Oct. 20, 1989	McClinton, Delbert	I,D	April 21, 1989
May, Phil/Pretty Things	DA	Nov. 17, 1989	McCormick, Gayle/Smith	I,D	Dec. 1982
Mayall, John	I, D	Sept. 3, 1993	McGriff, Jimmy	I, D	Mar. 20, 1992
Mayall, John Bluesbreakers		July 1982	McGuire, Barry	I, D	Nov. 13, 1992
Mayall, John Bluesbreakers	I,D	Feb. 23, 1990	McVie, Christine	I	Sept. 18, 1992
Mayfield, Curtis and the Impressions	I, D	April 2, 1993	Meat Loaf	D	Oct. 23, 1987
Mayfield, Curtis/Impressions	I,D	June 1983	Meat Loaf	D	Oct. 23, 1987
Mayfield, Curtis/Impressions		Dec. 7, 1984	Meat Puppets	I, D	April 28, 1995
Mayfield, Curtis/Impressions	I	Jan. 25, 1991	Meaux, Huey P.	I	April 22, 1988
Mayfield, Curtis	I,D	July 4, 1997	Meaux, Huey P.	I	June 3, 1988
Mayfield, Percy	D	March 14, 1997	Meaux, Huey P.	I	Sept. 9, 1988
Mayne, Roger/Ugly Ducklings	I,D	May 1980	Meaux, Huey P.	I	March 29, 1996
Mc Call, Cash	D	Aug. 14, 1987	Medley, Bill	I	March 4, 1994
Mc Call, Cash		Dec. 1, 1989	Medley, Bill/Righteous Brothers	I,D	May 11, 1984

Name	Code	Date
Mountain	I, D	July 21, 1995
Mudhoney discography		Apr. 17, 1992
Muldaur, Maria	ID	May 28, 1993
Mulligan, Dec/Beau Brummels	I,D	March 14, 1986
MultiMania! [by Jeff Tamarkin]		Dec. 8, 1995
Mumford, Eugene	D	April 6, 1990
Mumford, Eugene	DA	June 1, 1990
Mungo Jerry		Dec. 30, 1988
Murphy, Elliot	D	Sept. 18, 1992
Murray Hill Records		June 7, 1985
Murray Hill Records/Bob Hyde	I	June 2, 1989
Murray The K (DJ)	I	Feb. 1981
Music Biz Seminars Deal With Current Issues		Jan. 17, 1986
Music Book Update Part 1		March 23, 1990
Music City Records	D	July 31, 1987
Music Club	I	May 9, 1997
Music I Love To Hate		May-June 1978
Music In Action: Fighting An Uphill Battle Against Censorship		Jan. 27, 1989
Music In The Air (Lou Dumont)		Feb. 1979
Music Machine/Sean Bonniwell	I,D	Aug. 29, 1986
Music Magazines		July 1976
Music Video Collecting	D	June 3, 1988
Musical Youth	I	March 1983
Musselwhite, Charlie	I, D	Mar. 20, 1992
Mystics, The	I,D	Nov. 1983
N		
Nadar, Richard	I	Feb. 1982
Nadar, Richard	I	Sept. 7, 1990
Napoleon XIV		Sept.-Oct. 1976
Napoleon XIV		Dec. 30, 1988
Narada Records/Terry Woods	I	Sept. 7, 1990
Nash, Johnny	D	Jan. 12, 1990
Nashville Nuggets (Robert Oermann)		April 1983
Nashville Nuggets (Robert Oermann)		June 1983
Nashville Nuggets (Robert Oermann)		Aug. 1983
National Elvis Presley Day?		Jan. 1982
Nazz/Stewkey Antoni	I,D	Feb. 1983
Needham, Max (Waxie Maxie)		Jan. 1978
Neil, Fred	I,D	April 26, 1996
Nelson Young		March 1979
Nelson Young		April 1979
Nelson, Nate/Flamingos	I,D	March 1978
Nelson, Rick	D	Aug. 1980
Nelson, Rick	I,D	Feb. 14, 1986
Nelson, Rick		April 11, 1986
Nelson, Rick		Aug. 28, 1987
Nelson, Rick		Feb. 26, 1988
Nelson, Rick		Aug. 28, 1987
Nelson, Sandy	I,D	March 1983
Nelson, Sandy		Sept. 1983
Nelson, Sandy	DA	Dec. 7, 1984
Nelson, Willie	I,D	Jan. 6, 1995
Nele Festival '87		July 31, 1987
New Millenium	I	May 9, 1997
New Orleans Jazz & Heritage Festival '88		July 1, 1988
New Orleans Rock & Roll	D	Feb. 1981
New Riders Of The Purple Sage		May 8, 1987
New Riders Of The Purple Sage		May 8, 1987
New Synthesizer Rock: Before ELP	D	Aug. 24, 1990
New Vaudeville Band		Dec. 30, 1988
New Wave Floods Mainstream		May 1981
New York Dolls	D	March 11, 1988
New York's 10 Best Record Stores		Feb. 27, 1987
Newbury, Mickey	D	April 6, 1990
Newhart, Bob	D	Nov. 1979
Newman, Randy	D	Nov. 1981
Newman, Randy	D	Sept. 1, 1995
Newton, Wayne	I	June 21, 1996
Nexus: A Fusion Song Cycle Based On Songs/Poetry Of Richard P Havens		Nov. 1982
Nightcaps/Billy Joe Shine	I,D	June 1980
Nightcaps/Billy Joe Shine	D	Dec. 1981
Nighthawk Records		Aug. 3, 1984
Nighthawks, The	I	Sept. 1980
Nilsson, Harry	I	May 11, 1984
Nilsson, Harry	I, D	April 29, 1994
Nine Inch Nails	D	Aug. 4, 1995
Nine Nobles/Ron Courtney	I	May 9, 1986
Nirvana	D	Dec. 10, 1993
Nirvana		Feb. 14, 1997j
Nirvana/Kurt Cobain's Birthday	I,D	Feb. 14, 1997
Nirvana/Kurt's Suicide Circus		Feb. 14, 1997
Nirvana (original, brit. group, not the grunge group		April 14, 1995
Nirvana discography		Apr. 17, 1992
Nitty Gritty Dirt Band/Jimmie Fadden/Jimmy Ibbotson	I,D	Feb. 9,1990
Nitty Gritty Dirt Band/Jimmie Fadden/Jimmy Ibbotson	DA	March 23, 1990
Nitzsche, Jack	I	June 17, 1988
Nixon, Mojo	I	Aug. 10,1990
Nixon, Richard (a "Dickography"		May 27, 1994
Noone, Peter/Herman's Hermits	I	March 1981
Norfolk Jazz Quartet	D	Sept. 1979
North Texas Roundup		March 16, 1984
Notations	D	Jan. 1979
Notes From Downunder (Glenn Baker)		Sept. 14, 1984
Notes From Downunder (Glenn Baker)		Dec. 21, 1984
Now Is The Time To Become A Record Collector/Investor		April 1983
NRBQ	I,D	Jan. 1982
NRBQ	D	May 18, 1990
Number One Songs On The 4th Of July	D	July-Aug. 1978
Nutmegs	D	July 31, 1987
O		
O'Jays	D	June 19, 1987
O'Jays, The	D	June 19, 1987
O'Jays, The	D	Dec. 28, 1990
O'Leary, Reparata/Reparata & The Delrons	I,D	April 1983
O'Leary, Reparata/Reparata & The Delrons	DA	Dec. 7, 1984
O'Neill, Jimmy	I	July 1, 1988
O'Neill, Jimmy	I	Sept. 21, 1990
O. V. Wright	D	Dec. 18, 1987
Oasis		Feb. 16, 1996
Obit: Hull, Alan		Dec. 22, 1995
Obit: Stanshall, Vivian		April 14, 1995
Obit: Abe Neff		July 6, 1984
Obit: Abe Olman		March 2, 1984
Obit: Ace Buddy		March 17, 1995
Obit: Acuff, Roy		Dec. 25, 1992
Obit: Ahbez, Eben		May 26, 1995
Obit: Al Cohn		March 25, 1988
Obit: Al Dexter		March 16, 1984
Obit: Al Haig		Jan. 1983
Obit: Al Sears		May 18, 1990
Obit: Albert Grossman		April 11, 1986
Obit: Albert Johnson		Feb. 1, 1985
Obit: Albert White		Feb. 1984
Obit: Alberta Hunter		Dec. 7, 1984
Obit: Alberta Hunter		March 15, 1985
Obit: Alex Harvey		April 1982
Obit: Alex Korner		March 16, 1984
Obit: Alex Sadkin		Oct. 23, 1987
Obit: Alexander, Arthur		July 9, 1993
Obit: Allan Jaffe		April 24, 1987
Obit: Allen Collins		Feb. 23, 1990

Obit: Allen, Lee	Nov. 25, 1994	Obit: Bonnie M. Dodd	Feb. 1, 1985
Obit: Allin, GG	Aug. 6, 1993	Obit: Boris Schwarz	March 2, 1984
Obit: Almeida, Laurindo	Sept. 1, 1995	Obit: Boudleaux Bryant	Aug. 14, 1987
Obit: Alvin Robinson	May 5, 1989	Obit: Boyce, Tommy	Dec. 23, 1994
Obit: Amos Milburn	March 1980	Obit: Boyce, Tommy correction	Jan. 6, 1995
Obit: Andres Segovia	July 17, 1987	Obit: Boyd, Bill	March 31, 1995
Obit: Andrew Brown	Feb. 14, 1986	Obit: Boyd, Eddie	Sept. 16, 1994
Obit: Andrews, Darnell "D-Boy"	July 7, 1995	Obit: Breaux, Zachary	April 25, 1997
Obit: Andy Gibb	April 8, 1988	Obit: Brent Mydland	Aug. 24, 1990
Obit: Ann Sheldon	April 26, 1985	Obit: Brian Marnell	Dec. 1983
Obit: Annie Mc Fadden	Aug. 1982	Obit: Briggs, David	Jan. 5, 1996
Obit: Antrell, Dave "Doc"	April 28, 1995	Obit: Brilleaux, Lee	May 13, 1994
Obit: Archie Bleyer	April 21, 1989	Obit: Brook Benton	May 20, 1988
Obit: Arnold, Jack	May 1, 1992	Obit: Brown, Albert "Pud"	July 5, 1996
Obit: Art Blakey	Nov. 16, 1990	Obit: Brown, Oscar	Sept. 27, 1996
Obit: Art Lund	July 13, 1990	Obit: Buckley, Jeff	July 4, 1997
Obit: Art Pepper	Aug. 1982	Obit: Budd Johnson	Dec. 7, 1984
Obit: Art Satherley	March 28, 1986	Obit: Buddy Rich	June 5, 1987
Obit: Arthur Schwartz	Oct. 12, 1984	Obit: Bull Moose Jackson	Nov. 3,1989
Obit: Arvella Gray	Dec. 1980	Obit: Burbank, Charles	July 21, 1995
Obit: Ashman, Matthew	Feb. 16, 1996	Obit: Burrello, Tony	Oct. 30, 1992
Obit: Aug., Joseph "Mr. Google Eyes"	Nov. 13, 1992	Obit: Byers, Bill	June 21, 1996
Obit: B. Mitchell Reed	May 1983	Obit: Cage, John	Sept. 18, 1992
Obit: Baker, Bill	Sept. 30, 1994	Obit: Cal Tjader	Aug. 1982
Obit: Baker, LaVern	May 9, 1997	Obit: Caldwell, Toy	April 2, 1993
Obit: Balasaraswati	May 11, 1984	Obit: California, Randy	Feb. 14, 1997
Obit: Barbara Cowsill	May 10, 1985	Obit: Calloway, Cab	Dec. 23, 1994
Obit: Barker, Danny	April 29, 1994	Obit: Calvin Jackson	Feb. 28, 1986
Obit: Barry Sadler	Dec. 15, 1989	Obit: Campbell, Choker	Sept. 17, 1993
Obit: Barton, Alan	April 28, 1995	Obit: Campbell, John	July 23, 1993
Obit: Bass, Ralph	June 20, 1997	Obit: Carl Jones	April 25, 1986
Obit: Baxter, Les	March 1, 1996	Obit: Carl White	July 1980
Obit: Beatrice Smith	Sept. 1983	Obit: Carmen Dragon	May 25, 1984
Obit: Ben Ellison	April 13, 1984	Obit: Caroline Franklin	June 17, 1988
Obit: Bennett, Wayne	Jan. 22, 1993	Obit: Carroll, Johnny	April 28, 1995
Obit: Benny Goodman	Aug. 15, 1986	Obit: Charles Mingus	April 1979
Obit: Benton, Buster	March 29, 1996	Obit: Charles R. Mc Nally	Aug. 30, 1985
Obit: Berry, Richard	Feb. 28, 1997	Obit: Charles, Tommy	Nov., 8, 1996
Obit: Bert Kaempfert	Aug. 1980	Obit: Charlie Allen	July 13, 1990
Obit: Bessie Jones	Dec. 7, 1984	Obit: Charlie Parker	July 13, 1990
Obit: Big Joe Williams	May 1983	Obit: Cheatham, Doc	July 4, 1997
Obit: Big Leon Brooks	April 1982	Obit: Chet Baker	July 1, 1988
Obit: Big Twist (Larry Nolan)	April 20, 1990	Obit: Chouinard, Bobby	April 25, 1997
Obit: Big Willie Mabon	D July 5, 1985	Obit: Chris Wood	Oct. 1983
Obit: Bill Harris	Feb. 10, 1989	Obit: Christopher Adler	Feb. 1, 1985
Obit: Bill Justis	Sept. 1982	Obit: Chuck Willis	Nov. 23, 1984
Obit: Bill Kenny	Oct. 1978	Obit: Churchill Kohlman	Sept. 1983
Obit: Bill Mounce	Nov. 9, 1984	Obit: Clark, Dave	Sept. 1, 1995
Obit: Bill Pickering	May 10, 1985	Obit: Clarke, Michael	Jan. 21, 1994
Obit: Billy Bowen	Dec. 1982	Obit: Claude Hopkins	April 13, 1984
Obit: Billy Fury	April 1983	Obit: Clifton Chenier	Jan. 15, 1988
Obit: Billy "Tiny" Moore	Feb. 12, 1988	Obit: Cobain, Kurt	May 13, 1994
Obit: Blackwell, Ed	Nov. 13, 1992	Obit: Cole, David	March 31, 1995
Obit: Blandon, Richard	Feb.7, 1992	Obit: Collin Walcott	Feb. 1, 1985
Obit: Bo Gentry	Sept. 1983	Obit: Collins, Albert	Jan. 7, 1994
Obit: Bob Astor	March 15, 1985	Obit: Condello, Mike	Sept. 29, 1995
Obit: Bob Hite	May 1981	Obit: Connolly, Brian/The Sweet	March 14, 1997
Obit: Bob Jennings	July 6, 1984	Obit: Cootie Williams	Oct. 25, 1985
Obit: Bob Marley	July 1981	Obit: Cordell, Denny	March 31, 1995
Obit: Bob Morris	March 1982	Obit: Cornell Gunther	April 6, 1990
Obit: Bob "Bobalu" Lewis	March 13, 1987	Obit: Count Basie	D May 25, 1984
Obit: Bobby Day	Sept. 7, 1990	Obit: Cousin Joe (Pleasant Joseph)	Dec. 1, 1989
Obit: Bobby Mitchell	May 5, 1989	Obit: Covington, Robert	March 29, 1996
Obit: Bobby Nunn	Dec. 19, 1986	Obit: Creenberg, Chuck	Nov. 24, 1995
Obit: Bogue, Merwyn "Ish Kabibble"	July 8, 1994	Obit: Crosby, Bob	April 16, 1993
Obit: Bolian, Jesse	Oct. 28, 1994	Obit: Crosby, Gary	Sept. 29, 1995
Obit: Bolin, Tommy	Jan. 5, 1996	Obit: Curless, Dick	July 7, 1995

Obit: Cymbal, Johnny "Derek"	June 11, 1993	Obit: Estella "Mama" Yancey	June 20, 1986
Obit: Dairo, I.K.	March 29, 1996	Obit: Ethel Azama	May 11, 1984
Obit: Dale Edwards	Jan. 1983	Obit: Ethel Merman	March 16, 1984
Obit: Dale Shelnut	July 1983	Obit: Eubie Blake	April 1983
Obit: Dallas Taylor	Feb. 27, 1987	Obit: Eugene Ormandy	May 24, 1985
Obit: Daniel, Nathan I	Feb. 3, 1995	Obit: Eurreal "Little Brother" Montgomery	Oct. 25, 1985
Obit: Danny Rapp	May 1983	Obit: Ewan Mac Coll	Dec. 15, 1989
Obit: Dave Gordon	Dec. 19, 1986	Obit: Farrell, Wes "Sloopy"	May 10, 1996
Obit: Dave Prater	May 6, 1988	Obit: Feather, Leonard	Oct. 28, 1994
Obit: David Blue	Feb. 1983	Obit: Felix Pappalardi	June 1983
Obit: David Lynch	Feb. 1981	Obit: Fernando Corena	Feb. 1, 1985
Obit: David Martin	Sept. 25, 1987	Obit: Flemons, Wade	March 4, 1994
Obit: David Rogers	Dec. 1983	Obit: Floyd Smith	July 1982
Obit: David Rose	Oct. 5, 1990	Obit: Fontenot, Canray	Sept. 1, 1995
Obit: David Torbert	May 1983	Obit: Ford, Clarence	Sept. 16, 1994
Obit: Davis, James "Thunderbird"	Mar. 6, 1992	Obit: Fowler, Wally	July 8, 1994
Obit: Deafose, John	Oct. 28, 1994	Obit: Francia White	Dec. 7, 1984
Obit: Dean Paul Martin	May 8, 1987	Obit: Franklin, Melvin	March 31, 1995
Obit: Dee Clark	Jan. 11, 1991	Obit: Fred Martin	Oct. 10, 1986
Obit: Del Rubio, Eadie	March 14, 1997	Obit: Freddy Martin	Feb. 1984
Obit: Del Shannon	March 9, 1990	Obit: Freed, David	June 21, 1996
Obit: Dennis Hoffman	Aug. 30, 1985	Obit: Freeman Gosden	Feb. 1983
Obit: Dennis Wilson	Feb. 1984	Obit: Galbraith, Art	April 16, 1993
Obit: Dexter Gordon	June 15, 1990	Obit: Gale, Eric	July 8, 1994
Obit: Dickie Goodman	Jan. 12, 1990	Obit: Gallagher, Rory	July 21, 1995
Obit: DiMarino, Laura	Dec. 20, 1996	Obit: Garcia, Frankie "Cannibal"	March 15, 1996
Obit: Dixon, Willie	Mar. 6, 1992	Obit: Garcia, Jerry	Sept. 15, 1995
Obit: Dock Green	May 5, 1989	Obit: Gary Morrison	Dec. 4, 1987
Obit: Dolores Warren	Aug. 30, 1985	Obit: Gary Usher	June 29, 1990
Obit: Don Costa	March 1983	Obit: Gatton, Danny	Nov. 11, 1994
Obit: Don Ewell	Oct. 1983	Obit: Gene Ramey	Feb. 1, 1985
Obit: Don Gant	May 8, 1987	Obit: Gene Ramey	April 26, 1985
Obit: Don Paul Yowell	Feb. 1, 1985	Obit: George Bruns	Sept. 1983
Obit: Don Ray	May 10, 1985	Obit: George David Rock	June 3, 1988
Obit: Don Reno	Dec. 7, 1984	Obit: George Duvivier	Sept. 27, 1985
Obit: Don Reno	Feb. 1, 1985	Obit: George Mc Curn	Sept. 27, 1985
Obit: Donald James Addrisi	March 15, 1985	Obit: George Thill	Feb. 1, 1985
Obit: Donnie Elbert	March 24, 1989	Obit: Georgeanna Marie Tillmen Gorden	July 1980
Obit: Dopsie, Rockin' (Alton Rubin)	Oct. 1, 1993	Obit: Gil Evans	May 6, 1988
Obit: Dorsey, Thomas	March 5, 1993	Obit: Gilbert, Kevin	Sept. 27, 1996
Obit: Doug Wray	July 6, 1984	Obit: Gillespie, Dizzy	Feb. 5, 1993
Obit: Douglas, Steve	May 28, 1993	Obit: Gilmore, John	Sept. 29, 1995
Obit: Duffey, John	Jan. 31, 1997	Obit: Gloria Stavers	May 1983
Obit: Dupree, Jack	Feb. 21, 1992	Obit: Ginsberg, Allen	May 23, 1997
Obit: Earl "Fatha" Hines	July 1983	Obit: Goettel, Dwayne	Sept. 29, 1995
Obit: Easdale, Brian	March 29, 1996	Obit: Goldman, Albert	April 29, 1994
Obit: Eazy-E (Eric Wright)	April 28, 1995	Obit: Gordon, Irving	Jan. 3, 1997
Obit: Eckstine, Billy	April 16, 1993	Obit: Gordon Jenkins	July 20, 1984
Obit: Ed Kirkeby	Nov. 1978	Obit: Gottlieb, Lou	Aug. 16, 1996
Obit: Eddie Taylor	April 25, 1986	Obit: Greenhill, Manny	May 24, 1996
Obit: Eddie Thomas	Oct. 10, 1986	Obit: Grolnick, Don	July 5, 1996
Obit: Eddie Vinson	Aug. 26, 1988	Obit: Guzman, Eddie	Sept. 13, 1993
Obit: Eddie "Lockjaw" Davis	Dec. 5, 1986	Obit: Gwynn Cornell	March 15, 1985
Obit: Edmonton, Jerry	April 15, 1994	Obit: Hal Worthington	April 20, 1990
Obit: Edward Elkins	Feb. 1, 1985	Obit: Hamilton, Dan	Feb. 17, 1995
Obit: Edward Freche	May 12, 1995	Obit: Hammie Nixon	Nov. 23, 1984
Obit: Edwards, Bernard	May 24, 1996	Obit: Harold Arlen	June 20, 1986
Obit: Edwin Morrison	April 10, 1987	Obit: Harrison, Wilbert	Dec. 9, 1994
Obit: Elgart, Les	Sept. 1, 1995	Obit: Harry Carlson	May 23, 1986
Obit: Elizabeth Cotton	Aug. 14, 1987	Obit: Harry Chapin	Sept. 1981
Obit: Ellington, Mercer	March 29, 1996	Obit: Harry James	Sept. 1983
Obit: Ellison, Jim	Aug. 2, 1996	Obit: Harry Mills	Sept. 1982
Obit: Emily Remler	July 13, 1990	Obit: Harry Truitt	May 10, 1985
Obit: Ernest Tubb	Oct. 12, 1984	Obit: Hartman, Dan	April 29, 1994
Obit: Ernie Freeman	June 1982	Obit: Hawkins, Erskine	Dec. 24, 1993
Obit: Ervin, Difosco "Dee" [Big Dee Irwin]	Nov. 24, 1995	Obit: Hawkins, Ted	Feb. 17, 1995
Obit: Esquerita	Aug. 28, 1987	Obit: Hazel, Eddie	Feb. 19, 1993

Obit: Helen Donohoe Braun	Feb. 1, 1985	Obit: Joe Banashak	Dec. 20, 1985
Obit: Helen Mortenson Roberts	July 6, 1984	Obit: Joe Liggins	D Sept. 25, 1987
Obit: Hemphill, Julious	May 26, 1995	Obit: Joe Rapaso	March 24, 1989
Obit: Herbert Magidson	April 25, 1986	Obit: Joe Tex	Oct. 1982
Obit: Herman "Sunny" Chaney	May 5, 1989	Obit: Joe Turner	Jan. 17, 1986
Obit: Hillel Slovak	Aug. 26, 1988	Obit: Joe Val	Aug. 30, 1985
Obit: Hinton, Eddie	Sept. 1, 1995	Obit: Joel Turnero a.k.a Joe Turner/Skip Layne	Nov. 20, 1987
Obit: Hoagy Carmichael	Feb. 1982	Obit: John Cipollina	June 30, 1989
Obit: Hogan, Silas	May 27, 1994	Obit: John Felton	July 1982
Obit: Hollis Gray	July 6, 1984	Obit: John Gilston	July 20, 1984
Obit: Hoon, Shannon	Nov. 24, 1995	Obit: John Hammond, Sr.,	Sept. 11, 1987
Obit: Hopkins, Douglas	Jan. 21, 1994	Obit: John Henre "Blind John" Davis	Dec. 6, 1985
Obit: Hopkins, Nicky	Oct. 28, 1994	Obit: John Jordan	Aug. 26, 1988
Obit: Horace Heidt	Jan. 2, 1987	Obit: John Richbourg	April 11, 1986
Obit: Horatio "Ray" Duran	March 1981	Obit: John Ritchie (Sid Vicious)	April 1979
Obit: Houston, David	Jan. 21, 1994	Obit: John Wallace	Oct. 1978
Obit: Howard Allen Reed	June 1981	Obit: Johnnie Lee Wills	Dec. 7, 1984
Obit: Howard Dietz	Oct. 1983	Obit: Johnnie Louise Richardson	Dec. 30, 1988
Obit: Howard Greenfield	April 25, 1986	Obit: Johnny Desmond	Dec. 20, 1985
Obit: Hoyle Nix	Oct. 25, 1985	Obit: Johnny Guarnieri	April 26, 1985
Obit: Hubert Finlay	March 16, 1984	Obit: Johnny Hartman	Nov. 1983
Obit: Hugh Bryant	Oct. 23, 1987	Obit: Johnny Marks	Oct. 25, 1985
Obit: Hugo Peretti	June 20, 1986	Obit: Johnny Ray	March 23, 1990
Obit: Humphrey, Percy	Sept. 1, 1995	Obit: Johnny "Little Sonny" Jones	Jan. 26, 1990
Obit: Humphrey, Willie	July 8, 1994	Obit: Johnson, Allen	Nov. 24, 1995
Obit: Hyatt, Walter	June 21, 1996	Obit: Johnson, Marv	June 25, 1993
Obit: Hyman, Phyllis	Aug. 4, 1995	Obit: Johnson, Willie Lee "Guitar"	April 28, 1995
Obit: Ian Stewart	Jan. 17, 1986	Obit: Jon Poulos	Sept. 1980
Obit: Ina Ray Hutton	April 13, 1984	Obit: Jonathan Jo Jones	Oct. 25, 1985
Obit: Ingram, Ripley	May 26, 1995	Obit: Jones, Michael "Busta"	Feb. 16, 1996
Obit: Ira Gershwin	Oct. 1983	Obit: Jones, Tommy "Madman"	June 24, 1994
Obit: Irving Klein	May 11, 1984	Obit: Joseph Barthelemy	Jan. 11, 1991
Obit: Irvings Mills	Aug. 30, 1985	Obit: Juan Tizol	July 20, 1984
Obit: Ives, Burl	May 26, 1995	Obit: Jules Bihari	Feb. 1, 1985
Obit: J. Caleb Ginyard	Oct. 1978	Obit: Jump Jackson	May 10, 1985
Obit: J. Fred Coots	Aug. 30, 1985	Obit: June "Curley" Moore	April 25, 1986
Obit: J.B. Hutto	Sept. 1983	Obit: Kahn, John	July 5, 1996
Obit: Jack "Jive" Schafer	May 11, 1984	Obit: Kai Winding	July 1983
Obit: Jack, Wolfman (Robert Weston Smith)	Aug. 4, 1995	Obit: Karen Carpenter	April 1983
Obit: Jackson, Oliver	July 8, 1994	Obit: Kate Smith	Aug. 15, 1986
Obit: James Booker	Feb. 1984	Obit: Kate Wolf	Feb. 13, 1987
Obit: James Faye "Roy" Hall	April 13, 1984	Obit: Kay Kyser	Aug. 30, 1985
Obit: James Faye "Roy" Hall	May 11, 1984	Obit: Kay, Connie	Jan. 6, 1995
Obit: James Honeyman Scott	Aug. 1982	Obit: Ken Threadgill	May 8, 1987
Obit: James Jamerson	Oct. 1983	Obit: Ken Winslow	Aug. 30, 1985
Obit: James L. Riddle	Feb. 1983	Obit: Kendricks, Eddie	Oct. 30, 1992
Obit: Janet Vogel	May 1980	Obit: Kendricks, Eddie	Nov. 13, 1992
Obit: Janet Vogel Rapp	June 1980	Obit: Kennedy, Frankie	Nov. 25, 1994
Obit: Jarrett, James "Pigmeat"	Nov. 24, 1995	Obit: Kenneth Eglin	April 13, 1984
Obit: Jay Lerner	Aug. 15, 1986	Obit: Kenny Clarke	April 26, 1985
Obit: Jeanine Deckers	May 24, 1985	Obit: Kermit Chandler	April 1981
Obit: Jefferson, Carl	April 28, 1995	Obit: Kermode, Richard	March 29, 1996
Obit: Jeneva Campbell	July 6, 1984	Obit: Keyes, Jimmy	Sept. 1, 1995
Obit: Jesus Maria Sanroma	Feb. 1, 1985	Obit: King, Albert	Jan. 22, 1993
Obit: Jethro Burns	March 10, 1989	Obit: Kirk Mc Gee	Feb. 1984
Obit: Jim Berlowitz	Oct. 12, 1984	Obit: Kripp Johnson	July 27, 1990
Obit: Jimmy Cross	March 1979	Obit: Kyu Sakamoto	Sept. 27, 1985
Obit: Jimmy Gately	May 24, 1985	Obit: Lafayette Leake	Dec. 14, 1990
Obit: Jimmy Gately	Aug. 2, 1985	Obit: Lamar Williams	March 1983
Obit: Jimmy Holiday	April 10, 1987	Obit: Lamour, Dorothy	Nov. 22, 1996
Obit: Jimmy Kaku	May 11, 1984	Obit: Lance Smart	March 1979
Obit: Jimmy Lyons	Feb. 1, 1985	Obit: Lance, Major	Oct. 28, 1994
Obit: Jimmy Mundy	July 1983	Obit: Lane, Ronnie/Small Faces	July 4, 1997
Obit: Jimmy Springs	Jan. 1, 1988	Obit: Lane, Ronnie/Small Faces & The Faces	July 18, 1997
Obit: Jimmy Wakely	Dec. 1982	Obit: Lange, Bob	Oct. 28, 1994
Obit: Jobim, Antonio Carlos	Jan. 6, 1995	Obit: Larry Clinton	Aug. 30, 1985
Obit: Joe Albany	March 25, 1988	Obit: Larry Stock	July 20, 1984

Obit: Larry Williams	March 1980	Obit: Miller, J.D.		May 10, 1996
Obit: Larry "Big Twist" Nolan	April 20, 1990	Obit: Miller, Jimmy		Nov. 25, 1994
Obit: Laury, Lawrence "Booker T."	Nov. 24, 1995	Obit: Miller, Roger		Nov. 27, 1992
Obit: Lawrence Odell Holley	Aug. 30, 1985	Obit: Mississippi Johnny Waters		April 10, 1987
Obit: Lawson, Yank	March 31, 1995	Obit: Modugno, Domenico		Sept. 16, 1994
Obit: Leary, Timothy	July 5, 1996	Obit: Molly O'Day		Feb. 12, 1988
Obit: Leckenby, Derek "Lek"	July 8, 1994	Obit: Molly O'Day		March 25, 1988
Obit: Lee Dorsey	Jan. 2, 1987	Obit: Monk Higgins		Oct. 10, 1986
Obit: Lee Dorsey	Jan. 30, 1987	Obit: Montana Band		Sept. 11, 1987
Obit: Lee Gaines	Oct. 23, 1987	Obit: Montana, Patsy		June 7, 1996
Obit: Lee Rosenberg Burrows	Aug. 30, 1985	Obit: Moody Jones		June 17, 1988
Obit: Lenny Breau	Oct. 12, 1984	Obit: Morris Levy		June 29, 1990
Obit: Lenny Breau	Nov. 23, 1984	Obit: Morrison, Sterling		Oct. 27 1995
Obit: Leo Robin	March 15, 1985	Obit: Moses Asch		Dec. 19, 1986
Obit: Leon Mc Auliffe	Oct. 7, 1988	Obit: Muddy Waters		July 1983
Obit: Leonard Allen	Aug. 30, 1985	Obit: Mulligan, Gerry		March 1, 1996
Obit: Leonard Bernstein	Nov. 16, 1990	Obit: Murad, Jerry		July 5, 1996
Obit: Leonard Rose	March 15, 1985	Obit: Murray The K		April 1982
Obit: Leonard "Baby Doo" Caston	Dec. 18, 1987	Obit: Murray, Dee		Feb. 21, 1992
Obit: Leroy Kirkland	June 17, 1988	Obit: Myers, Louis		Oct. 28, 1994
Obit: Les, Don	Oct. 28, 1994	Obit: Napoleon Gagnon		Oct. 12, 1984
Obit: Lester Bangs	June 1982	Obit: Nash, Jim		Nov. 24, 1995
Obit: Lewis Rachmil	May 11, 1984	Obit: Nat Tarnopol		Feb. 12, 1988
Obit: Lightnin' Hopkins	April 1982	Obit: Nate Nelson		Oct. 12, 1984
Obit: Lila May Ledford Pennington	Aug. 30, 1985	Obit: Nathaniel Wilson		July 1981
Obit: Linda Creed	May 23, 1986	Obit: Neil Bogart		July 1982
Obit: Linda Smeage	April 27, 1984	Obit: Nelson, Willie	I, D	Jan. 6, 1995
Obit: Lloyd Glenn	Aug. 30, 1985	Obit: Nesuhi Ertegun		Nov. 3, 1989
Obit: Lonnie Hillyer	Aug. 30, 1985	Obit: Nico (Christa Paffgen)	D	Aug. 26, 1988
Obit: Louis De Jesus	Dec. 7, 1984	Obit: Nilsson, Harry		Feb. 18, 1994
Obit: Louis Keppard	April 25, 1986	Obit: Nolan Strong		July-Aug. 1977
Obit: Lucas, Harold	March 4, 1994	Obit: Nolan, Jerry		Feb. 21, 1992
Obit: Lucille Armstrong	Dec. 1983	Obit: Norman Petty		Sept. 14, 1984
Obit: Luke Kelly	March 16, 1984	Obit: Nyro, Laura		June 6, 1997
Obit: Lytle, Johnny	Feb. 16, 1996	Obit: O'Kelly Isley		May 9, 1986
Obit: Mabel Mercer	July 6, 1984	Obit: O. B. Mc Clinton		Jan. 15, 1988
Obit: MacGregor, Byron	Feb. 3, 1995	Obit: Ollie Mc Laughlin		April 27, 1984
Obit: Mancini, Henry	July 22, 1994	Obit: Onio Wheeler		July 20, 1984
Obit: Mann Curtis	Feb. 1, 1985	Obit: Overbea, Danny		June 24, 1994
Obit: Marcia Vance	Dec. 16, 1988	Obit: Owen, Donnie		Dec. 9, 1994
Obit: Marcus Price	Nov. 23, 1984	Obit: Panozzo, John		Aug. 16, 1996
Obit: Mark Dinning	May 9, 1986	Obit: Parker, Col. Tom		Feb. 28, 1997
Obit: Marty Robbins	Feb. 1983	Obit: Paskow, Bruce Jay		Feb. 18, 1994
Obit: Marvin Gaye	April 27, 1984	Obit: Pass, Joe		June 24, 1994
Obit: Mary Ann Eager	April 27, 1984	Obit: Paul Bascomb		Jan. 16, 1987
Obit: Mary Lou Williams	July 1981	Obit: Paul Butterfield		June 19, 1987
Obit: Maurice Goldman	May 11, 1984	Obit: Paul Francis Webster		May 11, 1984
Obit: Maxine Sullivan	June 5, 1987	Obit: Paul Glass		May 23, 1986
Obit: Mc Kinley Mitchell	March 28, 1986	Obit: Paul Robi		May 5, 1989
Obit: McDaniel, Floyd	Sept. 1, 1995	Obit: Paul, Clarence		July 7, 1995
Obit: McGhee, Brownie	March 29, 1996	Obit: Payton, Lawrence		Aug. 1, 1997
Obit: McKinley, Ray	June 9, 1995	Obit: Pearl Bailey		Sept. 21, 1990
Obit: McLain, Dan	Dec. 22, 1995	Obit: Pearl, Minnie		April 12, 1996
Obit: McRae, Carmen	Dec. 9, 1994	Obit: Pearl, Raymond		April 25, 1997
Obit: McVoy, Carl	Feb. 7, 1992	Obit: Pee Wee Clayton		Aug. 30, 1985
Obit: Melvin, Harold	April 25, 1997	Obit: Pee Wee Crayton		Aug. 30, 1985
Obit: Melvoin, Jonathan/Smashing Pumpkins	Aug. 16, 1996	Obit: Perez Prado		Oct. 20, 1989
Obit: Memphis Slim	April 8, 1988	Obit: Pete De Freitas		Oct. 6, 1989
Obit: Memphis Slim	April 8, 1988	Obit: Pete Farndon		June 1983
Obit: Merle Travis	Dec. 1983	Obit: Peter Smart		Sept. 1983
Obit: Michael David "Blaze" Foley	March 24, 1989	Obit: Peter Tosh		Oct. 23, 1987
Obit: Michael Mann (Hollywood Fats)	Feb. 13, 1987	Obit: Pfaff, Kristen		July 22, 1994
Obit: Michael Smith	Dec. 1983	Obit: Pfeiffer, John		March 29, 1996
Obit: Michael "Mickey" Coppola	Nov. 9, 1984	Obit: Phil Lynott		Feb. 28, 1986
Obit: Mickey Katz	Aug. 30, 1985	Obit: Phil Lynott		March 14, 1986
Obit: Mike Bloomfield	April 1981	Obit: Philly Joe Jones		Oct. 25, 1985
Obit: Milewski, Greg	April 15, 1994	Obit: Pierce, Jeffrey Lee		May 10, 1996

Obit: Pointer, Noel	Feb. 3, 1995	Obit: Shelly Manne	Dec. 7, 1984
Obit: Polk C. Brockman	May 24, 1985	Obit: Shelton, Robert	Feb. 16, 1996
Obit: Pope, Joe/Tams	May 10, 1996	Obit: Shore, Dinah	April 15, 1994
Obit: Priscilla Bowman	Oct. 7, 1988	Obit: Sid Torin	Nov. 23, 1984
Obit: Professor Longhair (Henry Roeland Byrd)	May 1980	Obit: Sid Vicious (John Ritchie)	April 1979
Obit: Pullen, Don	May 26, 1995	Obit: Sill, Lester	Dec. 9, 1994
Obit: Ral Donner	July 6, 1984	Obit: Singing Nun	May 24, 1985
Obit: Randall Monaco	Aug. 30, 1985	Obit: Sippie Wallace	Dee. 5, 1986
Obit: Raney, Jimmy	June 23, 1995	Obit: Slim, Root Boy	July 23, 1993
Obit: Ray Cawley	Dec. 1980	Obit: Slim, Sunnyland	April 28, 1995
Obit: Ray Eberle	Dec. 1979	Obit: Smith, Fred "Sonic"	Dec. 9, 1994
Obit: Ray Smith	May 1980	Obit: Smith, Major Bill	Oct. 28, 1994
Obit: Redmond, Mike	Sept. 27, 1996	Obit: Smothers, Otis "Big Smokey"	Sept. 17, 1993
Obit: Reed, Dalton	Nov. 25, 1994	Obit: Sonny Stitt	Sept. 1982
Obit: Rev. Marvin J. Yancy	Aug. 2, 1985	Obit: Sonny Terry	May 9, 1986
Obit: Rex Gosden	Sept. 1983	Obit: Sonny Thompson	Oct. 20, 1989
Obit: Ric Grech	June 29, 1990	Obit: Sonny Til	Feb. 1982
Obit: Rich, Charlie	Sept. 1, 1995	Obit: Spector, Jerry	April 15, 1994
Obit: Richard Manuel	April 25, 1986	Obit: Spruill, "Wild" Jimmy	May 10, 1996
Obit: Richard Sohl	July 13, 1990	Obit: Stacy, Jess	Feb. 3, 1995
Obit: Richard Taylor	March 25, 1988	Obit: Stafford, Terry	May 24, 1996
Obit: Rick Canoff	Aug. 26, 1988	Obit: Stan Kenton	Dec. 1979
Obit: Rick Nelson	Jan. 31, 1986	Obit: Starr, Jack	Jan. 6, 1995
Obit: Ricky Wilson	Jan. 17, 1986	Obit: Starr, Maureen	Feb. 3, 1995
Obit: Riley, Teddy	Dec. 25, 1992	Obit: Starr, Ruby	March 31, 1995
Obit: Rinzler, Ralph	Aug. 5, 1994	Obit: Steve Brown	May 5, 1989
Obit: Robert B. Sour	May 24, 1985	Obit: Steve Clark	Feb. 8, 1991
Obit: Robert Blackwell	May 24, 1985	Obit: Steve Wahrer	March 10, 1989
Obit: Robert Jones	Oct. 1982	Obit: Stevie Ray Vaughan	Sept. 21, 1990
Obit: Robert Morgan	Aug. 30, 1985	Obit: Stinson, Bob (Replacements)	March 31, 1995
Obit: Robert Shad	May 24, 1985	Obit: Stiv Bators	July 13, 1990
Obit: Rod Mc Nelly	March 27, 1987	Obit: Stregmeyer, Doug	Sept. 29, 1995
Obit: Rodney K. Albin	Oct. 12, 1984	Obit: Styne, Jule	Oct. 28, 1994
Obit: Rodney, Red	July 8, 1994	Obit: Sun Ra	July 9, 1993
Obit: Roger Bowling	Feb. 1983	Obit: T.C. Lu	May 11, 1984
Obit: Roger Gambill	May 24, 1985	Obit: T.C. "Son" Lansford	Sept. 8, 1989
Obit: Roger Gambill	Aug. 2, 1985	Obit: Tasha Thomas	Feb. 1, 1985
Obit: Rogers, Shorty	Dec. 9, 1994	Obit: Taylor, Art	March 31, 1995
Obit: Rollie Culver	Feb. 1, 1985	Obit: Teddy Wilson	Oct. 10, 1986
Obit: Rollin Smith	April 26, 1985	Obit: Tex Williams	Feb. 14, 1986
Obit: Ronald Kass	Dee. 5, 1986	Obit: Thad Jones	Oct. 24, 1986
Obit: Ronald Self	Nov. 1981	Obit: Thelonious Monk	April 1982
Obit: Ronnie Dyson	Dec. 14, 1990	Obit: Theodore Dudley Saunders	May 1981
Obit: Ronson, Mick	June 11, 1993	Obit: Thiele, Bob	March 15, 1996
Obit: Roosevelt Sykes	Sept. 1983	Obit: Thomas James "Sun"	Aug. 20, 1993
Obit: Ross Marino	March 25, 1988	Obit: Thomas, Jon	Jan. 6, 1995
Obit: Rothchild, Paul	May 12, 1995	Obit: Thompson, Don	June 24, 1994
Obit: Roy Brown	July 1981	Obit: Thore Jederby	April 13, 1984
Obit: Roy Buchanan	D	Sept. 9, 1988	Obit: Thurston Harris	June 15, 1990
Obit: Roy Elridge	April 7, 1989	Obit: Tim Hardin	Feb. 1981
Obit: Rozsa, Miklos	Sept. 15, 1996	Obit: Tim Mc Intire	June 20, 1986
Obit: Rudy Vallee	Aug. 15, 1986	Obit: Tino Rossi	Dec. 1983
Obit: Russel, Bill	Sept. 18, 1992	Obit: Tito Gobbi	April 27, 1984
Obit: Ruth Polsky	Oct. 24, 1986	Obit: Tom Clancy	Dec. 14, 1990
Obit: Salina Belvin Washington	Feb. 14, 1986	Obit: Tom Evans	Feb. 1984
Obit: Sam Chatmon	April 1983	Obit: Tom Fogerty	Oct. 19, 1990
Obit: Sam Theard	Feb. 1983	Obit: Tom Jans	July 6, 1984
Obit: Sammy Kaye	July 17, 1987	Obit: Tommy Jarrell	May 10, 1985
Obit: Sarah Vaughan	May 4, 1990	Obit: Tony Stratton-Smith	May 8, 1987
Obit: Sax Mallard	Oct. 24, 1986	Obit: Trummy Young	Dec. 7, 1984
Obit: Sayles, Johnny	Oct. 1, 1993	Obit: Tucker, Luther	July 23, 1993
Obit: Scandariato, Tom	March 31, 1995	Obit: Twitty, Conway	July 9, 1993
Obit: Scott, Raymond	March 18, 1994	Obit: Ty Hunter	April 1981
Obit: Selena (Selena Quintanilla Perez)	May 12, 1995	Obit: Valenti, Dino	Dec. 23, 1994
Obit: Seymour, Phil	Sept. 17, 1993	Obit: Van Dyke, Earl	Oct. 30, 1992
Obit: Shakur, Tupac	Oct. 11, 1996	Obit: Vanleer, Jimmy	Aug. 16, 1996
Obit: Sharrock, Sonny	July 8, 1994	Obit: Ventura, Charlie	Feb. 21, 1992

Parker, Maceo	I, D	May 26, 1995	Peter, Paul & Mary/Mary Travers	D	March 30, 1984
Parker, Robert	I,D	April 10, 1987	Peter, Paul & Mary/Mary Travers	DA	June 21, 1985
Parker, Robert	I,D	April 10, 1987	Petersen, Paul		Dec. 1, 1989
Parks, Van Dyke	I,D	April 1983	Peterson, Dick/Blue Cheer	I,D	May 23, 1986
Parks, Van Dyke		Oct. 1983	Peterson, Dick/Kingsmen	D	Aug. 1983
Parks, Van Dyke	DA	Dec. 7, 1984	Petty, Norman	I	May-June 1978
Parks, Van Dyke	I,D	Feb. 2, 1996	Petty, Norman	I	Sept. 14, 1984
Parris, Fred/Five Satins	I,D	May 1979	Petty, Norman	I	July 18, 1986
Parrot Records		March 18, 1994	Petty, Norman	I,D	July 18, 1986
Parsons, Gram		April 1982	Petty, Tom	I,D	July 13, 1990
Parsons, Gram		Sept. 1982	Petty, Tom		Aug. 24, 1990
Parsons, Gram		Dec. 1983	Petty, Tom	DA	Sept. 21, 1990
Parsons, Gram		Jan. 1984	Phil Upchurch Combo	I	Dec. 30, 1988
Parsons, Gram	D	Feb. 1984	Philles Records/Danny Davis	I	June 17, 1988
Partridge, Andy/X T C	I,D	May 5, 1989	Phillips, Glenn	I	Feb. 16, 1996
Pastels, The	D	April 1979	Phillips, Michelle/Mama's & Papa's	I,D	Sept. 1980
Patti And The Lovelites	D	June 1981	Phillips, Phil	I	July 10, 1992
Patton, Charley	D	Mar. 20, 1992	Phillips, Phil (John Baptiste)	I	April 25, 1986
Paul and Paula	I	Oct. 16, 1992	Phillips, Phil (John Baptiste)	I	Dec. 1, 1989
Paul Whiteman/Kraft Music Hall		June 1979	Phillips, Sam	I	July 31, 1987
Paul, Billy		Dec. 1, 1989	Phillips, Sam	I	Aug. 14, 1987
Paul, Frank/Casa Grande Records	I	Jan. 1980	Phillips, Sam	I	Aug. 28, 1987
Paul, Les	I,D	Dec. 18, 1987	Phillips, Sam		Feb. 26, 1988
Paul, Les	I,D	Feb. 26, 1988	Phillips, Sam	I	Nov. 22, 1996
Paul, Les		April 22, 1988	Phillips, Wilson		June 1, 1990
Paul, Les	DA	May 6, 1988	Phoenix Connection		March 25, 1988
Paupers/Skip Prokop	I,D	June 30, 1989	Piaf, Edith	D	Dec. 18, 1987
Pavitt, Bruce/Sub Pop Records	I	June 2, 1989	Pickering, John/Picks	I,D	Sept. 14, 1984
Pavlik, Johnny (Powers)		Nov.-Dec. 1976	Pickering, John/Picks	I	Sept. 14, 1984
Paxton, Tom	D	Sept. 1980	Pickett, Bobby Boris		Dec. 30, 1988
Paxton, Tom	I,D	April 1983	Pickett, Wilson	I	June 5, 1987
Paxton, Tom	DA	Dec. 7, 1984	Picks/John Pickering	I,D	Sept. 14, 1984
Paxton, Tom	I, D	Nov. 13, 1992	Picks/John Pickering	I	Sept. 14, 1984
Payne, Bill/Little Feat	I,D	Dec. 2, 1988	Picture Sleeves & Colored Wax (Surf Music)	D	July 1981
Payola		Nov. 1980	Picture Sleeves: A Collecting Guide		March 30, 1984
Payola		Dec. 1980	Pierce, Don	I	May 11, 1984
Peaches & Herb	D	May 22, 1987	Pierre, Elsie/Pearls	I,D	Feb. 8, 1991
Peaches & Herb	D	May 22, 1987	Pinckney, Bill/Drifters	I	May-June 1978
Pearl Jam	D	Aug. 20, 1993	Pink Floyd		Jan. 15, 1988
Pearls/Pierre, Elsie	I,D	Feb. 8, 1991	Pink Floyd	D	Feb. 12, 1988
Peck, Ray/Kiderian Records	I	July-Aug. 1977	Pink Floyd	I, D	Jan. 8, 1993
Peebles, Ann	D	July 1, 1988	Pioneer Awards		April 25, 1997
Peebles, Ann	DA	Nov. 18, 1988	Pipes, The	D	April 1979
Peebles, Ann	D	July 1, 1988	Pipkins, The		Dec. 30, 1988
Peebles, Ann	DA	Nov. 18,1988	Pirates	D	Jan. 1, 1988
Peel, John		March 27, 1987	Pirates, The	D	Jan. 1, 1988
Peel, John		March 27, 1987	Pirating, Bootlegging: Taping Pirates Not Guilty Of Theft		Nov. 9, 1984
Pekar, Marty/Ambient Sound Records	I	March 1982	Pistilli, Gene	D	Dec. 1981
Pendarvis, Tracy	I, D	Apr. 3, 1992	Pitney, Gene		Jan. 1978
Pendergrass, Teddy	D	Dec. 16, 1988	Pitney, Gene	I,D	Jan. 1983
Pendergrass, Teddy	D	Dec. 16, 1988	Pitney, Gene		March 1983
Penguins/Cleve Duncan	I	Dec. 1, 1989	Pitney, Gene		Dec. 7, 1984
Penn, Dan	I	Sept. 2, 1994	Pitney, Gene	DA	April 11, 1986
Pennington, Ray	I,D	Jan. 1979	Pitney, Gene	I, D	Oct. 1, 1993
Pennington, Ray/King Records	I	Feb. 9, 1990	Pitt, Eugene/Jive Five	I,D	March 1982
Pere Ubu/David Thomas	I,D	Jan. 15, 1988	Pitt, Eugene/Jive Five	I,D	Aug. 12, 1988
Pere, Ubu/David Thomas	I,D	Jan. 15, 1988	Pittman, Barbara	I	July 14, 1989
Perkins, "Pinetop"	I, D	Mar. 20, 1992	Pittsburgh: You're Guide To The Steel City's Hottest		
Perkins, Carl		March 1978	Record Stores		Feb. 26, 1988
Perkins, Carl	I,D	June 1980	Planet Records		Jan. 1976
Perkins, Carl		Aug. 1980	Plant, Robert	I	Aug. 6, 1993
Perkins, Carl	I,D	Sept. 26, 1986	Plant, Robert/Led Zeppelin		Aug. 24, 1990
Perkins, Carl	I,D	Feb. 26, 1988	Platter Chatter (by Tim Neely)		Nov. 24, 1995
Perkins, Carl	I	June 15, 1990	Platter Chatter (by Tim Neely)		Dec. 22, 1995
Pet Shop Boys	D	Sept. 16, 1994	Platter Matter		
Peter And Gordon/Peter Asher	I,D	April 25, 1986	Platter Matter: 1904 Victor 14-Inch Record		Jan. 3, 1986
Peter, Paul & Mary	I,D	April 12, 1996	Platter Matter: 1908 Double-Sided Columbia Records		Jan. 31, 1986

Entry	Code	Date
Platter Matter: 1909 & 1926 Records: Casey At The Bat		April 11, 1986
Platter Matter: 1910 Pathe 20 Inch Disc		April 11, 1986
Platter Matter: 1929 Amos 'N Andy Radio Disc		March 28, 1986
Platter Matter: 1932 Paul Whiteman Picture Disc		Feb. 28, 1986
Platter Matter: De'Bonairs "Mothers Son" Ping 1000		Aug. 15, 1986
Platters	I,D	Feb. 21, 1992
Plaza Records	D	Sept. 1978
Poco	I, D	Aug. 20, 1993
Poco/Rusty Young	I,D	Aug. 2, 1985
Poco/Rusty Young		Nov. 8, 1985
Poco/Rusty Young	DA	Feb. 13, 1987
Poindexter, Buster	I	March 11, 1988
Pointer Sisters	D	April 10, 1987
Pointer Sisters	D	April 10, 1987
Police	D	April 30, 1993
Pomus, Doc	I	Nov. 1982
Pomus, Doc	I	June 1983
Pomus, Doc	I	Aug. 10, 1990
Poni-Tails/Toni Costabile	I	Dec. 1, 1989
Pons, Jim/Leaves	I,D	Aug. 1982
Pons, Jim/Leaves	DA	Sept. 1983
Pop Promotionals Through The Ages		Sept.-Oct. 1976
Pop Schlock: A Guide To Tasteless Records		Oct. 24, 1986
Pop, Iggy	I,D	Aug. 1982
Pop, Iggy and the Stooges	I, D	March 17, 1995
Popeye (The Dance)		Nov. 4, 1988
Popeye (The Dance)		Nov. 4, 1988
Popllama Records/Conrad Uno	I	June 2, 1989
Poppy Family/Terry Jacks	I,D	June 30, 1989
Popular Music Series In Prime Time TV: 1947-1985		July 5, 1985
Porky Chedwick		Feb. 1980
Porter, Bill	I	May 5, 1989
Porter, Bob		Aug. 28, 1987
Porter, Royce	I,D	Oct. 1983
Porter, Royce	DA	Feb. 15, 1985
Portland's 10 Best Record Stores		Sept. 9, 1988
Post, Jim/Friend And Lover	I	Dec. 1, 1989
Posters, Collecting Rare		Sept. 29, 1995
Potter, Jerry/Fascinators	I,D	Nov. 16, 1990
Power Pop: U.S. Power Pop: A Collectors Guide To Obscure Gems		Dec. 4, 1987
Power Pop	I,D	Jan. 5, 1996
Power Pop		Jan. 5, 1996
Pre-History Of Black Harmony Groups		March-April 1977
Pre-History Of Black Harmony Groups		Oct. 1977
Presidential Satire Records	D	Nov. 18,1988
Presley, Elvis		
Presley, Elvis		Feb. 26, 1988
Presley, Elvis: Also see For Elvis Fans Only		
Presley, Elvis: Archaeology And Garbology — The Early Days		Aug. 10,1990
Presley, Elvis: Big Record News		Jan. 18, 1985
Presley, Elvis: Bob Snyder Remembers Elvis		Oct. 1977
Presley, Elvis: British EP Discography 1957 -1982	D	Jan. 1983
Presley, Elvis: Business End Of An Elvis Mecca		Jan. 29, 1988
Presley, Elvis: CD Reissues Discograph		Aug. 7, 1992
Presley, Elvis: Colonel Parker Story		Nov. 1981
Presley, Elvis: Colonel Parker Story		Nov. 1981
Presley, Elvis: D.J. Fontana: Elvis' Drummer Capsulizes The King's Career	I	Aug. 14, 1987
Presley, Elvis: Death Of Elvis		Jan. 1984
Presley, Elvis: Del Puschert's Friend...Elvis Presley		July-Aug. 1977
Presley, Elvis: Dorsey Shows		Jan.-Feb. 1977
Presley, Elvis: Elvis & The Press	I	Jan. 29, 1988
Presley, Elvis: Elvis At The Garden		Aug. 7, 1992
Presley, Elvis: Elvis At The Louisiana Hayride		Aug. 3, 1984
Presley, Elvis: Elvis Book Update		Aug. 10, 1990
Presley, Elvis: Elvis Book Update		Aug. 7, 1992
Presley, Elvis: Elvies Died For Our Sins		Jan. 3, 1997
Presley, Elvis: Elvis Discography Of The '80s	D	March 30, 1984
Presley, Elvis: Elvis In The Projects/Jimmy Denson	I	Aug. 10, 1990
Presley, Elvis: Elvis Is Eternal		Oct. 1977
Presley, Elvis: Elvis Lives		Aug. 26, 1988
Presley, Elvis: Elvis Lives (On CD, On Video And In Print)		Jan. 13, 1989
Presley, Elvis: Elvis Lives: The Posthumous Releases 1977-1989	D,	Aug. 11, 1989
Presley, Elvis: Elvis LPs (His Most Collectible)		Jan. 29, 1988
Presley, Elvis: Elvis Novelty Records	D	Jan. 1983
Presley, Elvis: Elvis Novelty Records	DA	Dec. 7, 1984
Presley, Elvis: Elvis on CD part one		Feb. 3, 1995
Presley, Elvis: Elvis on CD part two		Feb. 17, 1995
Presley, Elvis: Elvis on RCA	D	Feb. 3, 1995
Presley, Elvis: Elvis On TV		Jan. 29, 1988
Presley, Elvis: Elvis On TV Part 2		Aug. 26, 1988
Presley, Elvis: Elvis On Vik		Jan. 1981
Presley, Elvis: Elvis Presley Compact Disc Discography And Price Guide	D	Jan. 13, 1989
Presley, Elvis: Elvis Sun Promo (The Second Rarest Disc) /Gary Johnson	I,	Sept. 22, 1989
Presley, Elvis: Elvis Tributes	D	Jan. 1981
Presley, Elvis: Elvis Under The Counter (Bootlegs)		Oct. 23, 1987
Presley, Elvis: Elvis' Rarest Recording		Aug. 26, 1988
Presley, Elvis: Elvis' Rarest Recording		Sept. 23, 1988
Presley, Elvis: Elvis, Doc And Mojo Nixon	I	Aug. 10, 1990
Presley, Elvis: Elvis: Radio Shows	D	Aug. 11, 1989
Presley, Elvis: Elvis:The '68 Comeback	D	Jan. 1980
Presley, Elvis: Elvis:The '68 Comeback	DA	April 1980
Presley, Elvis: Even The "King" Went To High School		July 1979
Presley, Elvis: Facts Behind The Elvis Recording Sessions		April 11, 1986
Presley, Elvis: Four Rock Greats Talk About The 'King'		Aug. 30, 1985
Presley, Elvis: From Elvis In Memphis (Sun Records)	D	Aug. 26, 1988
Presley, Elvis: Getting The Ink 1954 - 1955		Jan. 1982
Presley, Elvis: Gold Standard Series 45s and EPs		Aug. 7, 1992
Presley, Elvis: Golden (and not so Golden) Records		Jan. 21, 1994
Presley, Elvis: Growing Up With Elvis, Interv. with George Klein		Aug. 7, 1992
Presley, Elvis: Guide To Books About Elvis		Aug. 30, 1985
Presley, Elvis: Guide To The Films Of Elvis		Aug. 3, 1984
Presley, Elvis: His Generosity Lives On Through Charitable Club Contributions		Jan. 16, 1987
Presley, Elvis: His Private Meeting With President Nixon		Jan. 16, 1987
Presley, Elvis: His Rare Worldwide Jackets & Sleeves		Aug. 14, 1987
Presley, Elvis: Hy Gardner Interview	I	Aug. 10,1990
Presley, Elvis: In the '50s		Aug. 7, 1992
Presley, Elvis: In the '60s		Jan. 21, 1994
Presley, Elvis In the 70's		Jan. 19, 1996
Presley, Elvis: Itinerary For 1954 And 1955		Sept. 1981
Presley, Elvis: Jay Thompson's Interview With Elvis	I	Jan. 1981
Presley, Elvis: Joan Deary: Listening To Unreleased Elvis Tunes	I	Jan. 1983
Presley, Elvis: King And Them		Aug. 10, 1990
Presley, Elvis: Legend Of A King		Aug. 10, 1990
Presley, Elvis: Leiber And Stoller: The Elvis Connection	D	Aug. 14, 1987
Presley, Elvis: Looking At "This Is Elvis"		Jan. 1982
Presley, Elvis: Mc Cormick-Elvis Whiskey Decanters		Jan. 1983
Presley, Elvis: Meeting Elvis in Killeen		Feb. 3, 1995
Presley, Elvis: Million Dollar Quartet Session		Aug. 26, 1988
Presley, Elvis: National Elvis Presley Day?		Jan. 1982
Presley, Elvis: Non Soundtrack Sessions		Aug. 7, 1992
Presley, Elvis: Paul Dragon		March 1978
Presley, Elvis: Provenance Of Elvis Presley's Sun Songs		Jan. 1983
Presley, Elvis: Quintessentially Essential Elvis		Jan. 3, 1997
Presley, Elvis: Rarest Elvis Disc Leased To Sun/Ed Leek /Sidney Singleton	I	Sept. 22, 1989
Presley, Elvis: RCA Versus Elvis		Jan. 18, 1985
Presley, Elvis: RCA's Man In Charge Of Elvis:		

Rooftop Singers	D	Aug. 12, 1988	Sahm, Doug/Sir Douglas Quintet		July 15, 1988
Rooftop Singers	D	Aug. 12, 1988	Sahm, Doug/Sir Douglas Quintet	DA	Aug. 26, 1988
Rosenberg, Marv/Safaris	I,D	Sept. 25, 1987	Sain, Oliver	I,D	Oct. 21, 1988
Rosie And The Originals/Rosie Hamlin	I	Dec. 1, 1989	Sain, Oliver	I,D	Oct. 21, 1988
Rotary Connection	D	June 17, 1988	Saints	D	Feb. 7, 1992
Rotary Connection	DA	Dec. 2, 1988	Sakamoto, Kyu		Jan. 30, 1987
Rotary Connection	D	June 17, 1988	Sakamoto, Kyu		Jan. 30, 1987
Roth, David Lee	D	Feb. 13, 1987	Sam & Dave	D	Jan. 2, 1987
Roth, David Lee	I	Jan. 13, 1989	Sam & Dave	D	Jan. 2, 1987
Rough Trade Records/Robin Hurley	I	Nov. 4, 1988	Sam The Sham & The Pharoes		May 1976
Roulette Records Trivia Contest		Aug. 1982	Sam The Sham & The Pharoes		March 15, 1985
Roulette Records Trivia Contest Answers		Nov. 1982	Samuels, Jerry		Sept.-Oct. 1976
Rounder Records		Nov. 4, 1988	San Francisco Remembered	D	Sept. 1983
Route 66 Records	D	May 1980	Sanders, Sonny	I,D	May 1980
Route 66 Records/Jonas Bernholm	I	June 2, 1989	Sandmen, The	D	April 1979
Rowland, Ken & Dexys Midnight Runners	I	April 1983	Sands, Tommy	I,D	April 25, 1986
Rowland, Ken & Dexys Midnight Runners		Dec. 30, 1988	Sands, Tommy		July 4, 1986
Roxy Music	D	Sept. 4, 1992	Sands, Tommy	DA	Nov. 21, 1986
Roxy Music	I	July 5, 1996	Santana/Carlos Santana	I,D	March 24, 1989
Roy Harper	I, D	Aug. 18, 1995	Santana/Santana, Carlos	I,D	March 24, 1989
Royal Teens	D	July 1979	Santo & Johnny/Santo Farina	I,D	Dec. 6, 1985
Royal, Billy Joe	I,D	Oct. 1981	Sapphire Records/Lou Welsch	I	Feb. 15, 1985
Royal, Billy Joe	I	June 29, 1990	Sapphire Records/Lou Welsch	DA	Jan. 17, 1986
Royals	D	Aug. 12, 1988	Sar Records	D	Aug. 26, 1988
Royaltones	D,DO	July 5, 1985	Sarg Records		Sept. 17, 1993
RPM Records		March 18, 1994	Satintones	I,D	April 1982
Rubin, Jan/Rubinoos	I,D	May 24, 1985	Saunders, Merl	I,D	Nov. 2, 1990
Rubin, Jan/Rubinoos	DA	Feb. 13, 1987	Savage Rose	D	Sept. 1981
Rubinoos/Jan Rubin	I,D	May 24, 1985	Savoy Brown/Kim Simmonds	I,D	Oct. 6, 1989
Rubinoos/Jan Rubin	DA	Feb. 13, 1987	Sawyer, Ray/Dr. Hook	I,D	April 1981
Rubinoos/Jan Rubin	I,D	May 24, 1985	Saxon, Sky/Seeds	I,D	June 5, 1987
Rubinoos/Jan Rubin	DA	Feb. 13, 1987	Sayles, Johnny	I,D	Nov. 1979
Ruby & The Romantics		Dec. 1, 1989	Scaggs, Boz	D	July 17, 1987
Ruffin, David	D	June 16, 1989	Scaggs, Boz	D	July 17, 1987
Ruffin, Jimmy	I,D	Nov. 16, 1990	ScepterWand REcords		Aug. 21, 1992
Ruhland, Robert (DJ)		May 1976	Schickele, Peter	I, D	Feb. 5, 1993
Rumblers, The	D	Nov. 1980	Schneider, Cowboy Carl/Mar Vel Records	I	Nov. 1981
Run D.M.C.	D	April 24, 1987	Schwartz, Bernard/Time/Edit Records	I,D	Sept. 7, 1990
Rundgren, Todd	I,D	March 29, 1996	Schwarz, Brinsley	D	May 20, 1988
Rush, Bobby	D	July 31, 1987	Score Records	D	Aug. 1979
Rush, Bobby	D	July 31, 1987	Score Records	DA	Nov. 1979
Rush, Otis	I,D	April 1982	Scorpions	I,D	May 19, 1989
Rush, Otis	D	Dec. 18, 1987	Scotland: Sound Of Young Scotland	D	May 1982
Rush, Otis	DA	Feb. 26, 1988	Scott, Freddie	I, D	March 5, 1993
Rush, Otis	D	Dec. 18, 1987	Scott, Jack	D	Sept.-Oct. 1976
Rush, Tom	D	Jan. 1980	Scott, Jack	I,D	April 1981
Rush, Tom	DA	April 1980	Scott, Jack	I,D	Nov. 1983
Rush, Tom	I,D	July 3, 1987	Scott, Jack	DA	July 20, 1984
Rush, Tom	I,D	July 3, 1987	Scott, Linda	I,D	Feb. 27, 1987
Rushen, Patrice	I,D	Jan. 26, 1990	Scott, Linda	I,D	Feb. 27, 1987
Rushen, Patrice	DA	May 4, 1990	Scott, Little Jimmy	I, D	Sept. 4, 1992
Russell, Leon	D	Nov. 1982	Scratchie Records	I	May 9, 1997
Russell, Tom	I,D	Oct. 25, 1985	Seals and Crofts	I, D	May 28, 1993
Rutles, The	D	July 29, 1988	Seals, Son	D	Jan. 15, 1988
Rutles, The	DA	Nov. 4, 1988	Searchers/John Mc Nally	I,D	June 1981
Rutles, The	I	Nov. 8, 1996	Seattle Heavy Rock	D	Apr. 17, 1992
Rydell, Bobby	I,D	Aug. 1979	Seattle Metal	D	Apr. 17, 1992
Ryder, Mitch	I,D	May 20, 1988	Seattle's Record Stores		March 25, 1988
Ryder, Mitch	DA	Aug. 12, 1988	Sebastian, John		Feb. 12, 1988
Rykodisc		Dec. 4, 1987	Sebastian, John	I,D	Nov. 3, 1989
			Sebastian, John		Feb. 12, 1988
S			Sebastian, John/Lovin Spoonful	I,D	July 1982
Sade		Nov. 20, 1987	Sebastian, John/Lovin Spoonful	DA	Sept. 1983
Safaris/Marv Rosenberg	I,D	Sept. 25, 1987	Sedaka, Neil	I	May 25, 1984
Sagittarius/Gary Usher/Curt Boettcher	I,D	Nov. 2, 1990	Sedaka, Neil	DA	March 29, 1985
Sahm, Doug	D	April 22, 1988	See For Miles Records/Colin Miles	I	June 2, 1989
Sahm, Doug/Sir Douglas Quintet	I,D	April 22, 1988	Seeds/Sky Saxon	I,D	June 5, 1987

Entry	Code	Date	Entry	Code	Date
Sgt. Pepper's Lonely Hearts Club Fans (Charles Reinhart)		Aug. 1982	Siegel, Jay/Tokens	I,D	Oct. 1981
Sgt. Pepper's Lonely Hearts Club Fans (Charles Reinhart)		Nov. 1982	Silhouettes, The		Dec. 30, 1988
Sgt. Pepper's Lonely Hearts Club Fans (Charles Reinhart)		Jan. 1983	Silkie		Dec. 1, 1989
Sgt. Pepper's Lonely Hearts Club Fans (Charles Reinhart)		March 1983	Sill, Lester	I	June 17, 1988
Sgt. Pepper's Lonely Hearts Club Fans (Charles Reinhart)		May 1983	Simmonds, Kim/Savoy Brown	I,D	Oct. 6, 1989
Sgt. Pepper's Lonely Hearts Club Fans (Charles Reinhart)		July 1983	Simmons, Gene/Kiss	I	June 29, 1990
Sgt. Pepper's Lonely Hearts Club Fans (Charles Reinhart)		Sept. 1983	Simon & Garfunkel	D	Sept.-Oct. 1976
Sgt. Pepper's Lonely Hearts Club Fans (Charles Reinhart)		Nov. 1983	Simon & Garfunkel		Oct. 1983
Sgt. Pepper's Lonely Hearts Club Fans (Charles Reinhart)		Dec. 1983	Simon, Lowrell	D	April 1982
Sgt. Pepper's Lonely Hearts Club Fans (Charles Reinhart)		Feb. 1984	Simon, Paul		Oct. 1983
Sgt. Pepper's Lonely Hearts Club Fans (Charles Reinhart)		March 2, 1984	Simon, Paul	I	Apr. 3, 1992
Sgt. Pepper's Lonely Hearts Club Fans (Charles Reinhart)		March 30, 1984	Simply Red/Mick Hucknall	I	June 3, 1988
Sgt. Pepper's Lonely Hearts Club Fans (Charles Reinhart)		April 27, 1984	Sims, Gerald	D	Dec. 1978
Sgt. Pepper's Lonely Hearts Club Fans (Charles Reinhart)		May 25, 1984	Sinatra, Frank	D	July 14, 1989
Sgt. Pepper's Lonely Hearts Club Fans (Charles Reinhart)		June 22, 1984	Sinatra, Frank Jr.	D	Aug. 26, 1988
Sgt. Pepper's Lonely Hearts Club Fans (Charles Reinhart)		Aug. 3, 1984	Sinatra, Frank Jr.	D	Aug. 26, 1988
Sgt. Pepper's Lonely Hearts Club Fans (Charles Reinhart)		Sept. 14, 1984	Sinatra, Nancy	D	Jan. 2, 1987
Sgt. Pepper's Lonely Hearts Club Fans (Charles Reinhart)		Oct. 26, 1984	Sinatra, Nancy	DA	Feb. 13, 1987
Sgt. Pepper's Lonely Hearts Club Fans (Charles Reinhart)		Dec. 7, 1984	Sinatra, Nancy	DA	Sept. 9, 1988
Sgt. Pepper's Lonely Hearts Club Fans (Charles Reinhart)		Jan. 18, 1985	Sinatra, Nancy	D	Jan. 2, 1987
Sgt. Pepper's Lonely Hearts Club Fans (Charles Reinhart)		Feb. 15, 1985	Sinatra, Nancy	DA	Feb. 13, 1987
Sgt. Pepper's Lonely Hearts Club Fans (Tim Watson)		May 1981	Sinatra, Nancy	DA	Sept. 9, 1988
Sgt. Pepper's Lonely Hearts Club Fans (Tim Watson)		Sept. 1981	Singer/Songwriter: Song Revival Revolution Of The '70s:		
Sha Na Na/Jocko/Denny/Santini	I,D	June 1979	Tapping The Musical Roots Of Rock	D	Nov. 1979
Sha Na Na/Jon Bauman	I	Aug. 1981	Singleton, Sidney/Rarest Elvis Disc Leased To Sun	I	Sept. 22, 1989
Shadows Of Knight/Jim Sohns		Nov. 1977	Siouxsie & The Banshees		Feb. 1981
Shadows Of Knight/Jim Sohns	I	July 18, 1986	Sir Douglas Quintet/Augie Meyers	I,D	April 22, 1988
Shalamar		Jan. 2, 1987	Sir Douglas Quintet/Doug Sahm	I,D	April 22, 1988
Shand, Terry/Castle Communications Records	I	Sept. 7, 1990	Sir Douglas Quintet/Doug Sahm		July 15, 1988
Shangri-Las	D	Oct. 9, 1987	Sir Douglas Quintet/Doug Sahm	DA	Aug. 26, 1988
Shangri-Las	D	Oct. 9, 1987	Sister Sledge	D	Aug. 28, 1987
Shannon, Del	I	July 1976	Sisters Of Mercy	D	Nov. 11, 1994
Shannon, Del	D	July 1981	Sixties: Top 100 Most Valuable Rock Records		
Shannon, Del	D	Dec. 1981	Of The '60s	D	May 6, 1988
Shannon, Del	I,D	Oct. 1983	16 RPM		Oct. 9, 1987
Shannon, Del	I,D	March 23, 1990	Sixties Albums: A Basic Guide To Collecting	D	Nov. 22, 1985
Sharpe, Ray	I	July 18, 1986	Sixties Alive In Tyhe '70s		Feb. 1979
Shaw, Artie	I, D	May 29, 1992	Sixties R&B		
Shaw, Greg/Bomp Records	I	Sept. 7, 1990	Sixties R&B: Hank Ballard	I	Aug. 12, 1988
Shaw, Sandie		March 27, 1987	Sixties R&B: William Bell	I,D	Feb. 13, 1987
Shaw, Sandie	I,D	April 10, 1987	Sixties R&B: Bobby Bland	I,D	Jan. 16, 1987
Shear, Jules	I, D	Apr. 3, 1992	Sixties R&B: Capitols/Ollie Mc Laughlin		
Sheila E (Escovedo)	I,D	Sept. 23, 1988	(Record Label Owner)	I,D	June 3, 1988
Sheridan, Tony	I	Nov. 25, 1994	Sixties R&B: Chambers Brothers	D	March 25, 1988
Sherman, Allan	D	Sept. 11, 1987	Sixties R&B: Clifton Chenier	D	Jan. 1, 1988
Sherman, Allan	D	Sept. 11, 1987	Sixties R&B: Chicago Contribution To Dance		
Shimmy-Disc Records/Mark Kramer	I	Sept. 7, 1990	(The Uncle Willie)	D	Jan. 29, 1988
Shindig	I	Sept. 21, 1990	Sixties R&B: Tony Clarke	D	Jan. 30, 1987
Shine, Billy Joe/Nightcaps	I,D	June 1980	Sixties R&B: Wayne Cochran	D	Dec. 16, 1988
Shine, Billy Joe/Nightcaps	D	Dec. 1981	Sixties R&B: G.L. Crockett	D	April 8, 1988
Shirelles/Mickey Harris	I	Sept. 1980	Sixties R&B: James Davis	I,D	April 22, 1988
Shirelles/Shirley Alston	I,D	Jan. 1984	Sixties R&B: Sugar Pie De Santo	D	July 3, 1987
Shocking Blue		Dec. 30, 1988	Sixties R&B: Fascinations	D	March 27, 1987
Shoes	D	Oct. 9, 1987	Sixties R&B: Gorgeous George	D	Sept. 9, 1988
Shoes, The	I,D	July 1980	Sixties R&B: Slim Harpo	D	March 11, 1988
Shoes, The	D	Oct. 9, 1987	Sixties R&B: Richie Havens	I	Sept. 25, 1987
Shorts (Ed Engel)			Sixties R&B: Jennell Hawkins	I	Nov. 20, 1987
Shorts: Castaways		July-Aug. 1977	Sixties R&B: Clarence Frogman Henry	I,D	May 22, 1987
Shorts: Fontella Bass		July-Aug. 1977	Sixties R&B: Jessie Hill	I,D	Oct. 21, 1988
Shorts: Johnny Oct.		Sept. 1977	Sixties R&B: Ron Holden	I,D	Sept. 11, 1987
Should You Become A Record Show Dealer?		March 9, 1990	Sixties R&B: Howlin' Wolf	D	June 5, 1987
Showmen/Norman Johnson	I,D	Nov. 16, 1990	Sixties R&B: Deon Jackson	I,D	Sept. 23, 1988
Shrieve, Michael/Santana	I	March 24, 1989	Sixties R&B: Elmore James	D	July 17, 1987
Shrieve/Santana, Michael	I	March 24, 1989	Sixties R&B: Elmore James	DA	Oct. 23, 1987
Shute, Bill/Fifth Estate	I,D	Feb. 1981	Sixties R&B: Jewels	D	Jan. 2, 1987
Sidney, Rockin (Simien)	D	Oct. 25, 1985	Sixties R&B: Chris Kenner	D	Feb. 12, 1988
Sidney, Rockin (Simien)	DA	Feb. 13, 1987	Sixties R&B: Larks/Don Julian	I,D	Aug. 26, 1988

Entry	Code	Date	Entry	Code	Date
Sixties R&B: Little Eva	I,D	May 20, 1988	Sixties Rock: Spooky Tooth/Jimmy Miller	I,D	Dec. 2, 1988
Sixties R&B: Little Eva	DA	Aug. 12, 1988	Sixties Rock: Thunderclap Newman		Oct. 21, 1988
Sixties R&B: Barbara Lynn	D	March 13, 1987	Sixties Rock: Tim Hardin	D	April 10, 1987
Sixties R&B: Sam Maghett	D	Jan. 15, 1988	Sixties Rock: Tom Jones	D	June 3, 1988
Sixties R&B: Cash Mc Call	D	Aug. 14, 1987	Sixties Rock: Tom Rush	I,D	July 3, 1987
Sixties R&B: Johnny Moore	D	Oct. 9, 1987	Sixties Rock: Tradewinds	D	Aug. 14, 1987
Sixties R&B: Robert Parker	I,D	April 10, 1987	Sixties Rock: Woodstock Music Festival		Aug. 28, 1987
Sixties R&B: Popeye (The Dance)		Nov. 4, 1988	Skinny Puppy	I,D	Sept 27, 1996
Sixties R&B: Jimmy Reed	D	Oct. 23, 1987	Skyliners	I	Sept. 25, 1987
Sixties R&B: Roscoe Robinson		Feb. 27, 1987	Skyliners/Jimmy Beaumont	I,D	Sept. 1981
Sixties R&B: Swan Silvertones		June 19, 1987	Slade	D	April 24, 1987
Sixties R&B: Johnnie Taylor	I,D	June 17, 1988	Slade	D	April 24, 1987
Sixties R&B: Little Johnny Taylor	I,D	Aug. 28, 1987	Slash/Guns N' Roses	I,D	May 19, 1989
Sixties R&B: Little Johnny Taylor	DA	Oct. 23, 1987	Slay, Frank	I,D	Oct. 1983
Sixties R&B: Ted Taylor	D	July 31, 1987	Sledge, Percy		July-Aug. 1978
Sixties R&B: Ted Taylor	DA	Oct. 23, 1987	Sledge, Sister	D	Aug. 28, 1987
Sixties R&B: Uncle Willie (The Dance)	D	Jan. 29, 1988	Sleeper		Feb. 16, 1996
Sixties R&B: Junior Wells	D	Nov. 6, 1987	Sless, Barry/Cowboy Jazz	I	Aug. 1982
Sixties R&B: Johnny Williams	D	April 24, 1987	Slick, Grace	I,D	April 1982
Sixties R&B: Lee Shot Williams	I,D	Dec. 2, 1988	Slim, T. V. (Oscar Wills)		March-April 1977
Sixties R&B: Jackie Wilson	D	Dec. 4, 1987	Slits	D	March 1981
Sixties R&B: Brenton Wood	I,D	May 8, 1987	Sloan, P.F.	I,D	Oct. 25, 1985
Sixties R&B: Brenton Wood	DA	Oct. 23, 1987	Sly and the Family Stone	D	Feb. 18, 1994
Sixties R&B: O. V. Wright	D	Dec. 18, 1987	Small Faces	I,D	June 21, 1996
Sixties Rock			Small, Millie		Dec. 1, 1989
Sixties Rock: 1965 A Year Of Satisfaction	D	May 20, 1988	Smith, Arlene/Chantels	I,D	Jan. 15, 1988
Sixties Rock: Allan Sherman	D	Sept. 11, 1987	Smith, Clarence		Feb. 26, 1988
Sixties Rock: Beacon Street Union/John Lincoln	I,D	Dec. 18, 1987	Smith, Herbie	I,D	Dec. 1983
Sixties Rock: Blind Faith		March 27, 1987	Smith, Homer/Southernaires		June 21, 1985
Sixties Rock: Bob Dylan		July 1, 1988	Smith, Huey Piano	D	June 1982
Sixties Rock: Bob Lind	D	Nov. 20, 1987	Smith, Huey Piano	DA	Jan. 1983
Sixties Rock: Bob Seger	D	June 5, 1987	Smith, Huey Piano	DA	Aug. 1983
Sixties Rock: Bobby Marchan	I,D	Sept. 25, 1987	Smith, Jimmy	D	June 30, 1989
Sixties Rock: Boby (Bobby) Curtola	I,D	April 8, 1988	Smith, Mack Allen	I,D	Oct. 1983
Sixties Rock: Chantays/Brian Carman/Bob Spickard	I,D	Dec. 16, 1988	Smith, Mack Allen	DA	Feb. 15, 1985
Sixties Rock: Crispian St. Peters	I,D	Nov. 4, 1988	Smith, Major Bill	D	June 1982
Sixties Rock: Detroit's '60s Rock Scene		Dec. 4, 1987	Smith, Major Bill	I,D	May 24, 1985
Sixties Rock: Fever Tree	D	April 22, 1988	Smith, Marvin/El Dorados/Artistics	D	July 1980
Sixties Rock: Frank Sinatra Jr.	D	Aug. 26, 1988	Smith, Mike/Dave Clark Five	I	Nov. 1982
Sixties Rock: Hey Joe (The Song)		Jan. 15, 1988	Smith, Mike/Dave Clark Five	I	Oct. 21, 1988
Sixties Rock: Holy Modal Rounders	D	Oct. 23, 1987	Smith, Mike/Paul Revere & The Raiders	I	April 20, 1990
Sixties Rock: Janis Joplin		March 13, 1987	Smith, Patti	D	Sept. 9, 1988
Sixties Rock: Jerry Lee Lewis		April 24, 1987	Smith, Patti Group/Lenny Kaye	I	May 1980
Sixties Rock: John Fred	I	March 25, 1988	Smith, Ray		Sept. 1979
Sixties Rock: Johnny Rivers		June 19, 1987	Smith, Robert O./Thorndike Pickledish Choir	D	Nov. 1980
Sixties Rock: Kyu Sakamoto		Jan. 30, 1987	Smith, Warren		Oct. 9, 1987
Sixties Rock: Linda Scott	I,D	Feb. 27, 1987	Smith, Warren		May 15, 1992
Sixties Rock: Lou Rawls	D	July 1, 1988	Smith/Gayle Mc Cormick	I,D	Dec. 1982
Sixties Rock: Love		Feb. 13, 1987	Smithereens	I,D	Dec. 15, 1989
Sixties Rock: Magicians	D	Nov. 6, 1987	Smithsonian/Folkways Records		Aug. 6, 1993
Sixties Rock: Mc5	D	Sept. 9, 1988	Smothers Brothers	D	Sept. 1979
Sixties Rock: Merry-Go-Round	D	Feb. 12, 1988	Smut Smiff/Rockats	I	Dec. 1980
Sixties Rock: Moby Grape		July 17, 1987	Snyder, Harry	I,D	May 1980
Sixties Rock: Nancy Sinatra	D	Jan. 2, 1987	Soft Machine	D	Oct. 6, 1989
Sixties Rock: Nancy Sinatra	DA	Feb. 13, 1987	Sohns, Jim/Shadows Of Knight		Nov. 1977
Sixties Rock: Nancy Sinatra	DA	Sept. 9, 1988	Sohns, Jim/Shadows Of Knight	I	July 18, 1986
Sixties Rock: Norma Tanega	I,D	Jan. 29, 1988	Soileau, Floyd/Flat Town Music Group	I	Nov. 4, 1988
Sixties Rock: Paul Butterfield	D	July 31, 1987	Somerville, David/Diamonds	I	March 2, 1984
Sixties Rock: Peggy March	I,D	Sept. 23, 1988	Sommer, Bert		April 7, 1989
Sixties Rock: Pirates	D	Jan. 1, 1988	Sommers, Joanie	D	Sept. 1981
Sixties Rock: Rip Chords		May 8, 1987	Song Revival Revolution Of The '70s: Musical Roots Of Rock	D	Nov. 1979
Sixties Rock: Roger Miller	D	May 22, 1987	Songs About The Numbers Game	D	March 30, 1984
Sixties Rock: Ronny & The Daytonas/Bucky Wilkin	I,D	Jan. 16, 1987	Sonic Youth	D	Aug. 28, 1987
Sixties Rock: Rooftop Singers	D	Aug. 12, 1988	Sonic Youth	I, D	Sept. 16, 1994
Sixties Rock: Rotary Connection	D	June 17, 1988	Sonnier, Jo-El	I,D	Nov. 1983
Sixties Rock: Scott Mc Kenzie	D	March 11, 1988	Sonnier, Jo-El	DA	May 24, 1985
Sixties Rock: Shangri-Las	D	Oct. 9, 1987			

Name	Code	Date	Name	Code	Date
Stereolab/Tim Gane	I	Nov. 8, 1996	Supergrass		Feb. 16, 1996
Stevens, Cat	D	Nov. 6, 1987	Supreme Court Rules On Bootleg Shipments		Aug. 16,1985
Stevens, Cat	D	Nov. 6, 1987	Supremes, The		Nov. 6, 1987
Stevens, Cat		April 7, 1989	Supremes, The		Feb. 26, 1988
Stevens, Dodie	I,D	Nov. 1978	Supremes, The	I,D	April 8, 1988
Stevens, Dodie	DA	Feb. 1979	Supremes, The	DA	July 1, 1988
Stevens, Shakin'	D	Oct. 1983	Supremes, The/Mary Wilson	I,D	Sept. 1983
Stevens, Shakin'	D	Oct. 1983	Supremes, The/Mary Wilson	DA	Dec. 1983
Stewart, Billy	D	Oct. 1982	Supremes, The: The Story Of Florence Ballard	D	Sept. 1983
Stewart, Eric/Mindbenders/Hotlegs/10 CC	I,D	Jan. 16, 1987	Supremes, The: The Story Of Florence Ballard	DA	Dec. 1983
Stewart, Eric/Mindbenders/Hotlegs/10 CC	DA	Feb. 27, 1987	Surf Records		Aug. 21, 1992
Stewart, Ian/Rolling Stones	I	May 1983	Surf: Southern California Surf Revival Music		July 1983
Stewart, John	D	April 1979	Surfaris, The	D	Aug. 1980
Stewart, John	DA	Apr. 3, 1992	Surfaris, The (Not The Wipeout Surfaris)	D	Jan. 1981
Stewart, Rod	D	May 15, 1992	Survey Souvenirs (Kal Raudoja)		
Stiff Records		Nov. 4, 1988	Survey Souvenirs: Chum (1/10/66)		Jan. 1979
Stinson, Tommy	I	Oct. 25, 1996	Survey Souvenirs: Chum (11/21/60)		Nov. 1978
Stipe, Michael/R.E.M.	I,D	July 31, 1987	Survey Souvenirs: Chum (12/15/58)		Dec. 1978
Stoker, Gordon/Jordanaires	I	Jan. 1979	Survey Souvenirs: Chum (2/16/59)		Feb. 1979
Stoker, Gordon/Jordanaires	I	March 1981	Survey Souvenirs: Chum (5/27/63)		May 1979
Stoker, Gordon/Jordanaires	I	Aug. 11, 1989	Survey Souvenirs: Whil (6/26/61)		June 1979
Stolen Records And The Law		Nov. 1983	Surveying Rock In Buffalo		Feb. 1980
Stoller, Leiber and	I	April 28, 1995	Sutcliffe, Pauline	I	Nov. 25, 1994
Stoller, Mike		Aug. 1981	Swamp Dogg (Jerry Williams Jr.)	I	Jan. 1982
Stoller, Mike		Oct. 26, 1984	Swamp Pop: An Introduction		Jan. 1982
Stone Pony, The (club)	I	March 17, 1995	Swamp Pop Music	I	Aug. 16, 1996
Storm, Warren	I,D	April 26, 1985	Swan Silvertones		June 19, 1987
Storm, Warren		Feb. 14, 1986	Swan Silvertones		June 19, 1987
Storm, Warren	DA	Feb. 13, 1987	Sweden's New Underground		May 8, 1987
Strange Case Of "Hula Love"		March 2, 1984	Sweet	D	Nov. 20, 1987
Strangeloves	I, D	Mar. 6, 1992	Sweet	D	Nov. 20, 1987
Strangest Of Strange (And Good Luck Finding Them)		Dec. 29, 1989	Sweet, The	I,D	Feb. 28, 1997
Stranglers, The	D	June 5, 1987	Sweet, Phil		Nov. 1983
Strawberry Alarm Clock	D	April 29, 1994	Sweet, Rachel	D	July 1, 1988
Strawbs, the	D	Aug. 21, 1992	Sweet, Rachel	D	Jan. 1983
Stray Cats, The		July 1981	Sweet, Rachel	DA	Sept. 1983
Stray Cats, the	I, D	March 4, 1994	Sweet, Rachel	DA	Dec. 7, 1984
Streisand, Barbra	D	March 5, 1993	Sweet, Rachel	D	Jan. 1983
String Records		April 1980	Sweet, Rachel	DA	Sept. 1983
String-A-Longs	D	Nov.-Dec. 1976	Sweet, Rachel	DA	Dec. 7, 1984
Strong, Nolan/Diablos		July-Aug. 1977	Sweet, Rachel	DA	July 1, 1988
Strong, Nolan/Diablos	D	Jan. 3, 1986	Sweet, Rachel	DA	Nov. 18,1988
Strong, Nolan/Diablos		June 20, 1986	Sweetwater	I, D	June 9, 1995
Struck, Nolan	D	Aug. 12, 1988	Swingin' Medallions/John Mc Elrath	I	Dec. 1, 1989
Struck, Nolan	D	Aug. 12, 1988	Sylvers	D	Dec. 4, 1987
Sub Pop Records discography		Apr. 17, 1992	Sylvers	D	Dec. 4, 1987
Sub Pop Records/Bruce Pavitt	I	June 2, 1989	Sylvia, Margo/Tune Weavers	I,D	Feb. 8, 1991
Sue Records		May 12, 1995	Syncopaters	D	June 1980
Suede		Feb. 16, 1996			
Suede	I,D	Feb. 28, 1997	T		
Sugar Hill	I	May 10, 1996	Talking Heads	I, D	Dec. 25, 1992
Sullivan, Ed		Sept. 1981	Tallent, Gary	I	July 3, 1987
Sullivan, Ed		Oct. 1981	Talmy, Shel	I	July 13, 1990
Sullivan, Ed		July 1982	Tamblyn, Larry/Standells	I	April 8, 1988
Sullivan, Eddie	D	April 1981	Tamla Records Discography	D	May-June 1977
Sullivan, Niki/Buddy Holly & The Crickets	I,D	Sept. 1978	Tamla Records Discography	D	July-Aug. 1977
Sullivan, Niki/Buddy Holly & The Crickets	I,D	Sept. 14, 1984	Tams		Dec. 1, 1989
Summer, Donna	D	March 11, 1988	Tams, the	I, D	Aug. 5, 1994
Summer, Donna	D	March 11, 1988	Tanega, Norma	I,D	Jan. 29, 1988
Summer, Donna	D	May 1, 1992	Tanega, Norma	I,D	Jan. 29, 1988
Summers, Gene	I,D	Feb. 1982	Taping Pirates Not Guilty Of Theft		Nov. 9, 1984
Summers, Gene	DA	May 1982	Tarheel Slim (Alden Bunn)	D	Feb. 12, 1988
Sun Ra	D	Jan. 22, 1993	Taste Of Country (Bob Jinkerson)		
Sun Records Rhythm Section		July 14, 1989	Taste Of Country: Slim Whitman	D	Feb. 1978
Sun Records: Tour Of Sun Records Studios		Jan. 1983	Tavares		Nov. 20, 1987
Sundazed Records/Bobby Irwin	I	Sept. 7, 1990	Tavares		Nov. 20, 1987
Sunrays	I, D	May 15, 1992	Taylor, Dick/Pretty Things	I,D	Oct. 6, 1989

Name	Code	Date	Name	Code	Date
Taylor, Dick/Pretty Things	I,D	Oct. 20, 1989	Thomas, Carla	DA	March 11, 1988
Taylor, Dick/Pretty Things	DA	Nov. 17, 1989	Thomas, David/Pere Ubu	I,D	Jan. 15, 1988
Taylor, Johnnie	I,D	June 17, 1988	Thomas, Irma	I,D	June 1983
Taylor, Johnnie	I,D	June 17, 1988	Thomas, Irma	I,D	June 1983
Taylor, Koko	I,D	Jan. 1982	Thomas, Irma		Aug. 1983
Taylor, Koko	D	May 20, 1988	Thomas, Irma	DA	Dec. 7, 1984
Taylor, Little Johnny	I,D	Aug. 28, 1987	Thomas, Rufus	I,D	June 15, 1990
Taylor, Little Johnny	DA	Oct. 23, 1987	Thomas, Rufus	DA	Nov. 2, 1990
Taylor, Little Johnny	I,D	Aug. 28, 1987	Thompson, Dennis/Mc5	I,D	May 1979
Taylor, Little Johnny	DA	Oct. 23, 1987	Thompson, Hayden	D	Oct. 1979
Taylor, Ray		March 1982	Thompson, Richard/Fairport Convention		May 8, 1987
Taylor, Ted	D	July 31, 1987	Thorndike Pickeldish Choir/Robert O. Smith	D	Nov. 1980
Taylor, Ted	DA	Oct. 23, 1987	Thornton, Mae, Willie (Big Mama)	I,D	Oct. 1983
Taylor, Ted	D	July 31, 1987	Thornton, Mae, Willie (Big Mama)	D	April 21, 1989
Taylor, Ted	DA	Oct. 23, 1987	Thorogood, George	I	Nov. 1982
Teardrop Explodes		June 1981	Three Dog Night	I, D	Nov. 26, 1993
Techniques Of Effective Advertising		June 29, 1990	Three Dog Night/Cory Wells/Danny Hutton	I,D	April 27, 1984
Teddy Bears	D	April 10, 1987	Three Flames/Tiger Haynes	I,D	April 1980
Teddy Bears/Annette Kleinbard	I	June 17, 1988	Three O'Clock	I	March 2, 1984
Tee Set		Dec. 30, 1988	Three O'Clock	I	March 2, 1984
Teenagers/Jimmy Merchant	I,D	March 1982	Three Sharps And A Flat	I,D	March 1980
Television (The Group)	D	Nov. 4, 1988	Thunder, Johnny	I	Dec. 1, 1989
Television (The Group)	D	Nov. 4, 1988	Thunder, Johnny	D	March 11, 1988
Television Boogie		Dec. 21, 1984	Thunderclap Newman		Oct. 21, 1988
Tempo, Nino	I	June 17, 1988	Thunderclap, Newman		Oct. 21, 1988
Tempo, Nino	I,D	Feb. 22, 1991	Tieken, Freddie	I,D	July 1981
Tempo, Nino & April Stevens		Dec. 1, 1989	Til, Sonny/Orioles	I	Feb. 1982
Tempo, Nino & April Stevens	D,DO	Feb. 22, 1991	Til, Sonny/Orioles	D	April 6, 1990
Temptations	D	Oct. 1980	Tillotson, Johnny	I,D	Oct. 1983
10CC	I,D	April 11, 1997	Tillotson, Johnny	DA	Feb. 15, 1985
10 CC/Graham Gouldman/Eric Stewart	I,D	Jan. 16, 1987	Tilt And Jam Records	D	Nov. 4, 1988
10 CC/Graham Gouldman/Eric Stewart	DA	Feb. 27, 1987	Tim/Kerr	I	May 9, 1997
Ten Years After/Alvin Lee/Ric Lee/Leo Lyons	I,D	Oct. 6, 1989	Time Records: Schwartz, Bernard/Time/Edit Records	I,D	Sept. 7, 1990
Ten Years After/Alvin Lee/Ric Lee/Leo Lyons	DA	Dec. 29, 1989	Time, The	D	Sept. 25, 1987
Tennstedt, Klaus	I,D	April 27, 1984	Time-Life Records		Sept. 17, 1993
Tenth Avenue Revisited (New York City)		March 27, 1987	Time/Edit Records/Bernard Schwartz	I,D	Sept. 7, 1990
Terranova, Joe/Danny & The Juniors	I	Nov.-Dec. 1976	Timmins, Margo/Cowboy Junkies	I	June 30, 1989
Terry, Joe/Danny & The Juniors	I,D	May 9, 1986	Tiny Tim	I,D	Oct. 1981
Texas Blues		April 22, 1988	Tiny Tim	I	Sept. 21, 1990
Texas Record Stores		April 22, 1988	Tiny Tim	I	Jan. 3, 1997
Texas Record Stores		Oct. 5, 1990	Together Records		Sept. 17, 1993
Thayer, Frank		Feb. 1979	Tokens, The	D	May 22, 1987
Thee Midnighters	D	Feb. 1982	Tokens/Jay Siegel	I,D	Oct. 1981
Thee Midnighters	DA	June 1982	Tolby, Sean/Chocolate Watch Band	I,D	Sept. 1983
Thiele, Bob	I	Dec. 11, 1992	Tom And Jerrio	D	Feb.1979
Thin Lizzy	D	Oct. 21, 1988	Tommy James and the Shondells	I, D	March 6, 1992
Thin Lizzy	D	Oct. 21, 1988	Tommy Tucker	D	Aug. 18, 1995
Things Got Groovy At The Drive-In Movie		Sept. 8, 1989	Toots & The Maytals	I,D	Dec. 1982
Thinking Out Loud (Bob Grasso)		Feb. 1976	Top 100 Most Valuable Rock Records Of The '60s		May 6, 1988
Thinking Out Loud (Bob Grasso)		March 1976	Top 40 Radio (Larry Sharp)		March+April 1977
Thinking Out Loud (Bob Grasso)		May 1976	Top 40 Radio (Larry Sharp)		May-June 1977
Thinking Out Loud (Bob Grasso)		Sept.-Oct. 1976	Top 40 Radio (Larry Sharp)		July-Aug. 1977
Thinking Out Loud (Bob Grasso)		Nov.-Dec. 1976	Top 40 Radio (Larry Sharp)		Nov. 1977
Thinking Out Loud (Bob Grasso)		Jan.-Feb. 1977	Top 40 Radio (Larry Sharp)		Dec. 1977
Thinking Out Loud (Bob Grasso)		March+April 1977	Top 40 Radio: Gene Nobles		Sept. 1977
Thinking Out Loud (Bob Grasso)		May-June 1977	Tork, Peter/Monkees	I,D	May 1982
Thinking Out Loud (Bob Grasso)		Oct. 1977	Tornadoes (Us Surf Group)	D	Jan. 1980
Thinking Out Loud (Bob Grasso)		Jan.1979	Toronto Peace Festival/John Brower	I	Feb. 24,1989
Thinking Out Loud: Bootleg Records		Issue #6	Torrence, Dean	I	July 1983
Thinking Out Loud: Kiddie Picture Disc		Oct. 1979	Toscanini		Jan. 7, 1993
Thinking Out Loud: Little Richard		July 1976	Tosh, Peter	I,D	April 1982
Thinking Out Loud: TV DJ's		Feb. 1978	Tower Of Power/Emilio Castillo	I,D	March 24, 1989
13th Floor Elevators	D	March 13, 1987	Townsend, Ed		Dec. 30, 1988
Thomas, B J	I,D	Dec. 1981	Trade Winds Five/Rick Miller	I,D	Aug. 3, 1984
Thomas, B J		Feb. 1982	Tradewinds	D	Aug. 14, 1987
Thomas, B J	DA	March 1982	Tradewinds	D	Aug. 14, 1987
Thomas, Carla	I,D	Feb. 13, 1987	Traffic/Jim Capaldi	I,D	April 13, 1984

Translator	I	Dec. 1983	UFO/Phil Mogg	I,D	May 1979
Translator	I	Dec. 1983	Ugly Ducklings	D	June 30, 1989
Trapeze	I, D	Nov. 11, 1994	Ugly Ducklings/Roger Mayne	I,D	May 1980
Trashmen/Dal Winslow	I	Sept. 22, 1989	Uncle Willie (The Dance)	D	Jan. 29, 1988
Travers, Mary/Peter, Paul & Mary	I,D	March 30, 1984	Uncle Willie (The Dance)	D	Jan. 29, 1988
Travers, Mary/Peter, Paul & Mary	DA	June 21, 1985	Union Gap/Gary Puckett	I,D	Dec. 1979
Trends In Recorded Television Themes	D	Sept. 1979	Unit 4 + 2	D	Oct. 21, 1988
Trends In Recorded Television Themes	DA	Nov. 1979	United Records	D	Feb. 13, 1987
Trends In Recorded Television Themes	DA	Dec. 1979	Uno, Conrad/Popllama Records	I	June 2, 1989
Treniers	D	Feb. 1978	Usher, Gary/Sagittarius/Millenium	I,D	Nov. 2, 1990
Tri-Phi Records	D	Nov. 1978			
Tri-Phi Records	DA	Jan. 1979	**V**		
Troggs/Reg Presley	I,D	July 1980	Vagrants, The	I,D	July 1981
Troggs/Reg Presley	DA	April 1981	Valadiers/Jerry Light	I,D	Nov. 16, 1990
Trower, Robin	D	Oct. 6, 1989	Valens, Ritchie		Nov.-Dec. 1976
Trumpet Records/Lillian Mc Murry	D	Jan. 1980	Valens, Ritchie	D	Jan. 2, 1987
Trumpet Records/Lillian Mc Murry	DA	April 1980	Valens, Ritchie	D	Feb. 10, 1989
Trumpet Records/Lillian Mc Murry	DA	July 6, 1984	Valentino, Sal/Beau Brummels	I,D	March 14, 1986
Trumpet Records/Lillian Mc Murry	DA	Feb. 1, 1985	Valentino, Tony/Standells	I	April 8, 1988
Tubb, Ernest	I,D	Sept. 1982	Valley Girl Soundtrack		Nov. 27, 1992
Tucker, Bob/Bill Black Combo	I,D	March 1981	Valley, Jim/Paul Revere & The Raiders	I	April 20, 1990
Tucker, Tommy		Sept. 8, 1989	Valli, Frankie/Four Seasons	I	Aug. 1983
Tune Weavers/Margo Sylvia	I,D	Feb. 8, 1991	Van Der Graaf Generator	D	March 9, 1990
Turbans		Dec. 1, 1989	Van Der Graaf Generator	DA	April 6, 1990
Turks/Gaynel Hodge	I,D	Feb. 8, 1991	Van Der Graaf Generator	DA	April 20, 1990
Turner, Big Joe	I	Nov. 1982	Van Eaton, Jimmy	I	July 14, 1989
Turner, Big Joe	D	Jan. 17, 1986	Van Halen	D	Feb. 13, 1987
Turner, Big Joe	DA	April 11, 1986	Van Meeredonk, Ben/Back-Trac Records	I,D	Jan. 3, 1986
Turner, Big Joe		April 26, 1988	Van Zandt, Little Steve	I	Feb. 1983
Turner, Ike		July-Aug. 1977	Van Zandt, Little Steve	I	Nov. 9, 1984
Turner, Ike	I,D	Nov. 3, 1989	Van Zandt, Townes	I,D	Oct. 5, 1990
Turner, Ike and Tina: River Deep, Mountain High		June 17, 1988	Van Zandt, Townes	I	Feb. 14, 1997
Turner, Tina	D	Oct. 23, 1987	Vance, Kenny/Jay & The Americans/Eddie & The Cruisers	I	Aug. 1, 1986
Turnero, Joel		Sept. 11, 1987	Vandellas, Martha Reeves and the	I, D	March 3, 1995
Turntable, Choosing A		Sept. 27, 1985	Vanguard Records/Kent Crawford	I	Sept. 7, 1990
Turtles/Mark Volman		April 1980	Vanilla Fudge/Mark Stein	I,D	Nov. 1981
Turtles/Mark Volman/Howard Kaylan	I,D	Dec. 1982	Vanishing Imports		Jan. 16, 1987
Turtles/Mark Volman/Howard Kaylan		Feb. 1983	Vann, Joey/Duprees	D	March 1, 1985
Turtles/Mark Volman/Howard Kaylan		Sept. 1983	Varese Vintage Records		May 12, 1995
Turtles/Mark Volman/Howard Kaylan	I	May 18, 1990	Various Artists Sing Bob Dylan	D	Dec. 1983
Turtles/Mark Volman/Howard Kaylan vs. De La Soul	I	May 18, 1990	Vaughan, Stevie Ray	D	April 21, 1989
TV DJ's		Feb. 1978	Vaughn, Ben	I, D	March 17, 1995
Tweeds, The	D	Aug. 1980	Vee Jay Stereo	I	May 1981
25 Years Of Country/Pop Music		April 1981	Vee Jay Story	I,D	May 1981
20/20		Oct. 1981	Vee Jay Story Part II	I,D	May 1981
20 Years Ago Today (Gary King)		May-June 1977	Vee, Bobby	I,D	March 1981
20 Years Ago Today (Gary King)		Sept. 1977	Vee, Bobby	I	Feb. 10, 1989
20 Years Ago Today (Gary King)		Dec. 1977	Vega, Suzanne	I	Aug. 12, 1988
Twilley, Dwight	D	March 9, 1990	Velvelettes, The	I,D	Sept. 12, 1986
Twin/Tone Records	D	Nov. 6, 1987	Velvet Underground	D	Oct. 7, 1988
Twist, The		Dec. 16, 1988	Venet, Nik		March 28, 1997
Twist, the		June 23, 1995	Ventures, The	I,D	July 1981
Twitty, Conway	D	July-Aug. 1978	Ventures, The		Oct. 1981
Twitty, Conway	D	March 1983	Ventures, The		Sept. 13, 1985
Twitty, Conway	DA	Oct. 1983	Ventures, The	DA	Feb. 13, 1987
Twitty, Conway	DA	Dec. 7, 1984	Vereen, George		Oct. 1978
Twitty, Conway	I,D	Nov. 30, 1990	Verve Records		March 18, 1994
2-Tone Records		May 12, 1995			
Tymes, The	I, D	Jan. 8, 1993	Vig, Butch	I	Oct. 27, 1995
			Village People/Jacques Morali	I,D	March 9, 1990
U			Villari, Guy/Regents	I,D	July 1980
U2		July 31, 1987	Vin cent, Gene	D	Nov. 26, 1993
U2	D	Nov. 30, 1990	Vincent, Gene		Nov.-Dec. 1976
U2	DA	Dec. 28, 1990	Vincent, Gene		Jan.-Feb. 1977
U2/Bono Vox	I,D	Nov. 30, 1990	Vincent, Gene		Dec. 1983
UB40		July 6, 1984	Vincent, Gene	D	Sept. 8, 1989
Ubu, Pere		Aug. 30, 1996	Vinyl Junkie (See "Report From Cub Koda" and "Cub Koda")		Jan. 10, 1992

Volk, Phil/Paul Revere & The Raiders	I	April 20, 1990	Watley, Jody	I	Oct. 9, 1987
Volman, Mark/Flo And Eddie		April 1980	Watson, Johnny "Guitar"	D	Feb. 2, 1996
Volman, Mark/Turtles	I,D	Dec. 1982	Watts, Charlie	I	March 27, 1987
Volman, Mark/Turtles		Feb. 1983	Watts, Charlie	ID	Sept. 18, 1992
Volman, Mark/Turtles	DA	Sept. 1983	Watusi, The		Oct. 1978
Vontastics	D	Jan. 1978	Wax Works (Bob Grossweiner) Rhino Records/		
Voorman, Klaus	I	Feb. 1984	Harold Bronson	I,D	Dec. 1982
Visconti, Tony	I	June 6, 1997	Wax Works (Ellen Zoe Golden) Attic Records	D	July 1982
Vox, Bono/U2	I,D	Nov. 30, 1990	Wax Works (George Moonoogian) Baron Records		March 1980
			Wax Works (J.j. Syrja) Flying Fish Records		Sept. 1980
W			Wax Works (Jeff Tamarkin)Accord/Townhouse Records	D	Sept. 1982
Wade, Adam	I,D	Dec. 1982	Wax Works (Martin Hawkins) Fernwood Records	D	Sept. 1981
Wade, Adam		Feb. 1983	Wax Works (Martin Hawkins) Flyright Records	D	July 1981
Wade, Adam		Sept. 1983	Wax Works (Martin Hawkins) String Records		April 1980
Wade, Adam	DA	Sept. 1983	Wax Works (Peter Grendysa) Route 66 Records	D	May 1980
Wadhams, Wayne/Fifth Estate	I,D	Sept. 21, 1990	Wax Works (Rick Whitesell) Blind Pig Records		Aug. 1980
Wagon Wheel Records		March 29, 1996	Wax Works (Rick Whitesell)Cowboy Carl Records	D	June 1980
Wahls, Shirley	I,D	Dec. 1981	Waxie Maxie (Max Needham)		Jan. 1978
Wailers	D	Nov.-Dec. 1976	Waxing On (Russ Shor)		May 1979
Wailers/Kenny Morrill	D	April 20, 1990	Waxing On (Russ Shor)		May 1980
Wailers/Kenny Morrill	DA	Aug. 10,1990	Waxing On (Russ Shor)		Sept. 1980
Wainwright, Loudon Iii	I,D	July 20, 1984	Waxing On (Russ Shor): Enrico Caruso		June 1980
Wainwritght, Loudon III	ID	June 25, 1993	Waxing On (Russ Shor): Louis Armstrong		Nov. 1979
Waite, John	D	Jan. 15, 1988	Waxing On (Russ Shor): New Orleans		Sept. 1979
Waits, Tom	D	July 18, 1986	Waxing On (Russ Shor): Paramount Record Label		July 1979
Walker, Jerry Jeff	D	April 22, 1988	Waxing On (Russ Shor): Paramount Record Label		Oct. 1979
Walker, Jerry Jeff	D	April 22, 1988	Waxing On (Russ Shor): The 20's Labels		Jan. 1980
Walker, Jerry Jeff	DA	July 1, 1988	Waxing On (Russ Shor): The 20's Labels	DA	July 1980
Walker, Jr. & The All Stars	I	Oct. 1981	Waxing On (Russ Shor): The 20's Labels Part 2		April 1980
Walker, Jr. & The All Stars	I,D	Nov. 16, 1990	Waxing On (Russ Shor): Vintage Colored Vinyl		Dec. 1979
Walker, T-Bone		Feb. 26,1988	Wayne, Gaylon	I,D	July 1980
Wallace, Sippie	I,D	Nov. 1982	Wayne, Thomas		Dec. 30, 1988
Wallace, Sippie	D	March 28, 1986	Weavers, The	D	Feb. 1982
Wallice, Ruth	I,D	May 9, 1997	Weavers/Gordon Jenkins	I,D	March 15, 1985
Walls, Van		May 9, 1986	Weavers/Gordon Jenkins		Feb. 13, 1987
Walt Disney Records		Sept. 17, 1993	Webb, Jimmy	I,D	Dec. 20, 1996
Walter, Little	D	April 16, 1993	Weil, Cynthia/Barry Mann	I,D	Aug. 1982
Walton, Mercy Dee		Feb. 23,1990	Weil, Cynthia/Barry Mann		Feb. 1983
War	D	March 9, 1990	Weil, Cynthia/Barry Mann	DA	Sept. 1983
War	DA	April 20, 1990	Weinberg, Max	I	Oct. 23, 1987
War	I, D	Sept. 2, 1994	Weinberg, Max	I	July 15, 1988
Ward, Anita		Dec. 1, 1989	Weir, Bob/Grateful Dead	I	Nov. 16, 1990
Ward, Walter/Olympics	I	Dec. 1, 1989	Weiss, David/Was (Not Was)	I,D	Dec. 16, 1988
Wardell, Don	I	Aug. 11, 1989	Weize, Richard/Bear Family Records	I	Nov. 7, 1986
Warner Brothers Records "Loss Leaders" LPs	D	Oct. 23, 1987	Weller, Freddy/Paul Revere & The Raiders	I	April 20, 1990
Warner Brothers Records "Loss Leaders" LPs	DA	Feb. 12, 1988	Weller, Paul/Jam	I	June 1981
Warwick, Dionne	I,D	Jan. 26, 1990	Wells, Cory/Three Dog Night	I,D	April 27, 1984
Warwick, Dionne	DA	Aug. 10, 1990	Wells, Junior	D	Nov. 6, 1987
Was (Not Was)/David Weiss	I,D	Dec. 16, 1988	Wells, Junior	D	Nov. 6, 1987
Was (Not Was)/Don "Was" Fagenson/David Weiss	I	Dec. 1983	Wells, Mary	I,D	Oct. 1980
Was (Not Was)/Don "Was" Fagenson/David Weiss	I	Dec. 1983	Wells, Mary		Dec. 1980
Was, Don	I	Aug. 19, 1994	Wells, Mary	DA	Feb. 1981
Washington Squares	I	May 25, 1984	Welsch, Lou/Sapphire Records	I	Feb. 15, 1985
Waterloo Revisited (Michael Dee)			Welsch, Lou/Sapphire Records	DA	Jan. 17, 1986
Waterloo Revisited: Jerry Samuels		Sept.-Oct. 1976	Welz, Joey	I,D	April 11, 1986
Waterloo Revisited: Napolean Xiv		Sept.-Oct. 1976	Werber, Frank/Kingston Trio	I	July 1981
Waters, John	I	May 18, 1990	Werber, Frank/Kingston Trio	I	Aug. 1981
Waters, Muddy	D	July 3, 1987	West Coast R&B		April 12, 1985
Waters, Muddy		July 1983	West, Tommy	D	Dec. 1981
Waters, Muddy	D	July 3, 1987	Westerberg, Paul		Nov. 25, 1996
Waters, Muddy		Feb. 26, 1988	Weston, Kim	I,D	Nov. 16, 1990
Watkins, Bill	I	Dec. 1978	Wexler, Jerry		Feb.26, 1988

ESSENTIALLY ELVIS:
THE ULTIMATE ELVIS ANTHOLOGY
by Dave Thompson

The perfect Elvis boxed set. There's no such animal, right? Short of being given a caseful of recordable CDs, and the keys to RCA's deepest vault, there's not an Elvis collector on earth who could be truly satisfied with what the label has offered, and that's not an indictment of the label, it's an indication of just how personally people take these things.

Goldmine's Neal Umphred hinted at a this back in January 1997, when he bemoaned the cancellation of what he described as proposed boxes documenting every version of "Hound Dog" the King ever recorded, and the similarly eclectic Elvis Sings For Pets (And Wild Critters Too) collection of Presley's zoological catalog.

To this catalog of devastation, we can now add the loss of In The Gateaux, a two disc box devoted to Elvis' songs about food: though the jokes are so old now, even the E.coli's have gone senile and died. There is no denying that Elvis liked his food, and scattered through his repertoire, conspiracy theorists have detected a thread which denies any suggestion that he was directionless for a decade or more.

Seamlessly sequenced with the very latest digital technology, In The Gateaux would have compiled a generously mouthwatering portion of Elvis' greatest culinary hits. Highlighted were the Behind Closed Doors bootleg outtakes o;f "Polk Salad Annie" and the less than hygienic "I Washed My Hands In Muddy Water"; the "Heartburn Hotel" variation of his first #1, recorded at the New Frontier Hotel in Las Vegas in May, 1956; "Clambake"; a Vegas performance of "Love Me Tender" (the medium rare version); "Crawfish"; "Blueberry Hill"; "Hot Dog"; a snatch of "got to go to lunch" dialog from take 8 of "Tonight Is So Right For Love"; and a fitting conclusion to such a repast, "Inherit The Wind." Certain Pacific Rim markets will also receive "Old Shep" (take 5).

Yes, there is indeed a thin line to be drawn between parody and passion, but the committed Elvis collector learned to walk it years back, in the days of Sings For Children (And Grown Ups Too) and any one of a dozen minor hits from the movies compilations. But the quest for the Holy Grail, the ultimate take of any given song, will never be fulfilled, simply because the ultimate take, like the ultimate box, just doesn't exist.

Or does it?

This project, which underwent upwards of a dozen changes in title before its current, unimaginative nomenclature was arrived at (Come Back Joanie was a longtime frontrunner, while both the 1950s and 1970s volumes were once titled Watch The Waistline), does not claim to plug that gap. It doesn't, in fact, claim much of anything. But sandwiched between the reprises of his greatest hits, and the once-more-around renditions of overhyped scarcities and rarities (exactly how rare is a previously unreleased out-take, once it's been released on a multi-million selling boxed set?), some primal glimpses of true collectors gold is visible.

Only glimpses, though: unreleased tracks are noted with an asterix. Despite the best intentions, many of the tracks here have been released, most commonly on the Elvis Aron Presley, Golden Celebration and Complete/Essential Masters boxed sets. Curiosity value is fine, but there is something we should remember regarding unreleased material, particularly material which remains unreleased after exhumations of that magnitude. And that is, there's often a very good reason for it remaining unreleased. But if Once More, The Ultimate Elvis is, as has already been suggested, the Presleyphile's answer to the Beatles' Anthology series, answer this. How many times have you played your copies of that?

Volume 1: From the Waist Up: The '50s

1: BLUES AFTER HOURS (live) (Flamingo, Memphis, 1951)
Elvis Presley was a familiar sight at the Flamingo, just off Beale Street, particularly on those nights when the Finas Newborne Orchestra's young guitarist, Calvin Newborne, took part in the Battle Of The Guitars. One night, according to Calvin, Elvis himself asked if he could join in; Calvin agreed, and handed over his instrument.

"The rhythm Finas played had him locked up so tight he couldn't have gotten out if he'd wanted to," Calvin marvels. "But he didn't want to. The audience went wild, it felt as though the entire building was shaking along with them.

"There was no such thing as rock'n'roll in 1951, but there were simply no other words that could describe what he did that night at the Flamingo. By the time he had finished, he had wrecked the house... and taken my guitar with it. Every string on my instrument had been broken, and even as Dad fished a new set out of his pocket, I knew that this was one guitar battle I wasn't going to win."

2: HUMES HIGH BAND PRESENTS ITS ANNUAL MINSTREL (live) (Humes Auditorium, 4/9/53)
In a room full of proud parents, surely someone thought to bring along a tape recorder, and capture little Johnny (or Jerry or Sidney or Glenn Yarborough) at their moment of triumph? Eighteen year old "Elvis Prestly" appeared 16th on the bill, sandwiched between the band's rendition of "Beautiful Ohio," and Jerry Blanton's tap dancing routine.

3: THAT'S WHEN YOUR HEARTACHES BEGIN (Memphis Recording Service, 4/53)
It has been described as the single most important day in rock-'n'roll history. Certainly it was the most important hour or so; that afternoon in April, 1953, when a young truck driver stopped by the Memphis recording service and cut a couple of songs for his mother, "That's When Your Heartaches Begin" and

"My Happiness." After he'd gone, the legend insists, studio boss Sam Phillips turned and asked who that mysterious vocalist was. Forty-five years later, with the original lacquer having finally surfaced and been leased to RCA, many collectors still ask that same question — with one speaking for many when he says, "there's a rumor going around that it's not Elvis singing on those tracks."

Interviewed for this article, Neal Umphred remarked, "if you're doing the 'essential' Elvis, there is no reason at all to include these songs." On the contrary, that rumor alone is the best reason in the world. What, after all, could be more tantalizing than the possibility there were Elvis impersonators going around, a full year before there was even an Elvis to impersonate?

4: I'LL NEVER STAND IN YOUR WAY
5: CASUAL LOVE AFFAIR (Memphis Recording Service, 1/4/54)
Like any other passing punter, Elvis paid $4 Sam Phillips for the privilege of recording his second acetate. The disc has never resurfaced.

6: WITHOUT YOU
7: RAG MOP (Memphis Recording Service, 1954)
Sometime in the early summer of 1954, "the kid with the sideburns," as MRS manager Marion Keisker called him, was invited in to the studio. Sam Phillips was casting around for someone to cover "Without You," a demo he'd just received from an unknown black singer from Nashville. The results, history insists without hearing them, were ridiculous. "Rag Mop" was no better. But Phillips was nothing if not persevering. "What in hell can you sing, then?" he demanded.
"Oh anything," Elvis replied. And he went on to prove it.

8: I REALLY DON'T WANT TO KNOW
9: I DON'T HURT ANYMORE (Scotty Moore's house, 7/4/54)
Elvis and Moore, with bassist Bill Black turning up later, spent Independence Day jamming through whatever songs they could think of: these recent hits by Eddy Arnold and Hank Snow included.

10: THAT'S ALL RIGHT (Sun Studios, Memphis, 7/5/54)
Author Nik Cohn said it all. Elvis' first record, a cover of the Big Boy Crudup classic, "was quite marvelous. His voice sounded edgy, nervous, and it cut like a scythe, it exploded all over the place. It was anguished, immature and raw. But above all, it was the sexiest thing that anyone had ever heard" (from *Awopbopaloobop Alopbamboom*, Paladin 1970; reissued Da Capo, 1996)

11: SATISFIED (Sun Studios, Memphis, 9/10/54)
Halting between takes of "I'll Never Let You Go," Elvis and the band ran through a 1.15 minute rendition of "Satisfied." RCA have, apparently, never been able to locate the performance, although it was documented on the tape boxes they received when they purchased Elvis' contract from Phillips.

12: BLUE MOON OF KENTUCKY (live) (Grand Ole Opry, 10/2/54)
It took 19 years for Elvis' first ever "proper" session to see the light of day, on the Bopcat bootleg "Good Rocking Tonight" (and another decade before RCA got in on the act). A matter of mere hours separated it from the familiar, released, cut, hours

during which the tentative Elvis heard on this original, countrified, take was replaced by a tougher, more confident, more rocking version. But still, Phillips was impressed. "Hell, that's different. That's a pop song now. That's good."
The producers of the Grand Ole Opry evidently agreed. As the local, Memphis "Commercial Appeal" reported, the Opry "never takes anyone but long-established stars. But Presley has already appeared...."

13: HOW DO YOU THINK I FEEL
14: YOU'RE A HEARTBREAKER
15: I'M LEFT, YOU'RE RIGHT, SHE'S GONE (Sun Studios, Memphis, 3/5/55)
Before getting down to the serious business of Elvis' next single, the band tried out a couple of songs; one ("You're A Heartbreaker") which had already been recorded shortly before Christmas. The official archives contain only a fragment of this rehearsal, Scotty Moore's guitar overdubs for "How Do You Think I Feel."
Two versions of "I'm Left..." were taped; oozing primal blues power, the initial attempt at Elvis' fourth Sun 45 first surfaced on the bootleg *The Rockin' Rebel Volume One*.

16: MONEY HONEY (take 5, take 6) (RCA Nashville, 1/10/56)
Elvis' first RCA session would produce his first gold record, the chilling "Heartbreak Hotel." The equally enjoyable, if lighter weight "Money Honey" would be included on his first EP; the released take was created from a marriage between this pair of takes.

17: I WANT YOU, I NEED YOU, I LOVE YOU (takes 14-17) (RCA Nashville, 4/11/56)
The released version of Elvis' second #1 combined takes 14 and 17; this sequence of increasingly confident (if error prone) takes illustrates the process by which they arrived at what proved to be perfection.

18: MARCH OF DIMES* (1956)
Elvis donates time, and his voice, to a brief charity commercial.

19: BLUE SUEDE SHOES MONOLOGUE (live) (New Frontier Hotel, Las Vegas 5/56)
"The night before last, on the stage of this place here, RCA Victor awarded me a gold record for the millionth sale of 'Heartburn Motel,' we're real proud of it cos it's made so much mon... it's done so well for itself; here's another one that's coming right up behind it, we hope it'll hit the million mark, this one here is called 'Get Out Of The Stables, Grandma'... no, it's called 'Blue Suede Shoes.' 'Blue Suede Something.'"

20: BLUE SUEDE SHOES
21: SHAKE RATTLE AND ROLL*
22: HEARTBREAK HOTEL
23: BLUE SUEDE SHOES (reprise) Milton Berle Show, 4/3/56)
While portions of this performance, filmed at the USS Hancock naval station in San Diego, were finally unearthed for 1984's "Golden Celebration" boxed set (CPM6 5172), the complete show has hitherto surfaced only on bootleg. It is, of course, a remarkable affair, as Elvis adapts instantly to both his surroundings and the audience, and turns in as racey a performance as

was probably imaginable back then.

24: HOUND DOG (Hudson Theater, NY, 7/1/56)

Elvis had been performing Jerry Lieber/Mike Stoller's "Hound Dog" for some months before he finally recorded it; indeed, he played it live on NBC's *Steve Allen Show* just a day before he took it into the studio.

For Lieber/Stoller, the session was the culmination of several months of hopes and dreams, and a fraught culmination as well. Stoller explained in a BBC interview, "'Hound Dog' was the first of our songs that Elvis recorded, although I didn't hear about it in the normal way. During July, 1956, I was coming back from Europe on a boat called the *Andrea Doria*, which sank. So I didn't arrive in New York on schedule, I came in on a freighter (about a day late), happy to be alive, and Jerry's first words to me were, 'Elvis Presley did "Hound Dog"!'"

25: TV GUIDE PRESENTS ELVIS PRESLEY (8/56)

It has been described, in the booklet accompanying *A Legendary Performer Volume 3* (RCA CLP1 3082) as "the most valuable record in the world." Neal Umphred's *A Touch Of Gold* Presley collecting guide, contrarily, ranks six other Elvis records higher in value. Either way, it's a bugger to find. In August, 1956, journalist Paul Wilder interviewed Elvis backstage at the Polk Theatre, Lakeland FL, with the ensuing disc being mailed out to select radio stations for promotional purposes: *TV Guide* was running a three part Elvis feature at the time.

Included in the four excerpts from the interview are Elvis' thoughts on his Pelvis nickname ("It's one of the most childish expressions I ever heard coming from an adult."), and a brief interview with Colonel Tom Parker, conducted while Elvis himself was (audibly) onstage, performing "Heartbreak Hotel."

"We are informed by RCA that this (record) represents the very first occasion on which the famous Presley voice has appeared on record... sans music," one of the two accompanying inserts remarked. "If this constitutes a collectors' item, make the most of it."

26: WE'RE GONNA MOVE* (20th Century Fox Stage 1, Hollywood, 8/24/56)

Recorded for the "Love Me Tender" soundtrack, this is the original performance of a strangely silly song, before the backing vocals, handclaps and (so irritating) fingersnaps were over-dubbed.

27: OLD SHEP (Radio Recorders, Hollywood, 9/2/56)

Unable to decide which of two versions of "Old Shep" (take 1, take 5) they preferred, Elvis forwarded both to RCA. The company opted for the later version, but early pressings of his second British album, *Elvis*, mistakenly used the first take (RCA HMV CLP 1105). It appeared in this country on the fifth disc of *The Complete 50s Masters* (RCA 66050).

28: LOVE ME TENDER (20th Century Fox Stage 1, Hollywood, 10/1/56)

This "extended" version of "Love Me Tender," featuring different lyrics and an extra verse, appeared over the end titles of the film version of Elvis' first movie. It appears on "Essential Elvis Volume 1"

29: YOU BELONG TO MY HEART
30: BROWN EYED HANDSOME MAN (Sun Studio, 12/4/56)

Be careful what you wish for, it might not be very good. The Million Dollar Quartet spent so much lurking in legend that when the tapes did finally begin creeping out, there was no way this ragtag jam full of religious and country performances could have lived up to the hype. This pair of tracks has been selected in memory of the mid-1970s bootleg promo 45 which aroused so much excitement with its delivery of one, and promise (on the forthcoming album) of a second, undocumented performance. The album never materialized, but no matter.

31: MEAN WOMAN BLUES
32: GOT A LOT O'LIVIN' TO DO
33: LOVING YOU (slow version) (Radio Recorders, Hollywood, 1/?/57 — 2/14/57)

This clutch of soundtrack performances were recorded for Elvis' second movie, *Loving You*, up to a month after tamer versions were taped for release on the accompanying album.

Mick Farren, author of the authoritative guide to ephemeral dementia, *The Hitch Hikers Guide To Elvis* (Collectors Guide Publishing), describes the finale version of "Got A Lot O'Livin' To Do" as "probably the closest to a live show by the young Elvis ever committed to film."

34: JAILHOUSE ROCK (take 5)
35: YOUNG AND BEAUTIFUL (solo version)
36: (YOU'RE SO SQUARE) BABY I DON'T CARE (basic track) (Radio Recorders, Hollywood, 4/30/57)
37: (YOU'RE SO SQUARE) BABY I DON'T CARE (completed take) (MGM 5/57)

The names Jerry Lieber and Mike Stoller are synonymous, today, with rock'n'roll at its most beautifully primal, and "Baby I Don't Care," written for the *Jailhouse Rock* soundtrack, proves why. With Mike Stoller pounding the piano, alongside Elvis' now regular studio band, the basic track oozes a passion which Elvis' vocal overdubs, at MGM in May, fought hard to retain. He managed it, though.

The same writing team also penned "Jailhouse Rock," of course, and with it launched a rock revolution which echoed around the world. Arguably one of the most influential songs ever written, two master takes of "Jailhouse Rock" were recorded; take 5, which engineer Thorne Nogar instructed should start fading at 1.50; and take 6, which would provide both the hit single and (with subsequent overdubs) the soundtrack version.

"Young And Beautiful" is the movie version, featuring a tender Elvis alone on guitar, as included on *The Complete 50s Masters* (RCA 66050)

38: HEARTBREAK HOTEL
39: I WAS THE ONE
40: I GOT A WOMAN
41: THAT'S WHEN YOUR HEARTACHES BEGIN (live) (Vancouver BC, 9/1/57)

Clocking in at under 5 minutes, this excerpt from one of Elvis' first foreign concerts first appeared on the *Got A Lot O'Living To Do* bootleg.

42: DANNY (Hollywood Radio Recorders, 1/23/58)

In later years, Elvis would describe his fourth movie, *King Creole*, as his favorite. Based upon Harold Robbins' boxing classic *A Stone For Danny Fisher*, the movie was originally titled *Danny*, and the songwriting team of Fred Wise and Ben Weisman dutifully came up with a title song.

The bulk of the soundtrack had already been recorded by this time, at a hectic session reaching across January 15/16; the January 23 session produced more out-takes than it did releasable material, with only "Young Dreams" and a second attempt at "King Creole" making it onto the final album. "Danny" was scrapped shortly after the movie title was changed (sheet music was published crediting the song as being featured in the renamed movie); it would not resurface for another two years, until Conway Twitty recorded it as "Lonely Blue Boy," for a 1960 hit. Elvis' own version would not see the light of day until 1978. (LP *A Legendary Performer Vol 3* RCA CPL1©3082, 1978)

43: KING CREOLE (take 3) (Radio Recorders, Hollywood, 1/15/58)

A storming alternate version included on *The Complete 50s Masters* (RCA 66050).

44: MY WISH CAME TRUE
45: DONCHA THINK IT'S TIME (takes 40, 47, 48) (Radio Recorders, Hollywood, 2/1/58)

Elvis had already recorded a somewhat limp "My Wish Came True" for a single, in September, 1957; obviously dissatisfied with the result, he used these sessions as an opportunity to redo the song, only to apparently lose interest again before it was completed.

The released version of "Doncha Think It's Time" was a splice of these three takes; take 40 has subsequently, if erroneously, been released, on the *Gold Records Volume 2* (RCA LPM 2075) collection.

46: I UNDERSTAND
47: HAPPY, HAPPY BIRTHDAY BABY
48: JUST A CLOSER WALK WITH THEE (Fadals, Waco TX, 1958)

An amateur recording from a private birthday party features Elvis at his most relaxed, clowning with friends, jamming on piano (Anita Wood handles vocals on two further tracks, "I Can't Help It" and "Who's Sorry Now"), and generally having a great time. There was, of course, no reason on earth for anybody to bother taping the event (RCA didn't even know it occurred), so its emergence on bootleg possibly ranks amongst the greatest vindications of that profession one could name. If the pirates hadn't preserved the tape, who would?

49: AIN'T THAT LOVING YOU BABY (take 11) (RCA Nashville 6/10/58)

The Complete 50s Masters unearthed this sparkling rocker for the "Rare And Rocking" fifth disc.

50: I GOT STUNG (RCA Nashville, 6/11/58)

The last song Elvis recorded for release during the 1950s.

VOLUME TWO: UNCONDITIONAL SURRENDER: THE SIXTIES

1: FAME AND FORTUNE
2: STUCK ON YOU

On March 26, 1960, Elvis visited the Fountainbleau Hotel in Miami to record his guest appearance on ABC's Frank Sinatra/Timex Show. He performed two songs he had recorded just five days earlier, 15 days after his discharge from the army, at his first studio date of the decade, before duetting with his host for the final song. The "Witchcraft"/"Love Me Tender" medley, of course, would close RCA's 1960s boxed set; the remainder, however, has never seen the light of day.

3: FEVER
4: IT'S NOW OR NEVER (RCA Nashville, 4/3/60)

"Fever" is the sinuously seductive final mix; "It's Now or Never," adapted from the Italian "O Sole Mia," appears minus the overdubbed percussion and piano, as sparse as a Venetian cafe, but strangely affecting as well.

5: ARE YOU LONESOME TONIGHT?
6: THE GIRL OF MY BEST FRIEND (RCA Nashville, 4/4/60)

With the rigors of military life firmly behind him, Elvis launched into possibly his most precocious period of recording yet, lurching with indescribable ease from the sublime to the ridiculous. This pair, of course, fit the former bill seamlessly.

7: WOODEN HEART (false start and complete) (4/27 — 28/60)

The soundtrack to *G.I. Blues* has encouraged some of the wildest speculation in Elvis' Hollywood catalog, thanks primarily to the sheer quantity and quality of out-takes which have surfaced since Presley's death; the initial attempt at "Wooden Heart" here would eventually resurface on 1983's *A Legendary Performer Volume 4* (RCA CPL1 4848).

Equally remarkable, of course, is the song's no-show performance in American chart terms; it eventually turned up as the b-side to the execrable "Puppet On A String" 45 (RCA 447 0650). British fans, however, made it Elvis' eighth #1 overall, and his third (out of four) in succession.

8: SURRENDER (RCA Nashville, 10/30/60)

When Doc Pomus and Mort Shuman lifted the melody line to "Come Back To Sorrento," and grafted their own "Surrender" lyric to it, maybe they figured no-one would notice. The song's Italian publisher did, and plans to release this remarkable record in Britain were put on hold for three months after its US appearance, while the matter of recompense was sorted out. The follow-up to the similarly Euro-themed "Wooden Heart" and "It's Now Or Never," "Surrender" became the fourth of four successive UK #1s for Elvis.

9: CRYING IN THE CHAPEL (RCA Nashville, 10/31/60)

Originally recorded during the sessions for Elvis' *His Hand In Mind* album, Artie Glenn's masterpiece of heartbroken religious iconography was left on the shelf for five years, until RCA — desperate to rekindle Elvis' dying chart career — took it down for an Easter 45. They were rewarded with a U.K. #1, and in America, his first Top Ten single in 18 months (RCA 447 0643).

Unfortunately, it would also prove to be his last for five years.

10: CAN'T HELP FALLING IN LOVE (Takes 20 -24) Radio Recorders, Hollywood, 3/23/61)
11: BEACH BOY BLUES (takes 1-3)

"Can't Help Falling In Love" was adapted from the French song "Plaisir D'Amour," and saw Elvis turn in one of his most sincere vocals for this 1961 #2. Take 20 offers a brief attempt at the first verse before Elvis extemporizes a complaint about falling out of tempo. Four similarly abortive attempts later, they got the song (almost) right.

The three takes of "Beach Boy Blues," also recorded for the *Blue Hawaii* movie soundtrack, first appeared on the *Beach To The Bayou* bootleg.

12: ALL SHOOK UP (live) (USS Arizona memorial Benefit, 3/25/61)

A stunning performance from a superlative concert.

Neal Umphred relates, "not counting television, this was the only live performance Elvis gave between 1957 and 1969. It was taped by somebody in the audience; it's a bad mono recording of Presley with a staggering band, DJ Fontana, Scotty Moore, Chet Atkins, Floyd Cramer, Boots Randolph, and Presley was in incredible form. It was officially released years after the boot came out (on the 1980 *Elvis Aron Presley* RCA CPL8 3699) boxed collection), and the official release was no worse or better than. Same source, same fidelity, but it's a must have for Presley fans."

At a time when the debate over even the historical value of bootlegs is heating up, there is not an iota of space here for doubt. Without the bootlegs which kept the tape circulating for 20 years before RCA picked it up, this performance would have been lost forever, and while RCA could argue that they had little reason to record the show (who, after all, could have predicted that Presley would wait so long, and change so dramatically, before his next gig), that very argument in its own way justifies bootlegging.

13: THAT'S SOMEONE YOU NEVER FORGET (RCA Nashville, 6/25/61)

It would be a year before this beautiful arrangement made it onto vinyl, on the aptly titled *Pot Luck* album (RCA LSP 2523).

14: LITTLE SISTER
15: HIS LATEST FLAME (RCA Nashville 6/26/61)

A wise choice for a single, this coupling became Elvis' last double sided smash (RCA 47-7908).

16: FOLLOW THAT DREAM (RCA Nashville, 7/5/61)
17: FOLLOW THAT DREAM RADIO SPOT

By 1961, Elvis was resolutely pursuing the title of "the American Cliff Richard." The previous year, he had covered "I Gotta Know," a song which Cliff had already made irredeemably his a year before that (it appears on *Cliff Sings*); his distinctly Cliff-like performance on the theme to his latest movie, then, came as no surprise. Indeed, one of Cliff's other rivals, homegrown star Billy Fury, only exacerbated the situation by telling *Melody Make**, "I reckon this is one of Presley's very best. What a song! This must go right up the charts here to #1." This alternate take was included on the *Elvis Aron Presley* box (RCA CPL8 3699).

18: A WHISTLING TUNE (takes 1-7) (Radio Recorders, Hollywood, 10/26 - 27/61)

The man was a singer. He was not a whistler. And across seven curtailed takes, he proves it.

19: SUSPICION (3/19/62)

In 1972, ex-Bonzo Dog vocalist, the late Viv Stanshall, would record what can only be called the definitive rendition of this masterpiece of paranoia. Elvis' version, which had at least proven adequate up until that point, simply left the building after hearing it.

20: MEMPHIS TENNESSEE (RCA Nashville, 5/27/63)
21: ASK ME (RCA Nashville, 5/28/63)
22: SLOWLY BUT SURELY (backing track) (RCA Nashville, 5/28/63)

These two songs, recorded during a mammoth three day session, were rejected by Elvis, and subsequently recorded the following January. It is difficult to appreciate Elvis' objections; as revealed on the *From Nashville To Memphis* box (RCA 66160), the original take of the Berry song, at least, was at least up to his contemporary standards, rattling along on express train tracks, and pulling some real yearning out of Elvis' voice; he can almost see Marie's house.

The backing track to "Slowly But Surely," meanwhile, exceeds even this by several light years; the fuzz guitar line which torments the melody could have stepped out of any garage, in any state, any time after 1965. Scotty Moore's development of that sound two years previous, and for an uncool, unhip, Elvis song yet, remains one of the unsung miracles of 60s pop.

23: CHEEK TO CHEEK (Radio Recorders, Hollywood, 7/9/63)

The *Viva Las Vegas* bootleg dates this brief (1.35) out-take to the soundtrack sessions for the movie of the same name.

24: FRANKIE AND JOHNNY (Radio Recorders, Hollywood, 5/65)

Asked what Elvis' last movie, *Harum Scarum*, was about, Colonel Parker replied, "I don't read the scripts." Elvis took a little more care about his performances, but only a little. Still, "Frankie And Johnny," the occasionally burlesque flavored theme to his next movie, has a certain swinging charm, with the non-album movie version punching the stakes up a little further.

25: DATIN' (take 12)
26: THIS IS MY HEAVEN (take 3) (Radio recorders, Hollywood, 8/2/65)

English producer Mickie Most recalls, "1964/65 was a really hot time for me, I had four or five records in the Top 10... and RCA was one company that was trying to acquire my services. I went to see them and they said that part of the deal would be that they'd like me to record Elvis Presley, and I declined immediately. He'd done the best stuff he was ever going to do, and there was no way I was going to be able to make records as good as those — it was like asking me to beat up Muhammad Ali."

Elvis' response has not been reported, but if the soundtrack to *Paradise Hawaiian Style* is anything to go by, he would not have argued too hard. Take 12 of "Datin'," as found on the *Elvis Aron Presley* box (CPL8 3699) proves he was having trouble even keeping a straight face.

The gently swaying "This is My Heaven," contrarily, is a gem. The released version was created from two separate takes, numbers six and eight; take three, however, could have saved them all a lot of bother if Elvis hadn't forgotten the final line, and then sung his confusion into the mike - "what is that last part?" A wonderfully human moment from a man who was now recording some awfully inhuman songs.

27: HELP!
28: YOU'RE MY WORLD (Bel Air, 8/27/65)

On August 27, 1965, Elvis got together with the Beatles in Bel Air. According to John Lennon, "we ate a lot, shot some pool and had a ball"; the impromptu five piece also switched on the tape recorder and jammed. The tape itself has never surfaced; the whole thing may have been a figment of Lennon's imagination. But what if it wasn't?

With Elvis alternating between drums and piano, they ran through a set which rumor, or at least wishful thinking, has translated into one of the greatest super sessions of all time: the Beatles' own "Help," and the Cilla Black showstopper "You're My World" are amongst the songs they laid down that evening.

29: TOMORROW IS A LONG TIME
30: LOVE LETTERS (RCA Nashville, 5/26/66)

Elvis sings Dylan, and RCA have a cow. Clocking in at almost twice the length of any past Elvis recording, 5.20 minutes, it wasn't "Like A Rolling Stone," but it might as well have been. Although it had nothing to do with the movie, the performance was one of several tracks from this session which would appear buried away on the *Spin Out* soundtrack (RCA LSP 3702), at a time when nobody really bought Elvis' soundtracks.

"Love Letters," meanwhile, is one of those slices of unadulterated mawkish slop in which Elvis was now so well versed, but which he magically steps out of stereotyping for, turning in a genuinely touching slab of sentimentality which it is impossible to tire of listening to.

31: LONG LEGGED GIRL (Radio Recorders, Hollywood, 6/66)

A boiling stunner from the *Double Trouble* soundtrack.

32: GUITAR MAN/WHAT'D I SAY (RCA Nashville 9/10/67)

The original unedited master of this irreverent country rocker jams into a few lines of "What'd I Say"; a highlight of the *From Nashville To Memphis* box (RCA 66160), it was a harbinger of the musical firestorm which was about to break.

33: YOU'LL NEVER WALK ALONE (RCA Nashville, 9/11/67)

Why this recording — the best known song from Rodgers and Hammerstein's *Carousel* musical — continues to be filed away with Elvis' secular recordings, remains a mystery; from Gerry & The Pacemakers to the Liverpool soccer team's supporters, who adopted it for their own matchday anthem, its religious intent is wholly in the eye of the beholder. Rather like the Bible, really.

34: DOMINIC (RCA Nashville, 1/15/68)

Having already released enough garbage to fill a satirically minded bootleg album (the legendary, posthumous, *Elvis' Greatest Shit* collection), RCA now started getting picky. "Dominic," recorded during the *Stay Away Joe* soundtrack sessions, was shelved for possessing insufficient quality to merit release. But "Old McDonald" was okay. The Singing Nun could not be reached for comment.

35: BABY WHAT'S WRONG/PETER GUNN
36: GUITAR BOOGIE (NBC Burbank, 6/68)
37: BLUE SUEDE SHOES
38: TRYING TO GET TO YOU
39: BABY, WHAT YOU WANT ME TO DO (NBC Burbank, 6/27/68)

Elvis' leatherjacketed reinvention for the benefit of NBC's cameras have spawned a number of bootlegs; although it produced the least number of used recordings, the 6 pm show offers up some of the best, as in loosest, of all the sessions, including a triumphant reading of "Trying To Get To You" — a song Elvis first tackled at his penultimate Sun Studios session; and a "Blue Suede Shoes" which RCA saw fit to splice with a later (June 29) per-

formance before release, on *This Is Elvis* (CPL2 4031). The released version of "Baby What You Want me To Do" (*A Legendary Performer Volume 2* RCA CPL1 1349), meanwhile, was edited down from the original performance.

40: WIFFENPOOF SONG/VIOLET (United Recorders, LA, 8/23/68)

A beautiful take of this peculiar coupling, so close as it is to "Love Me Tender," was included on Audiofon's four LP *Behind Closed Doors* (AFNS 66072-4) collection; an out-take from the *Trouble With Girls* soundtrack sessions, supervised by kitsch guitar hero Billy Strange, it was in fact an excerpt from a longer medley, featuring a variety of other vocalists, Marilyn Mason included (the same session, and indeed the same album, features Elvis and Mason duetting on the equally bizarre "Signs Of The Zodiac").

41: CHARRO (10/15/68)

This has to be one of the pre-Memphis Elvis' most impassioned performances, even if you can hear him grimacing through every spaghetti-westernized lyric. Kitsch guitar hero Billy Strange's epic title song to his latest (not so epic) movie, the tale of a lowdown dirty dog who's about to get what's coming to him, alive with spectral backing vocals and the rattle of tumbleweed blowing through the studio, "Charro" would be relegated to the b-side of 1969's "Memories" 45 (RCA 47-9731). It deserved much more.

42: A LITTLE BIT OF GREEN (American Studios, Memphis, 1/14/69)
43: INHERIT THE WIND (American Studios, Memphis, 1/15/69)
44: IN THE GHETTO (THE VICIOUS CIRCLE) (take four) (American Studios, Memphis, 1/20/69)

Even before Elvis arrived at American Studios in January, 1969, the word was that he was finally shrugging off the torpor of the past near-decade. The NBC TV special, of course, had served notice of his reformation; his return to his old home stomping grounds even more so. But even that paled against the open rebellion in which he was now delighting. RCA were certainly infuriated by his choice of studio, and even angrier when they found out the full title of the Mac Davis song he intended to release as his next single. At least they won that battle.

With Elvis' regular backing musicians left behind, producer Chip Moman had pieced together a remarkable houseband, led by guitarist Reggie Young, bassist Mike Leech and drummer Gene Chrisman, while recent recordings by the Boxtops and Dusty Springfield testified to the magical feel which the studio was capable of imparting. Moman added to this by his hands-on involvement in the material Elvis would tackle, and has gone on record claiming that an even stronger selection might have been possible, had Elvis' own publishing company chief, Freddy Bienstock, not raised so many financial objections.

Even this turned out to Elvis' advantage, however, as he continued his rehabilitation by announcing that henceforth, he — and only he — would control the songs he recorded. The puppet strings would, of course, reappear eventually, but for now, Elvis was in control, and his performance across the 32 songs recorded demonstrates just how firm his grip was.

"In The Ghetto" would make #3 in America and #2 in Britain, his biggest hit in either country since 1965. As featured on the *Nashville To Memphis* box (RCA 66160), take four is a far darker version than the released single (take 23), the absence of backing singers giving the arrangement, and Elvis' mournful vocal, a menacing quality far more in keeping with the song's subject matter.

45: LET US PRAY (movie version) (Decca recording Studio, Universal City, 3/6/69)
This version was planned for release, up until a second version was recorded, apparently in September.

46: MY BABE (live) (International Hotel, Las Vegas, 8/?/69)
47: SUSPICIOUS MINDS
48: WHAT'D I SAY?
49: YESTERDAY/HEY JUDE (medley) (live) (International Hotel, Las Vegas 8/21/69)
50: WORDS (live) (International Hotel, Las Vegas 8/22/69)
With the band seemingly intent on breaking into "Green Onions," and Elvis sounding tougher than he had in years, "My Babe" was one of several shimmering highlights on the From Memphis To Vegas package (RCA LSP 6020), but pales again against the pounding rendition included in Elvis Aron Presley (RCA CPL8 3699).
The cuts from the August 21 performance are included primarily to satisfy fans who are bored with the multitude of other versions from later in the engagement; that said, "Suspicious Minds" is as good as any live rendition Presley performed at this time, and the Beatles medley was no worse than any other. "Words" is the Bee Gees ballad, and appears on From Memphis To Vegas (RCA LSP 6020).

VOLUME THREE: A LOVELY LITTLE MOVER: THE SEVENTIES

1: ALSO SPRACH ZARATHUSTRA
2: SEE SEE RIDER (live) (Market Square Arena, Indianapolis, 6/26/77)
It takes a lot of nerve to open your show with the theme from *2001*, but Elvis pulled it off, even this late in the day. "See See Rider," part of his live show since 1970, burns with a rare intensity here, almost as if Elvis knew this was the last live show he would ever give.

3: THE WONDER OF YOU (International Hotel, Las Vegas, 2/18/70)
Elvis' first significant single of the new decade, sensibly cut in concert, gave him his first U.K. #1 in five years, and still sounds fresh, riding in on a triumphant overture before Elvis, who really does sound glad to be back, launches in with his most confidently majestic vocal in years.

4: THE FOOL (RCA Nashville, 6/4/70)
5: GOT MY MOJO WORKING/KEEP YOUR HANDS OFF OF IT
6: STRANGER IN THE CROWD (RCA Nashville, 6/5/70)
7: FADED LOVE (RCA Nashville, 6/6/70)
8: TOMORROW NEVER COMES (alternate take) (RCA Nashville, 6/7/70)
"The Fool" is an insistent bluesy pounder, with Elvis' best understated roar narrating the tale of the fool who let his baby go. James Burton's guitar motif, incidentally, was the inspiration behind another song on the session; it, too, was born about ten thousand years ago.
As representatives of one of the greatest Elvis sessions of all time,

the June 5 selections are included primarily because there are no good reasons why they shouldn't be, while "Faded Love" is present as an out-take first unveiled on the *Behind Closed Doors* bootleg. The rocking, James Burton dominated "Faded Love" appears, in marginally smoother form, on the *Elvis Country* album (RCA LSP 4460); it was also one of several songs selected in 1980 to be remixed and have their backing tracks rerecorded under the guidance of Felton Jarvis and Chip Young, ostensibly to appeal to a more modern audience. Ah, would that be, Punk Rockers? If so, this performance could have done the job in half the time, and with twice the authenticity.
Finally, the version of "Tomorrow never Comes" was found on the *Special Delivery* bootleg, and rocks just a little more harshly than the released version.

9: FROGGY WENT A COURTING (rehearsal) (MGM Studios, Culver City, 7/29/70)
Elvis sings for children, and the grown-ups can go whistle.

10: YOU'VE LOST THAT LOVING FEELING (Las Vegas rehearsal: 8/70)
Having been firmly locked into the Las Vegas routine earlier in the year, Elvis apparently resigned himself to his fate, working up a live set which was half old favorites, and half crowd pleasing crooners which could have given him no more pleasure than he derived from testing his voice against his most classic competition.
"You've Lost That Loving Feeling," a smash for the Righteous Brothers half a decade before, had hit the charts at a time when Elvis' own career was its lowest ebb; while Billy Medley and Bobbie Hatfield unleashed their lugubrious tones over Barry Mann and Cynthia Weill's finest four minutes, Elvis was tempting the same public with... "Do The Clam."
But who remembered the Righteous Brothers now?
Elvis's August rehearsals were remarkable enough for the tapes to be rolling all the way through, for both the *That's The Way It Is* movie, and RCA's archive: one rendition of "Loving Feeling" made it onto the silver box anniversary package; this slightly rawer run through appears on the movie.

11: BRIDGE OVER TROUBLED WATER (Las Vegas Hilton, dinner time show 8/20/70)
Elvis pounced upon Paul Simon's plaintive lament almost the instant it was released. His earliest live performances of the song are the best; this one has a gently aching quality which few others have matched.

12: THE IMPOSSIBLE DREAM (1971)
13: AN AMERICAN TRILOGY (1971)
There have been three indispensable renditions of "The Impossible Dream." One, by Belgian singer songwriter Jacques Brel, is in French. Another, a Christmas hit in Britain in 1992, was performed by Carter The Unstoppable Sex Machine. And the third can be found on the *Man From La Mancha* soundtrack. Elvis had nothing to do with any of them, but from the moment the song arrived in his live set, in Las Vegas in February, 1972, he at least proved that his ear for a great song remained unblemished. The Las Vegas version was originally released on *He Walks Beside Me* (RCA AFL1-2772) in 1978; what remains mystifying is why Elvis never took either this, or "An American Trilogy" into the studio with him... or if he did, why they never came out again. From a source so secret that there is not a shred of documentary

evidence to prove they exist, these takes indicate just how power-ful Elvis could be, if he only stopped trying to cut it on stage.

14: MERRY CHRISTMAS BABY (RCA Nashville, 5/15/71)
The ultimate Elvis Christmas blues boogie, recorded for the *Elvis Sings The Wonderful World Of Christmas* album (RCA LSP 4579).

15: DON'T THINK TWICE, IT'S ALRIGHT (RCA Nashville, 5/16/71)
The full, unedited take which appeared, as a dramatically cropped four minute edit, on the Walk A Mile In My Shoes box (RCA 66670).

16: MY WAY (piano mix) (RCA Nashville, 6/10/71)
Sensitive, and in many ways superior, though it was, the "Walk In My Shoes" arrangement of Elvis' interpretation of the Sinatra sig-nature could not help but bear comparison with the original per-formance. With the backing track stripped down to the piano alone, a version which grows progressively more bombastic the longer it goes on, is reduced back to the smokey nightclub feel which is still the song's ideal setting, and which Elvis alone of its most popular performers, at least appears to have sensed.

17: BURNING LOVE (RCA, Hollywood, 3/28/72)
Grateful as we all are for the boxed sets, it is undeniable that several of Elvis' most energetic later performances suffer irre-deemably from their transfer to the digital medium. Taken from a painstakingly crackly original 45, this is how "Burning Love" should sound. Fiery, fierce and a punch in the face.

18: ALWAYS ON MY MIND (RCA Hollywood, 3/29/72)
Achingly fragile, this was Elvis' Christmas 1972 British hit, and the prototype for a song which Britain's Pet Shop Boys would later bring to fruition.

19: SUSPICIOUS MINDS (live) (Madison Square Garden, 6/10/72)
The release, in 1975, of the Having Fun With Elvis On Stage album, painted a very distorted vision of Elvis, primarily via the insinuation that he only had fun when he was chatting to the crowd. Taken from the evening performance at MSG, this version of "Suspicious Minds" may not hold a candle to its studio coun-terpart, but it does illustrate in distinctly light-hearted mood. Half sung asides as the song moves along are, an exhortation to "stick it up your nose," and "I hope this suit doesn't tear up baby."

20: STEAMROLLER BLUES (live) (Anaheim 4/24/73)
A raucous stomp through Elvis' most recent, James Taylor com-posed, 45.

21: YOU DON'T HAVE TO SAY YOU LOVE ME (live) (Portland 4/27/73)
A triumphant rendition of the 1970 hit single.

22: HELP ME MAKE IT THROUGH THE NIGHT (live) (Nashville, 7/1/73)
Elvis' 1973 tour continued to produce some fine renditions of old favorites; in front of an adoring second-hometown crowd, he breathes new emotion into the hoary old Gladys Knight staple.

23: MYSTERY TRAIN
24: JAILHOUSE ROCK

25: DON'T BE CRUEL (live) (Las Vegas, 9/3/73)
It wouldn't be Elvis if you didn't get the hits; it wouldn't be Elvis if he didn't sound just a little tired as he sang them all again. Tonight in Las Vegas, maybe it wasn't Elvis.

26: I GOT A FEELIN' IN MY BODY (Stax Studio, Memphis, 12/10/73)
PROMISED LAND (Stax Studio, Memphis, 12/15/73)
Elvis goes disco! This exclusive remix medley was commissioned from U.K. dance specialists Motiv 8.‹j‹å

27: SPANISH EYES (live) (Las Vegas midnight show, 2/7/74)
28: PROUD MARY (live) (first show, Las Vegas International, 8/19/74)
29: THE FIRST TIME EVER I SAW YOUR FACE (live) (Las Vegas International, midnight show 8/21/74)
Elvis' Vegas residency through 1974 provoked a storm of bootlegs. These cuts are genuine stand-outs from a selection of these Vegas-centric offerings.

30: TEDDY BEAR (live) (Niagara Falls, 6/24/74)
Though Elvis probably wasn't aware of it, his resurrection of "Teddy Bear" in 1974 certainly resonated with any British mem-bers of the audience; a slightly reworded version of the song, with spot-on arrangement and vocal inflections, was selling Cresta soft drink on UK TV at the same time. It was frothy, man.

31: TIGER MAN (RCA Hollywood, 3/11/75)
The full, unedited take which appeared in truncated 3.05 form on Walk A Mile In My Shoes.

32: KILLING ME SOFTLY (live) (Nassau Coliseum, matinee per-formance 7/19/75)
An indescribably sweet performance from one of Elvis' best-loved, but least documented live shows.

33: AND I LOVE YOU SO (live) (Las Vegas Hilton, 12/14/75)
Perry Como never sounded like this!

34: SHE THINKS I STILL CARE (Graceland, Memphis, 2/2/76)
Elvis' legendary home studio recordings have all been released, to varying degrees of applause. This alternate take of one of the most familiar songs was later in seeing the light of day; it appeared on the *Guitar Man* compilation (RCA AAL1 3917), with a nasty, new, posthumously recorded, backing track. This is the original performance.

35: AMERICA (Graceland, Memphis, 2/?/76)
Popular history insists this rendition of Leonard Bernstein's *West Side Story* showstopper was erased shortly after it was recorded. Maybe it was, maybe it wasn't.

36: MOODY BLUE (Graceland, Memphis, 2/4/76)
Anybody chastising the latter day Elvis for not having kept up with modern musical fashions obviously never listened to this, the title track from his final album. Every ingredient of mid©70s pop is here, from the strings to the slight dance beat, and on to the motivational guitar.

37: WOODEN HEART
38: RETURN TO SENDER (live) (Sahara Hotel, Lake Tahoe, 5/76)
Two astonishingly animated performances, found on the bootleg The Entertainer.

39: WAY DOWN (backing track) (Graceland, Memphis, 10/29/76)
Incredibly, "Way Down" borrows its opening guitar rhythm from the bass motif which powers Pink Floyd's "One Of These Days." Not many people know that, but the backing track makes it crystal clear.

40: THERE'S A FIRE DOWN BELOW (Graceland, Memphis, 10/30/76)
The backing track was completed on this date; according to official records, Elvis never recorded a vocal. But he would have thought about it.

41: JAILHOUSE ROCK
42: YOU GAVE ME A MOUNTAIN
43: HOUND DOG (live) (Philadelphia 5/28/77)
At least four of the shows on Elvis' final tour were recorded by RCA, for releases across a spectrum of collections. This is one that got away.

44: UNCHAINED MELODY (live) (Rushmore Civic Center, 6/21/77)
Mick Farren is unequivocable in his support for this one. The bloated, sweaty rendition" of "Unchained Melody," from the *Great Performances* video cassette, with Elvis accompanying himself on the piano, gets his support "because, even fucked up as he was, he still had the power to give Bill Medley a vocal run for his money. In this clip, Elvis roared like a magnificently dying bull elephant and it should probably be recognized as his swansong." The falsetto which closes the lyric is still painful to contemplate.

45: A CHILD'S PRAYER (1977)
This Christmas song was written by English songsmith Alex Hughes — better known to the charts as ska artist Judge Dread. A copy of Hughes' demo made its way to Elvis via the Oakridge Boys; Colonel Tom called Hughes to say Elvis loved the song and wanted to record a version as a birthday present for Lisa Marie. Could Hughes change the lyrics accordingly?
Hughes complied, mailed the tape back to Presley, and waited.... Elvis died shortly after.
RCA is adamant that the song was never recorded. But if Elvis liked it enough to give to his daughter, he surely liked it enough to strum a few chords on the guitar, and sing a few lines of the lyric. And if he had a tape running while he did it..."A Child's Prayer" might well have been the last song Elvis ever recorded.

46: HOUND DOG
47: CAN'T HELP FALLING IN LOVE (live) (Market Square Arena, Indianapolis, 6/26/77)
The final songs, from the final live performance.

48: THE KING IS DEAD: NPR NEWS BROADCAST 8/16/77
49: THE BONES OF ELVIS
Nik Turner's Inner City Unit recorded their tribute to the King in 1982, a militaristic tattoo which projected the GI he once was onto the posthumous icon of Arthurian Americana that he became. Utterly irreverent, and damned near sacrilegious, it is nevertheless a fitting conclusion to any collection.
Well, it was either this, or Danny Mirror's "I Remember Elvis Presley."

50: ELVIS PRESLEY HAS LEFT THE BUILDING (live) (Market Square Arena, Indianapolis, 6/26/77)

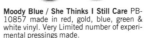

1998 Fan Club Directory

The following is a selected list of clubs and fanzines dedicated to recording artists. For more information about the clubs listed here, most require that you send them a self-addressed stamped envelope. For more information about fan clubs in general, including clubs formed in honor of actors, non-recording artists, sports figures, etc., we recommend that you contact the excellent National Association of Fan Clubs at 818-763-3280. The information contained here comes, more or less, verbatim from the clubs, is not individually verified by Goldmine, and Goldmine can not accept responsibility for any claims made by the clubs.

A

JOHN AGAR

The John Agar Fan Club
Attention: Scott Hughes, President
7901 Iroquois Ct.
Woodridge, IL 60517-3332

Hollywood's heartthrob since the 1940s and a favorite western and sci-fi film hero, John Agar has turned singer. For $3 annual dues, members receive an autographed snapshot and two newsletters telling the latest and best from and about John Agar. For a copy of the latest letter only, send $1.

LYNN ANDERSON

Lynn Anderson International Fan Club
Attention: Michael Dempsey
P.O. Box 90454
Charleston, SC 29410
Phone: 803-797-0802
Best time to call: Anytime

The Lynn Anderson fan club is the only official fan club for this legendary lady of country music. The club has been around since 1970 and offers its members an 8x10 autographed photo, biography, discography and quarterly newsletters.

ANTHRAX

NFC
Attention: Christine Vogel
P.O. Box 254
Kulpsville, PA 19443
Hotline: 215-721-6461

The Anthrax "NFC" is the official fan club offering a yearly membership. Membership includes special merchandise, photos, tour info and a backstage pass.

B

BACHMAN TURNER OVERDRIVE

Canadian Friends Of Mine
See Guess Who listing

SHIRLEY BASSEY

The Shirley Bassey Collectors Club
Attention: Arthur Rugg

35 Vasa Drive, R.D. #1
Hackettstown, NJ 07840
Phone: 201-691-1538
Best time to call: Between 6 and 11:00 p.m.

This official club was formed in 1989 to honor Shirley Bassey's career. It offers two 30-page newsletters per year. Membership spans 11 countries and provides photos, videos, audios, CDs and LPs. Dues are $15 U.S. and $20 non-U.S.

THE BEACH BOYS

Beach Boys Fan Club
Attention: President
P.O. Box 84282
Los Angeles, CA 90073

This club is an official Beach Boys fan club and has been in existence since 1976. The newsletter goes out five times a year. It is brief, contains the news only, but also has an extensive classified section. Send SASE for more information.

Endless Summer Quarterly
Attention: Lee Dempsey/David Beard
P.O. Box 470315
Charlotte, NC 28247
E-mail: esqeditor@aol.com

ESQ features exclusive interviews and articles, rare photos (many previously unpublished) reviews of new CDs and videos (commercial and underground) and up to the minute recording and personal information regarding Brian Wilson and the Beach Boys. Subscription costs $20 per year (foreign write first); sample issues cost $15.

Also see Mike Love and Dennis Wilson

THE BEATLES

Drive My Car Fabulous Fan Club
P.O. Box 159
Fairfax, VA 22030-0159

Good Day Sunshine
Attention: Matt Hurwitz
Phone: 310-391-0778
Best time to call: Anytime

This well-loved fanzine has been in publication since 1981. Every issue has 80 or more pages of Lennon/McCartney / Harrison / Starr news, reviews, collectors columns, exclusive photos, sales offers, ads and much more. Write or call for more information.

Liverpool Productions
Attention: Charles F. Rosenay!!!
315 Derby Ave
Orange, CT 06477
Phone: 203-865-8131
Best time to call: Anytime

Liverpool Productions lists Beatles conventions, tours to England, Beatles cruises and other related happenings.

Octopus's Garden
Attention: Beth Shorten
21 Montclair Avenue
Verona, NJ 07044
Phone: 201-239-7042
Best time to call: Evenings.
E-mail address: Beatles94@aol.com

This Beatles fanzine is published quarterly. Each issue is completely different as members are constantly bringing in new ideas. It features short stories, poetry, games, cartoons, news, opinion articles, etc. It encourages everyone to participate and to give their input.

Strawberry Fields Forum
Attention: Joe Pope
310 Franklin St. #117
Boston, MA 02210

Tokyo Beatles Fan Club
Attention Kenji Maeda
4-9-14, Honcho, Ageo-City
Santama 362
Japan
Phone: 048-773-4050

World Beatles Forum
Attention: Brad Howard
2440 Bank Street
P.O. Box 40081
Ottowa, Ontario KIVOW8
Canada

THE BEE GEES

Bee Gees Fan Club
Attention; Renee Schreiber
P.O. Box 2429
Miami Beach, FL 33140

Members of this club receive newletters with the latest info and current photos, contest with autographed prizes, membership card, color photos, black and white photos, a telephone hotline, bios, fact sheets, tour dates, television air-dates, listing of all clubs world-wide and, occasionally, tickets to shows.

BIG COUNTRY

All Of Us
Attention: James D. Birch
201 Gay Street, #4
Denton, MD 21629
Phone: (410)-479-0777
Best time to call: 10:00 a.m. to 1:00 p.m. EST, weekdays

olmine 1998 Annual Page 103

After 18 months of productive growth, AOU is now the official Big Country fan club for North America. AOU is recognized by the band and their management. The club publishes the Big Country fanzine which reprints articles about the band, features opinion pieces, fans' reviews, photos, interviews with the band and help in finding rare Big Country items. AOU is run by a dedicated fan who is committed to providing a quality publication.

Clint Black

Clint Black International Fan Club
Attnetion: Don Zullo
P.O. Box 299386
Houston, Texas 77299-0386
Phone: (713)-498-2734
Best time to call: Anytime

THE BLASTERS AND DAVE ALVIN

American Music and the Blasters Newsletter
Attention: Billy Davis
80-16 64th Lane
Glendale, NY 1138-6819
E-mail address: davistb@aol.com

This group provides a newsletter/ fanzine that is normally seven or eight pages long, covering the Blasters, Dave Alvin and related members. All artists are extremely active in supporting and participating in the contents. Tour dates, album releases, stories, merchandise availability is published 4-6 times a year. The club also provides post card mailing updates when necessary.

Tommy Bolin

Tommty Bolin Archives
Attention: Mike Drumm
P.O. 11243
Denver, CO 80211
Phone: (303)-331-2826
Fax:(303)-455-3040
Web address: www.tbolin.com

PAT BOONE

National Pat Boone Fan Club
Attention: Chris Bujnovsky, President
1025 Park Road
Leesport, PA 19533

The NPBFC is an official club and has been in existence since 1956. For $10 annually ($12 elsewhere), members receive quarterly newsletters (entitled Then and Now), a photo membership-card and a photo of Boone upon joining.

David Bowie

Crankin' Out
Attention Steve Pafford

P.O. Box 3268
London NW6 4NH UK
Phone: (44)-171-372-6130
Fax: (44)-171-328-7492

Crankin' Out, the International Bowie fan club endorsed by the man himself. For details send 2 International Reply Coupons.

JUNIOR BROWN

JUNIOR BROWN INTERNATIONAL FAN CLUB
P.O. Box 128203
Nashville, TN 37212

Join this official club and receive a membership kit which includes an 8 x 10 autographed photo of Brown, a biography, newsletter with concert schedule, official junior Brown fan club member badge and special merchandise offerings.

Savoy Brown

P.O. Box 855
Oswego, NY 13126

Free bi-annual newsletter!

ERIC BURDON

Eric Burdon Connection Newsletter
Attention: Phil Metzger
448 Silver Lane
Oceanside, NY 11572
E-mail: ebcn@i-2000.com

Rock and Roll Hall of Fame member Eric Burdon is a frequent contributor. Subscription rate is $20 per year and includes an 800# Hot-Line for residents of North America, 6 bi-monthly issues, photos, reviews, tour schedules, free subscriber ads, historical and current info. Fan participation is encouraged. Send $3 for sample issue. Make check out to Phil Metzger.

C

DAVID CASSIDY

Just David International David Cassidy Fan Club
Attention: Barbara Pazmino
979 East 42nd Street
Brooklyn, NY 11210

The Official David Cassidy fan club is celebrating its 23nd anniversary. Members get a trimonthly newsletter containing interviews, photos, a raffle, ads and a penpal section. Occasionally there's an actual photo print to take out and keep. Newsletters are printed in English and German, combined. Includes handwritten messages from Cassidy. Send SASE for more information.

THE CASSIDYS

Friends Of The Cassidys
Attention: Cheryl Corwin
2601 E. Ocean Blvd, #404
Long Beach, CA 90803-2503
Phone: 310-433-7448
Best time to call: After 5:00 p.m. PST

The Friends began in 1977 as Friends of Shaun Cassidy, but expanded in 1993 to include the rest of the family. It oversees a yearly collection for the Leukemia Society, provides. its members with monthly newsletters and is supported by the family.

Cheap Trick

Cheap Trick Zine
Attention: Dana C. James
P.O. Box 98
Eagleville, TN 37060-0098

CTZine was born in May,1991 and is recognized by Cheap Trick and their management. This fanzine comes out every three months. Issues are $4, made payable to Cheap Trick fanzine.

LOU CHRISTIE

Lou Christie International Fan Club
Attention: Harry Young
P.O. Box 748
Chicago, IL 60690-0748.

The Lou Christie fan club was founded in 1977. The club publishes Lightning Strikes, a biannual 44-page fanzine packed with articles, news, reviews, photos and details, the inside story on'all aspects of Lou Christie, past present and future.
Members also receive lists of upcoming concerts, The club has contributed to the', making of the Rhino, Sequel and Varese Vintage Lou Christie reissues. Please send a SASE for information.

PETULA CLARK

The International Petula Clark Society
Attention: Bonnie O. Miller
50 Railroad Avenue
Madison, CT 06443

This is an international organization that features worldwide membership and publishes an in-depth quarterly newsletter. Petula and Company is the original and definitive organization and we are celebrating our 25th anniversary. The publication features concert and CD reviews, interviews, print articles and nostalgia. It also offers opportunities to purchase current CD releases, photos or memorabilia for sale by the membership. Members receive information on concert dates, CD releases, etc.

BRUCE COCKBURN

Gavin's Woodpile
Attention: Daniel Keebler
7321 131st Avenue, S.E.
Snohomish, WA 98290
Phone: 360-568-9543
Best time to call: From 9:00 a.m. to 10:00 p.m.

Gavin's Woodpile is a newsletter designed to increase the awareness of the work and music of Bruce Cockburn, as well as to share interviews, concert dates, etc. Information is provided by Cockburn's management and record company. An annual subscription is $10 U.S., $12 Canada, $15 elsewhere.

Debbie Collins

Debbie Collins Fan Club
Attention: Robin Bruce
P.O. Box 689
Hilliard OH 43026
Phone: (614)-487-1911
Fax: Same

THE COWSILLS

Cowsills Fan Club
Attention: Marsha Jordan
PO. Box 83
Lexington, MS 39095

This an official fan club that offers its members a quarterly newsletter. Annual dues are $10.

WARREN CUCCURULLO

(see DURAN DURAN)

BURTON CUMMINGS

Canadian Friends Of Mine
See Guess Who listing

D

The Charlie Daniels Band

Charlie Daniels Band Volunteers
17060 Central Pike
Lebanon, TN 37090
Phone: (615)-799-8923
Best time to call: Anytime

NEIL DIAMOND

The Diamond Connection Attention: June Allen
P.O. Box 2764
Witham, Essex CM8 2SF England

Phone: +44 (0)1376 500059
Fax: Same
Best time to call: Anytime

The Diamond Connection is published bimonthly and includes articles, wants and swaps, memorabilia, photos and the latest information on Diamond. Cost of the 'zinc is L2.50 for the U.K., $5 for the U.S. (a yearly subscription reduces the cost). For a sample copy please send a large self-addressed stamped envelope.

DION

Official Dion Fan Club
119 Hutton Street
Gaithersburg, MD 20877

Membership in this official club entitles one to an autographed photo, a quarterly newsletter with lots of information and an advance performance schedule and a membership card. Dues are $10 U.S., annually ($15 elsewhere).

OSCAR D'LEON

The International Oscar D'Leon Fan Club
Attention: Betsy Quillin, President
928 Myakka Ct., N.E.
St. Petersburg, FL 33702-2792
813-527-OSCAR

Oscar D'Leon is considered the "King Of Salsa." Send an SASE for more information.

Donovan

Donovan's Friends
P.O. Box 1119
London SW9 9JW
England, UK

Donovan's Friends (Ireland)
Attention:Maree Jewell
119 Coolamber Park
Knocklyon
Dublin 16
Ireland, UK

Hurdy Gurdy Man
P.O. Box 17
Rye
East Sussex TN31 6ZY
England UK

Meadowlight
P.O. Box 304
Ipswich IP9 1PD
England, UK
E-mail: donn@enterprise.net

THE DOORS

The Doors Collectors Club
Attention: Kerry Humphreys
P.O. Box 1441
Orem, UT 84059-1441
Phone: 801-224-7390
Fax: 801-224-5723
Best time to call: Anytime

The Doors Collectors Magazine is published four times a year. It includes a host of feature articles, including interviews with the surviving Doors members, Elektra's president, Jac Holzman, Morrison biographer Jerry Hopkins, as well as articles on collecting Doors memorabilia and more. Each issue contains the past quarter's Doors-at-auction report, bootleg reviews, letters to the editor, concert information for the surviving Doors members and tribute bands and much more.

Every summer the club sponsors a Los Angeles Feast Of Friends, which is a solid week of Doors-related activities usually culminating in a Doors member's performance. Subscription also includes a membership card. Rates are $20 a year U.S., $25 Canada and $30 elsewhere. Visa and Mastercard are accepted. For more information call toll free, 800-891-1736.

DURAN DURAN

Carnival: The Duran Duran Trade Magazine
Attention: Kimberly Blessing
930 Sassafrass Circle
West Chester, PA 19382

Carnival is known to many fans as the Goldmine of the Duran realm. It maintains the largest and most complete Duran Duran discography, printed yearly, available on the Internet, and approved by Duran themselves. Quarterly issues include information on releases, interviews with band members, answers to questions on collecting, contests for valuable memorabilia, and ads from distributors and fans alike. Inquiries sent by mail must include a SASE for a response.

Duck! The Duran Duran Humour Fanzine
Attention: Janet Stroppel
9159 Robinson Apt.2C
Overland Park, KS 66212
E-mail: DUCK!@wwgv.com
Web address: www.wwgv.com/britchez/duck!

The Duranie Connection
Attention: Kapil Mathur
E-mail: Http://www.chapman.edu/students /mather/duran.html

The Duranie Connection is a group of online Duran Duran fans who are affectionately called "Duranies." TDC's main focus is its World Wide Web page, which functions as an extended fanzine. However, it goes beyond a fanzine because it provides instant information. The Web page is updated almost daily so there is always new information to read or see. It holds the most complete collection of lyrics to the music of DD and related groups. TDC also has a concert guide which lists all shows that Duran Duran has ever done as well as all upcoming shows. There are also articles written by fans, exclusive interviews with Duran Duran and relatives and links to every Duran Duran source on the internet. You can also find lists of magazines with feature articles dedicated to the group, as well as sources for Duran merchandise. Best of all, it is 100 percent free. All one needs is access to the World Wide Web.

Icon Fan Club and Fanzine
Attention: Nancy Seman or Barbara Renaud
P.O. Box 158
Allen Park, MI 48101-0158
Phone: (313)-928-3368
Fax: (313)-928-7755
E-mail: theIcon@rust.net

The Krush Bothers
Attention: Claudia De Castro
Address: Rua Quirta das Palmeiras, 32
2780 Nova Oeras, Portugal

We publish a 'zine 4 times per year in the months of March, June, September and December. Each issue contains meeting reports with the band, things written by Duran themselves, all the latest news musically and privately, update photos, Duran drawings, concert reviews and loads more.

UMF
Attention: Tina L. Lawson
P.O. Box 975
Dayton, OH 45409-0975
E-mail: lawsontl@erinet.com
Web address: Http://www/.netaxs.com /people/puck/umf.html

UMF is a club for authors and artists inspired to create works after exposure to Duran Duran and its music. All submissions are accepted without censoring or editing, but a pool of editors is available to help critique and shape works if desired. Zines also include current information on Duran Duran and their side projects (such as the Power Station 11, TV Mania and the Neurotic Outsiders), facts about members ansd musical schedules, contests for autographed and official memorabilia, ads for other fanzines, and listings of current Duran Duran fan conventions. Any type of art, visual or written, is accepted. Please send a SASEfor more information,including methods of submission.

ZTV
Attention: Liz Owens
132 St. Andrew's Court
Mt. Laurel, NJ 08054
Phone: 818-509-1731
Fax: 201-779-8434
E-mail: ZTVDD@aol.com

ZTV is a 30-minute public access show devoted to Duran Duran and its offshoot groups. The show covers live and media events, interviews and skits. It airs in several cities across the country as well as some foreign countries. Episodes are available; $15 each or three for $30.
ZTV also has concert footage of Duran Duran and Nuerotic Boy Outsiders. Concerts are $25 each or both for $40. Checks should be made payable to Katie Sandstrom. If you'd like to see ZTV air near you, contact Sandstrom for more information.

Privacy: The Warren Cuccurullo Fan Club
Attention: Cyndi Glass
P.O. Box 593
Vincennes, IN 47591
E-mail: cglass@vunet.vinu.edu

This is the official club for Warren Cuccurullo. Privacy covers Warren's career and music in and beyond Duran Duran (Zappa, Missing Persons, solo career, etc.). It offers a membership kit, mail forwarding, question and answer segments and a fanzine which is usually 20-25 pages and is published quarterly. Send an SASE or International Reply Coupon for more information. Dues are $10 a year, U.S., $20 non-U.S. (U.S. funds only please).

E

Electric Light Orchestra

Face The Music
Wiener Platz 6
78048 Villingen
Germany

F

FISH

The Company North America
Attention: Eric D. Brooks
P.O. Box 20766
Castro Valley, CA 94546
E-mail: conapres@aol.com

This club is the official North American chapter of Fish's fan organization called "The Company" The fan club has been in existence since 1993. Membership includes four issues of both the Company North America fanzine (articles, reviews, photos, pen-pals, other contacts, etc.), and the FishNet Indie Review (other indie progressive and celtic rock), a color membership card, extra mailings and more. For a free copy of the FishNet Indie Review and other information, send a self addressed, stamped envelope.

The group also has an official live Fish/Marillion chat every Sunday at 8:00 p.m. EST on America Online in the Nightclub (keyword: Music Chat).

G

LESLEY GORE

Lesley Gore International Fan Club
Attention; Jack Natoli, President
P.O. Box 305
Pompton Plains, NJ 07444
Phone/ Fax: 201-616-1233
Best time to call: Evenings from 6-9:00 p.m. or on weekends.

This is the only authorized official for club for Lesley Gore and was establisher 31 years ago by the same person who is current-ly the president, with the full support and cooperation of Lesley Gore. Membership include a fan club package of photos, record lists and quarterly newsletters. Dues are $8.

The GRATEFUL DEAD

Relix
P.O. Box 94
Brooklyn, NY 11229
718-258-0009

This magazine also features several like groups, including Phish, Hot Tuna, the Allman Brothers, Rusted Root and much more. Relix has been in publication for 24 years. Call or write for sub-scription information.

The GUESS WHO

Canadian Friends Of Mine
Attention: Kevin C. Beyer
8645 24th Ave. Southwest
Jenison, MI 49428-9543
Phone: 616-667-1662
Fax: 616-667-1647
Best time to call: Anytime

CFOM is the only official Guess Who fan club and is 11 years old. Members get four newsletters a year, personal contact with the band members, information about offshoot band Bachman Turner Overdrive and Burton Cummings. Current information and tour dates are provided as well and additional flyers are sent out that list rarities for sale. The club is international.

H

HALL & OATES

Rock And Soul International
Attention: Diane Vaskas or Lori Allred
P.O. Box 450
Mansfield, MA 02048
Web address: http://www.webspan.net/~rsil/site/hall_oates.html

This official club is nine years old and its newsletter includes reviews, updates on band members, pictures, ads and pen pals.

BETH HART

Beth Hart Fan Club
Attention: Jerry Hill
P.O. Box 48214
Minneapolis, MN 55448-0214

This club's members share information, ideas and enthusiasm about the work of Beth Hart. The club includes up to-date information and special dispatches to its members. Please send a SASE when requesting information.

ANNIE HASLAM

The Annie Haslam Appreciation Society
Attention: Joanne (Jo) Shea
P.O. Box 12
Folsom, PA 19033
OR
Attention: Joseph (Joe) Franzen
Fax: (609)242-9403
E-mail: RgrJoe@AOL.com

Organized in 1990, this group is official and recognized by the artist. Anne Haslam provides outstanding involvement—she receives all correspondance and responds personally when time permits. The club currently offers a newsletter (about two a year) with postcard updates on concerts and career events. Heretofore, membership has been free. Yet, with the growth of the society, and with a 'zine (three a year) in development—a $10 annual fee is requested. Please write (enclose SASE), fax, or e-mail for membership info.

JIMI HENDRIX

Experience Hendrix-The Official Jimi Hendrix Fanzine
Attention: Steven Roby
P.O. Box 4459
Seattle, WA, 98014
Phone: 415-332-5800 ext.160
Best time to call: Anytime
Web address; www.jimihendrix.com

This is the only official Jimi Hendrix fanzine authorized by the family of Jimi Hendrix. Our premiere edition will be published in December 1996.

Jimi Hendrix Information Management Institute
Attention: Ken Voss
P.O. Box 20361
Indianapolis, IN 46220
Phone: (317)-257-JIMI
Best time to call: Evenings

JIMI accumulates and disseminates information regarding the legend and the legacy of rock guitarist Jimi Hendrix.

HUEY LEWIS & THE NEWS

Newsline 11
Attention: Debbie Parry
P.O. Box 99
Payson, UT 84651
E-mail address: debparry@juno.com
Newsline 11 offers its members a quarterly news letter and the cost to join is $10 per year U.S., $12.50 non U.S.

ENGELBERT HUMPERDINCK

Engelbert's 'Goils' Fan Club
Attention: Jeanne Friedl or Dot Gillberg
10880 Kader Drive
Cleveland, OH 44130

This is an official fan club that was formed in 1971. Its newsletter, Goil Talk, is bimonthly and reports on record releases, news of Humperdinck's career, itinerary info and all things pertinent to hi career. It is basically active in the Cleveland area, but has members worldwide and across the U. S. Its purpose is to support him in a dignified and responsible manner, always showing respect for his talent and person, wherever he appears.

Engel's Angels in Humperdinck Heaven
Attention: Jean Marshalek, President
3024 Fourth Avenue Carney
Baltimore, MD 21234-3208
Phone: 410-665-0744
Rest time to call: From 10:30 a.m.-10:00 p.m.

Founded in 1971, this non-profit group raises charity funds in Humperdinck's name, supports and promotes his career through meetings, video viewings, parties, attending concerts and purchasing all of his recordings and videos. Its award-winning newsletter, The Guardian Engel, is issued approximately seven times a year, as news is received from Humperdinck's office. Itineraries are mailed as soon as they come in. Dues are $10, U.S., per year, husbands $5 and $15 overseas

JULIO IGLESIAS

Friends Of Julio Iglesias
Attention: Isabel Butterfield, President
28 Farmington Avenue
Longmeadow, MA 01106
Phone: 413-567-0845
Best time to call: Evenings, before 8:00 or on weekends

This official fan club, honoring Julio Iglesias started in 1986. The club provides 3-4 newsletters a year, a tour schedule and regular updates as they become available, a photo and biography. Dues are $18 U.S., $21 Canada, $24 Europe and $28 Asia.

IRON BUTTERFLY

Iron Butterfly Information Network
Attention: Rick Gagnon
9745 Sierra Avenue
Fontana, CA 92335

This official club was formed in 1985. Send a self-addressed stamped envelope for a membership certificate or to have specific questions answered.

JONI JAMES

Joni James International Fan Club
Attention: Mr. Wayne Brasler
P.O. Box 7207
Westchester, IL 60154

The official international fan club for Joni James, this club dates back to the dawn of her recording career in 1952. James has always been generously involved in the club. Membership is free. Subscriptions to the club's newsletter, Joni, published four or more times a year, are available-write to the club for information about rates.
Joni includes news about James' latest activities, features about her career and abundant photos, many never before published. The club also accepts mail for Joni James and facilitates media

contacts with her.

JAN & DEAN

Surfun
Attention: Lori Brown
328 Sumner Avenue
Summer, WA 98390

The official Jan & Dean fan club has been celebrating the accomplishments (past, present and future!) of the "The Laurel and Hardy of the Surf Crowd" since 1987.
Membership includes up-to-date concert information, quarterly newsletters, a photo, biography, discography and more. Send a SASE for more information. Membership fees are $8 U.S., $9 to Canada and Mexico, and $12 elsewhere.

ELTON JOHN

East End Lights
Attention: Tom Stanton
P.O. Box 760
New Baltimore, MI 48047
Phone: 810-949-7900
Best time to call: 9-5:00

East End Lights publishes an international Elton John magazine, featuring fullcolor covers, interviews with band members, tour dates and great insider information. Dues are $26 per. year

Hercules International
Attention:Sharon Kalinoski
P.O. Box 398
LaGrange, IL
60525
Web address:
http://ourworld.compuserve.com/homepages/SHeimbecher

Founded in Germany in 1988, Hercules Int. publishes a quarterly fanzine, sponsors fan meetings and holds fundraisers for the Elton John AIDS foundation. The fanzine is available English, German, Italian and French. Membership is $40 per year. Club staff members do not receive monetary compensation.

AL JOLSON

International Al Jolson Society
Attention: Mrs. Dolores Kontowicz, Secretary
11520 W. James Ave.
Franklin, WI 53132
Phone: 414-529-2868
Best time to call: Days

This club has been in existence since April of 1950. It was formed with Jolson's permission before he died.
The club publishes The Jolson journal (and just recently published

their 85th volume) which contains stories on Jolson, many photos, articles by members, and an exchange column. It also issues four newsletters a year and has an annual convention that is held in different cities each time.

International Al Jolson Society
Attention: Otis R. Lowe, Director
2981 Westmoor Dr.
Columbus, OH 43204
Phone: 614-274-1507
Best time to call: Evenings, before 8:00

Serving Jolson admirers for seventeen years. Members recieve six news bulletins a year with membership, plus the issuing of many color photos throughout the year. Offering audio and video tapes, sheet music, books, LPs, CDs, photos and many other Jolson items. Want lists are welcomed. Dedicated to perpetuating the memory of Al Jolson throughout the world.

SHIRLEY JONES

Shirley Jones Fan Club
Attention: Martina Schade
2295 Maple Road
York, PA 17404

Membership in this club entitles you to a beautiful 8x10 photo, two 4x6 photos, a bio/fact sheet and credit list, membership card, four copies of Shirley's World, the official newsletter, and Jones's personal appearance schedule, which is updated regularly. Dues are $13 U.S., $16 Canada and $20 elsewhere.

K

DOUG KERSHAW

Doug Kershaw Fan Club
Attention: Gail Delmonico
P.O. Box 24762
San Jose, CA 95154

This club offers four newsletters, a biography and autographed 8x10. Membership costs $12 US and $14 international.

THE KINGSTON TRIO

Kingston Korner
Attention: Allan Shaw
6 South, 230 Cohasset Road
Naperville, IL 60540-3535
Phone: (630)-961-3559

This isn't an official fan club, and prefers to refer to itself as an information service. It circulates news of the group and makes itineraries and recordings available.

THE KNACK

The Knack Fan Club
Attention: Ethen Barborka
P.O. Box 1022
Provo, UT 84603

The Knack fan club sends its members a quarterly newspaper in which the members celebrate the past, present and future of the Knack. Fans can also buy sell or trade memorabilia in its Knick Knack department and it invites you to be a part of the Knack Knation.

L

FRANKIE LAINE

Frankie Laine Society of America
Attention: Helen Snow
P.O. Box 145
Lindenhurst, NY 11757-0145

The Frankie Laine Society has been in existence since 1949. It publishes three to five newsletters a year, offers members special discounts on videos, CDs, records and tapes and informs members of Laine's concerts and upcoming events.

ERNIE LANCASTER

Ernie Lancaster Fan Club
Attention: Vicki Newton, President
P.O. Box 629
Havre De Grace, MD 21078
Phone: 410-939-5864
Best time to call: From 7-10:00 p.m.

This a start-up fan club for Ernie Lancaster, guitarist extraordinaire and writer of 99 percent of the music for Root Boy Slim and the Sex Change Band. It's new, hot and happenin'! Be there! It's free! You can't quit this club!

LEAD BELLY

Lead Belly Society
P.O. Box 6679

Ithaca, NY 14851

Attention: The Lead Belly Society fosters the appreciation and celebration of Lead Belly's music through the publication of the quarterly Lead Belly Letter, videos about Lead Belly and other projects. The society was established in 1990.

BRENDA LEE

The Brenda Lee International Fan Club
Attention: Bob Borum
4720 Hickory Way
Antioch, TN 37013

The Brenda Lee International Fan Club is an official club, authorized by Brenda Lee, and has been in existence since March 1994. It offers its members four newsletters a year, which contain an intinerary and news on Lee's career and personal life. Members receive U.S. and foreign discographyies, and information about merchandise that's available: jackets, T-shirts, sweatshirts, videos, pictures and more. Membership is $12 U.S., $15 Canada and $18 foreign (in U.S. dollars).

THE LETTERMEN

The Letterman Fan Club
Attention: Sharon Stewart
P.O. Box 570727
Tarzana, Ca 91357-0727
Phone: 818-705-5326
Best time to call: Mondays, Wednesdays and Fridays, from 8:00 to 3:00 p.m.

Membership in this official, 17-year-old fan club includes biography information, discographys, touring schedules, and 8x10 autographed photo and quarterly eightpage newsletter. Dues are $13 initial membership with annual $10 renewals.

Liberace

The Liberace Club
Attention: Linda Claussen, President
1104 Kimberly Rd. #603
Bettendorf, IA 52722

Membership includes welcome packet of info/photos, club newsletters, birthday card on your special day, Christmas card, memorial tribute in February, and invitation to annual May Reunion for Liberace birthday celebration in Las Vegas. Annual membership dues of $20 payable each January.

LITTLE JIMMY & THE BAD BOYS

Little Jimmy & the Bad Boys International Fan Club
Attention: Charlie Wolf
P.O. Box 111604
Nashville, TN 37222

This is a brand new club, started in May, 1995, and has no dues at this time. Iea in the process of compiling a mailing list. Dues will start as soon as the group's first CD is released (estimated date: February, 1996).

LORETTA LYNN

Loretta Lynn Swap Shop
Attention: Lenny Mattison/Andy Comer
R.R. 1, Box 63A
Parish, NY 13131
Phone: 315-298-6860
Best time to call: Anytime

The club has been in existence since 1991. The membership kit includes four newsletters per year, etc. It offers members a way to swap, sell and buy Loretta Lynn memorabilia as well as reporting on past and present material regarding Loretta Lynn.

Mike Love

The Mike Love Fan Club
Attnetion: Patricia Ferelli
114 Gov. Winthrop Rd.
Somerville, MA 02145

This official fanclub began in 1990. It includes four quarterly newsletters with reviews, news and exclusive photos and interviews. New members recieve a free 8X10 color glossy of Mike Love.

LOWEN & NAVARRO

International Lowen and Navarro Fan Club
Attention: Sue
P.O. Box 19285

Alexandria, VA 22320
E-mail: fanclub@ix.netcom.com
Web address: Http://www.clark.net/pub/ hshaw/Lownav.html

Membership includes a subscription to the newsletter (Wire), an 8X10 autographed photo, 2 member-only bumper stickers, and a casette of L&N music put together just for Fan Club members!!!. Dues are $15 per year.

LYNYRD SKYNYRD

Lynyrd Skynyrd Fan Club
P.O. Box 120855
Nashville, TN 37212

Membership includes a specially designed club T-shirt, a band photo, biography and discography, current and vintage merchandise, an itinerary and four quarterly newsletters. The annual membership fee is $20 U.S., $25 non-U.S.

M

MADONNA

The Official Madonna Fan Club
Attn: Marcia Delvecc hio/Coordinator
8491 Sunset Blvd., #485
West Hollywood, CA 90069
E-mail: icon-mfc@primenet.com
Web address: www.madonnafanclub.com

This club, which is officially endorsed by Madonna, offers a quarterly magazine, Icon, membership kits and a mail-order catalog filled with over 400 Madonna collectibles. The club has been in existence for over six years. Membership is $29 domestic, $39 international.

BARRY MANILOW

Very Barry Kentuckiana Connection
Attention: Ann Harris
409 N. 28th Street
Louisville, KY 40212-1905
Phone: 502-772-0509
Best time to call: After 5:00 p.m.

This official club has been in existence for over 10 years and is a member of the National Association of Fan Clubs. The group gets together to "celebrate their friend Barry!"

JIM MARLBORO

Jim Marlboro International Fan Club
Attention: David W. Kelly
2011 State Ave. S.W.
Decatur, AL 35601

JOHNNY MATHIS

Reflections On Mathis
Attention: Melanie Slavin
P.O. Box 182
Jacksonville, NC 28541
Phone: 910-346-4983
Fax: (910)-346-8400
Best time to call: After 5:30 EST or leave message on machine.

This club is an official chapter, eight years old. It provides a quarterly newsletter with special event updates and lots of surprises throughout the year.

MELANIE

Melanie Mania
Attention: Richard Dozier
32 Brookfield Lane
South Setauket, NY 11720
Phone: 516-696-7039
Best time to call: Daytime
E-mail address: Rchrdxx@aol.com

Melanie Mania is a collectors club. We also have some up to date information on Melanie concerts and recordings.

The Mills Brothers

The Mills Brothers Society
Attention: Daniel R. Clemson
604 N. Market St.

Mechanicsburg, PA 17055-2727

KATY MOFFAT

Katy Moffat World Headquarters
P.O. Box 334
O'Fallon, IL 62269-0334

The MONKEES

Head Of The Monkees
Attention: Teresa Jones
262 Baltimore Avenue
Baltimore, MD 21222

Membership includes four issues of "HTM" News, membership card, fact sheets, pencil, sticker, folder and club certificate. Membership is $10 a year.

Monkeein' Around
Attention: Janet Marie Davis
41297 C.C. Road
Ponchatoula, LA 70454

The newsletter of this club, started in 1988, contains a main news section, a "Fan Talk' section, articles from members, games, a pen pal directory, birthday section and occasional recipes.

ANNE MURRAY

The Anne Murray Collectors Club
Attention: Rita Rose
1618 Park Ridge Way
Indianapolis, IN 46229
317-633-9269

The Anne Murray Collectors Club specializes in locating Murray's recordings on vinyl, as well as sheet music, photos, tapes, tour books and other memorabilia. Its newsletter is issued four times a year.
Nazareth
Naz-Net
Headrest, Street End Lane
Broad Oak, Heathfield
East Sussex, TN21 BTU
England
Web address:
http://shell.idt.net/~rockso19/nazareth.html

Chuck Negron

Attention: Kathy Reese
P.O. Box 54990
Portland, Oregon 97294
E-mail: Http://www.Negron.com
Web address: Http://www.Negron.com

Chuck Negron—singer extraordinaire!!!!! (former lead singer of Three Dog Night). His first solo album asks, "Am I Still In Your

Heart"...you bet he is!!! Annual dues are $20 or $25 US funds for foreign members, membership includes quarterly newsletter, tour updates, hand signed photo of Chuck, a backstage pass and much more! You can also join us for our weekly chat on America On Line Thursday evenings at 7 p.m.acific time in the private room called Negron Chat, or check out our library on Compuserve in Fan Club Forum B, Go World Negron.

MICHAEL NESMITH

Dedicated Friends
Attention: Donna Bailey
1807 Millstream Drive
Frederick, MD 21702
Phone: 301-694-8064

This club is recognized and approved by Mr. Nesmith. Members receive four newsletters with color photos and information directly from Michael regarding his current career activities. Members are encouraged to be actively involved in this club's efforts to honor and support Michael's solo career and his work with the Monkees. Our club is a proud sponsor of the current campaign to induct the Monkees into the Rock and Roll Hall of Fame. One year membership is $12 U.S., $17 non-U.S.

NEW COLONY SIX

The New Colony Six Fan Club
Attention: Jerry Schollenberger
24435 Notre Dame
Dearborn, MI 48124

This official fan club, which provided the liner notes for both Rhino's and Sundazed's New Colony Six retrospectives, sends out show lists and is compiling a definitive international discography. Please send a SASE for more information.

OLIVIA NEWTON-JOHN

Hopelessly Devoted
Olivia Newton-John Fan Club
465 S. Poplar Street, #1110
Hazleton, PA 18201

The Hopelessly Devoted Olivia Newton-John fan club was founded in late 1991. The club has issued over 400 memberships and holds an annual convention. The 1996 convention will be in Pittsburgh, PA. Membership includes a biography on Olivia, color 8x10 photo, color photo membership card and four issues of the newsletter. U.S. membership is $20, Canada/Mexico $25, and elsewhere $30. (U.S. funds only, please.)

O

ROY ORBISON/Vintage Rock 'n Roll

In Dreams
Attention: Bert Kaufman
484 Lake Park #80
Oakland, CA 94610
Phone: 510-444-0805
Best time to call: early/late
Web address: http://www.gpage.com/host/indreams/shtml

More than just a fan club, In Dreams is a magazine/society supporting Orbison first and foremost, but also vintage rock 'n' roll (circa 1955-'64 primarily). Eight years in existence and supported by Orbison Productions, it offers multi-media stuff, interviews, reviews and a pen pal section in its 30-100-page approximately quarterly newsletter.

P

JOHN PATRICK

John Patrick Fan Club
Attention: Laurie Ewld
2140 W. Cass City Road
Unionville, MI 48767

The John Patrick fan club has been in existence for nine years. It offers its members an 8x10 picture of Patrick and a newsletter three times a year.

PEARL JAM

Release
Attention: Markus Wawzyniak
410 Gilbert Street, Apartment A
Bryan, TX 77801-3407

Release is a fanzine for Pearl jam with readers all over the world. The zine is published twice a year with the fourth issue to be out by the end of 1995. Every issue (and back issues are still available) features show reviews, discography, collectible corner, articles on PJ side projects and tons of high quality photographs. Release is saddle stapled and printed on high quality paper. Release costs $6 per issue, or $24 for a two year subscription.

PINK FLOYD

Brain Damage
Attention: Jeff Jensen or Steve Edwards
P.O. Box 109
Westmont, IL 60559
For nearly a decade, Brain Damage has been dedicated to the fans of Pink Floyd, Roger Waters, and Syd Barrett. Each issue is packed with timely, informative and entertaining articles along with rare fullcolor pictures, book, video and CD reviews, Q&A's and much more. Brain Damage is great for casual fans, Floyd fanatics and serious collectors alike.
Subscribers receive a free mini-poster with each issue. $28 for U.S., Canada and Mexico (six issues), or $5 for sample issue.

Elsewhere: $40 or $7 for sample.

GENE PITNEY

Gene Pitney International Fan Club
Attention: David P. McGrath
6201 39th Avenue
Kenosha, WI 53142

Gene Pitney's only fan club has been active for over 30 years. It currently has close to 2,000 members in 11 different countries. Pitney participates in all of the activities of the club.
It puts out three 16-page newsletters annually, which carry stories about Pitney, concert reviews, a regular letter from Pitney, merchandise for sale like videos, Tshirts, etc. It also holds a convention in the U.K. every two years.

ELVIS PRESLEY

Elvis Arkansas Style Fan Club
Attention: Beverly Rook
P.O. Box 898
Mabelvale, AR 72103
Phone: 501-455-1273
Best time to call: Before 10:00 p.m.

This official fan club makes Elvis information available to its members and works with the Make A Wish Foundation. Send a SASE for more information.

Elvis's Teddy Bear Fan Club
Attention: Mary Ann Parisi
744 Caliente Drive
Brandon, FL 33511
Phone: 813-684-6522
Best time to call: Weekends

This club, started in May, 1976, provides newsletters every three months and is recognized by Graceland. Membership is $6 domestic, $8 foreign

The Elvis Beat
Attention: Troy Yeary
2716 Terry Drive
Richmond, VA 23228

The Elvis Beat offers a free quarterly newsletter to U.S. fans. Four 32-cent stamps are requested, but not required. Non-U.S. membership is $5. The unique newsletter features the latest Elvis news, reviews, and more, This club is registered at Graceland.

True Fans For Elvis Fan Club of Maine
Attention: Dot Gonyea, President
62 Lowell Street
South Portland, ME 04106

This club has been in existence since the spring of 1977 when Elvis was making his first appearance in Maine on May 24 at the Augusta Civic Center. The club was formed on the steps of the Civic Center while waiting in line for tickets for two days. It publishes four newsletters a year with information from the Elvis world and also all the activities taking place in Maine. It is a very social club and raises money year round in Elvis's memory: It supports several associations dedicated to medical research as well as Meals On Wheels, Elvis Presley Memorial Trauma Center, Camp Sunshine and many other worthwhile causes.

We Remember Elvis
Attention: Priscilla A. Parker, President
1215 Tennessee Ave.
Pittsburgh, PA 15216-2511

Members receive a membership kit with the most recent club newsletter, three 8x10 black and white photos of Elvis, stationery, a membership card, information booklet about the club and much more. It publishes six newsletters a year and works to keep the memory of Elvis alive through its works of charity. Membership in this official Elvis fan club, established in 1982, costs $10 a year.

Louis Prima

Louis Prima Fans and Friends
1209 St. Charles Ave.
New Orleans, LA 70130

(The artist formerly known as) PRINCE

Uptown
Attention: Harold Lewis
P.O. Box 43
Cuyahoga Falls, OH 44222
E-mail address: editorial@uptown.se
Web address: http://www710.univ-lyon.fr/~burzlaff/uptown.html
Uptown, beginning its sixth year, is a quarterly fan magazine produced by some of the leading "Princeologists" in the world. Regular features include tour reports, color photos and exclusive interviews with Prince associates, past and present, plus all of the latest news.

PROCOL HARUM

Procol Harum Appreciation Society
Attention: Patrick Keating

8415 W. 89th Street
Overland Park, KS 66212

Since 1990, this club has kept members abreast of tour information, concert reports and new releases from the group. New members may join for $10 and receive everything to date that's been offered by the club.

Dave Prowse

The Official International Dave Prowse Fan Club
Attention: Max Peterson
508 Maplewood Ave.
Wilson, NC 27893
Phone: (919)-291-9468
OR
12 Marshlea Rd.
London SE1 1HL
England
Phone: 0171-407 5650
Fax: 0171-403 8326

Q

R

EDDY RAVEN

Eddy Raven International Fan Club
Attention: Sheila Futch
P.O. Box 2476
Hendersonville, TN 37077

This official club is 10 years old. Members receive an 8x10 photo, button, membership card, quarterly newletters, a biography, fact-sheet, discography, letters and the club makes tapes and t-shirts available. Membership costs $10 per year.

LOU RAWLS

The Lou Rawls National Fan Club
Attention: Dottie Taylor, President
904 Iverson Dr.
Great Mills, MD 20634-2530

This club is official. Membership is $15. Write for more details.

HELEN REDDY

Helen Reddy Fan Club-East
Attention: Lorraine Breault

204 Thunder Circle
Bensalem, PA 19020
Phone: 215-702-1421
Best time to call: Anytime

This club is officially recognized by Reddy and is ten years old. New members receive an autographed photo of Reddy, newsletters and postcard updates.
Lou Reed

Lou Reed Unofficial International Fan Club
Attention: Janis
P.O. Box 2392
Woburn, MA 01888
Phone: (617)-YELL-FUN
Best time to call: 11 a.m. to 11 p.m. EST

also see Velevet Underground

MARTHA REEVES

Martha Reeves Exclusive Newsletter
P.O. Box 1987
Paramount, CA 90723
Phone: 562-634-4676
Best line to call: Evenings, after 5 p.m.

This is the official fan club for Martha Reeves, the "legendary diva of Motown." The club provides members with one (color) trading card, information about Reeves's television, radio and live performances and special rates for exclusive photos and memorabilia.

R.E.M.

Country Feedback
Attention: Toni Sturtevant
RR1 North Road
Jefferso, NH 03583
This four-year-old fanzine includes original artwork, regular articles by the fans, contests, poetry, classic reprints and lots of photos, surprises and R.E.M. autographed items that are auctioned off for charity benefits. Subscriptions cost $4 per issue, $15 per year.

REO SPEEDWAGON

REO Pals International
Attention: Jordan Taylor, President
P.O. Box 410084
Melbourne, FA 32941-0084
Phone: 407-253-3712
Best time to call: Evenings/Weekends

This club is approved by REO Speedwagon and has been in existence since 1985. The club offers a detailed quarterly newsletter, including tour and studio updates, and offers an in-depth look at REO Speedwagon and its fans. Membership is $12 a year U.S., $18 overseas and Canada.

REO Speedwagon Fan Club
Attention: Kathy Stover
3017 Sowers Court
Topeka, Kansas 66604

HAPPY RHODES

Rhodeways-The International Happy Rhodes Medium
Attention: Sharon Nichols
P.O. Box 1233
Woodstock, NY 12498
Phone: 914-679-5795
Best time to call: Anytime
E-mail address: rhodeways@aol.com

Rhodeways is the only official Happy Rhodes (recording artist similar to Kate Bush) club/'zine. A one-year (four-issue) subscription is $17 U.S. and $20 non-U.S.
The 'zine is 16 pages, professionally printed on glossy stock with halftones (screened photos). Happy contributes artwork, articles or pictures to each issue.

CLIFF RICHARD

Cliff Richard Fan Club of America
Attention: Mary Posner
8916 N. Skokie Blvd. #3
Skokie, IL 60077

This club is affiliated with the International Cliff Richard Movement, which oversees dozens of Cliff fan clubs around the world. In addition to distributing the ICRM's bimonthly newsletter, Dynamite/International, it also publishes its own U.S. newsletter, The Cliff Connection, six times a year. The club can be reached by mail or by e-mail at CRFCUSA@aol.com.

SMOKEY ROBINSON
and the MIRACLES

Smokey Robinson and the Miracles Fan Club
Attention: Marie Leighton
8 Hillside Road
Marragansett, RI 02882-2821
Phone: 401-789-8992
Best time to call: From 5-8 EST
E-mail: SRMFC@edgenet.net
This club is the officially authorized fan club Smokey Robinson

and the Miracles. It publishes a quarterly newsletter and frequent bulletins. It offers itineraries, contests, exclusive special offers and news of other Motown artists.

TOMMY ROE

Tommy Roe International Fan Club
Attention: Theresa Ehler
P.O. Box 813
Owatonna, MN 55060-0813

This is the only official Tommy Roe fan club, and it is six-years-old. It provides its members quarterly newsletters with an itinerary, current news, photos, etc. New members receive an 8x10 photo, factsheet, biography, discography, membership card and a special gift from Roe. Dues are $12 U.S., $14 Canada and $17 elsewhere.

the ROLLING STONES

Gimme Shelter
Attention: David Conway
P.O. Box 163632
Austin, TX 78716

Gimme Shelter is the only monthly Stones fanzine in the world. It started in October, 1992. It is unofficial but has interviewed Ron Wood, Mick Taylor, Bobby Wood and original Stones bass player, Dick Taylor.

Visual Radio
Attention: Joe Viglione
P.O. Box 2392
Woburn, MA 01888

ROOT BOY SLIM

Root Boy Slim Memorial Fan Club
Attention: Duane Straub, Director
3834 Sheffield Circle
Danville, CA 94506
Phone: 510-736-1480
Fax: 510-736-7844
Best time to call: From 6:00 p.m. to 6:00 a.m.

People loved this man-and a bizarre man he was. Many have a special story about Root Boy Slim, most have more than one. This club is devoted to tracking down episodes and tie-ins to a man with the strangest of messages; untangling the web, removing the cloak... day by day, documenting and saluting the life and times of Root Boy Slim. Rare audios, videos, and much more. It's free. You can't quit this club!

RUSH

A Show Of Fans
Attention: Steve and Mandy Streeter
5411 E. State Street, #309
Rockford, IL 61108

Phone: 815-398-1250
Best time to call:Anytime

This is a fanzine for and by Rush fans. In ASOF readers will find original photos and artwork, a wide open feedback section for fans to sound off and interact, tour hook-up section, announcements, free classifieds for subscribers, stories of "brushes with greatness," up to date listings of new Rush memorabilia and all the latest news.

S

SANTANA

Santana International Fan Club
Attention: Kitsaun King
P.O. Box 881630
San Francisco, CA 94188-1630

Lifetime membership in the Santana International fan club costs $25. Members receive the quarterly newsletter, advance notice of concerts when possible, a Santana merchandise catalog and other special goodies.

PAT SHEA

Pat Shea International Fan Club
Attention: Carol MacDonald
P.O. Box 905
Orchard Park, NY 14127
Phone: 716-941-5675
Best time to call: Anytime
This official fan club was formed in 1989. Members receive a quarterly newsletter, membership card and certificate, a personally autographed photo, biography and merchandise offers. Membership costs $10 per year (Canada/foreign $12).

Jim Seibers

Jim Seibers Fan Club
P.O. Box 5345
Toledo, OH 43611
Phone: (419)-476-8722

FRANK SINATRA

International Sinatra Society
Attention: Dustin Doctor
P.O. Box 7176
Lakeland, FL 33807
Phone: 941-646-7650
Best time to call: From 9-5, CST

This is the best Sinatra fan club and the only mailing list that you need to be on to keep up with all the latest Sinatra info and product. The club's newsletter includes discussion about all the latest CD releases, videos and laser discs. There's also an alternate takes column, a collectors column, many photos and more.

PHIL SEYMOUR AND DWIGHT TWILLEY

Hearmore Seymour Twilley
Attention: Karen Momme
P.O. Boy 33151
Tulsa, OK 74153

This is the official fan club for Dwight Twilley and Phil Seymour, recognized by both artists, since 1987. It provides its members a newsletter, and merchandise when available. The fanzine is $4 per issue, U.S. and $6 overseas.

SIR DOUGLAS QUINTET, DOUG. SAHM AND AUGIE MEYERS

Sir Douglas Quintet-Doug and Augie
Attention: K.P. Kosub
P.O. Box 3248
Corpus Christi, TX 78463-3248
Phone: 512-287-3945
Best time to call: Anytime

This club has been the official fan club for the Sir Douglas Quintet since 1980. It offers its members updates on the Quintet and the Texas Tornados. It offers rare records, memorabilia, videos and collectibles for fans worldwide and is approved by Doug and Augie. The fee for membership is $10 and members receive one CD and two 45s by Doug and Augie. Send an SASE for details.

the SMITHEREENS

The Smithereens Fan Club
P.O. Box 35226
Richmond, VA 23235
E-mail: GirlLikeU@aol.com

This official club publishes a quarterly newsletter, 'Reen Thoughts, which includes articles written by the band members themselves. All members receive the newsletter for their $5 annual fee (Canadian and International members higher) as well as contest eligibility, special merchandise offers (T-shirts, beverage wrenches, buttons) and exclusive releases/recordings including a 1995 Holiday CD.

SPACEMEN 3

Dreamweapon
Attention: Matt Hunter
P.O. Box 2813
New Orleans, LA 70176
504-486-7211
Best time to call; After 9:30 p.m. CST

Now in its third year, Dreamweapon has networked fans of

Spacemen 3 and its side projects with tour information, merchandise offers and a resource for audio and video trades. While not an "official" club, band members are aware of the group and will probably be making contributions to the newsletter in 1997.

SPARKS

Sparks International Official Fan Club
Attention: Mary Martin, Secretary
Box 25038
Los Angeles, CA 90025

This fan club publishes six newsletters per year and also provides its members with a button badge and personally signed 8x10 glossy photo to new members. It is the only official club for Sparks and has been in existence since 1975.

RICK SPRINGFIELD

Rick's Loyal Supporters
Attention: Vivian Acinelli
4530 E. Four Ridge Road
Imperial, MO 63052
Fax: 314-942-9920
E-mail: 102506,1472@Compuserve.com
Web address: Http://ally.ios.com/~dawnb19

Established in 1989 and authorized and endorsed by Rick Springfield, this club offers a fan club package including a club folder, photos, membership card, updates on Rick (between newsletters, if necessary), bio, discography and filmography. The Newsletter averages 30 pages, has a classified section, stories, poems, puzzles, raffles, photos and occasional updates from Springfield. Membership costs $15 U.S., $17 Canada, $20 elsewhere.
Write, fax or e-mail for more information.

Rick Springfield Quarterly
Attention: Robin Gregg
4611 S. University Drive, Suite #206
Davie, FL 33328

Send SASE to R.S.Q. for more information.

BRUCE SPRINGSTEEN, SOUTHSIDE JOHNNY, other Jersey Shore Artists

Backstreets
Attention: Charles R. Cross
P.O. Box 51225
Seattle, WA 98115
Phone: 206-728-7603
Best time to call: 9:30-5:00, PST
E-Mail: Bossorders@aol.com
Wesite: Http:members.aol.com/joeroberts/

Backstreets is a magazine and information service for fans of Bruce Springsteen and other Jersey Shore artists. (There is no official fan club-Backstreets is probably the closest thing to it.)

The magazine has been around for 16 years, is published quarterly and is one of the largest and most respected fan organizations in the world. Subscriptions are $18 U.S., $25 non-U.S.

JIM STEINMAN

Rockman Philharmonic—The Jim Steinman Society for the Arts
Attention: Jacqueline Dillon
10 Cindy Lane
Wappingers Falls, NY 12590
Phone: 914-297-0731
Best time to call: Evenings, before 8:00

The Rockman Philharmonic is an official fan club. Membership is $20 U.S., $25 non-U.S. payable in U.S. funds to Jacqueline Dillon. It publishes a full-color magazine quarterly and sends special mailings as needed. The life and work of Jim Steinman (writer and producer of Meat Loaf, Bonnie Tyler, Sisters Of Mercy, Pandora's Box, Barbra Streisand, etc.), is explored at depth.

JOHN KAY and STEPPENWOLF

The Wolfpack Fan Club
Attention: Charlie Wolf, President
P.O. Box 1435
Franklin, TN 37065

Membership includes a welcome letter from John Kay, a biography, discography, Steppenwolf family tree, color photo (autographed), a window decal, a membership card and four quarterly issues of their newsletter, The Howl. The club is official and has been around for three years. Dues are $10 a year U.S., $15 non-U.S.

AR STEVENS & the RICOCHETTES

Ar Stevens & the Ricochettes Fan Club
Attention: Newell Shoup, Jr.
P.O. Box 18008
Fairground Annex
Des Moines, IA 50313

This is the official fan club, authorized by the band, and is starting its fourth year.
Membership is $8, renewals are $5 Members receive and 8x10 of the band and four newsletters per year.

T

Three Dog Night

See Chuck Negron

THUNDER ROAD

Thunder Road Fan Club
Attention: Barbara Gentry

5926 Seminary Road
Smyrna, TN 37167

This is the only official fan club for Thunder Road. It offers a free cassette to new members, tour updates and contests. It also sends a newsletter six times a year to all members.
It has been in existence for three years and has 100 percent participation from the band.

TRAVIS TRITT

Travis Tritt's Country Club
Attention: Liz Garrison
P.O. Box 2044
Hiram, GA 30141
Phone: 770-439-7401
Best time to call 9-5 EST

Write or call for more information.

TINA TURNER

Simply The Best Tina Turner Fan Club
Attention: Mark Lairmore
4566 S. Park Ave.
Springfield, MO 65810
Phone: 417-881-3746
Best time to call: After 6:00 p.m.
Fax: 417-865-7304

Tina Turner's fan club, organized six years ago, offers its members four quarterly newletters and organizes an annual meeting in Nutbush, TN every August. .Membership is $10 U.S., $14 non-U.S.

U

U2

U Stay 2
Attention: Mr. Sady Azefzaf and Ms. Dana McIntosh
5816 N. Sheridan Rd. Apt.2B
Chicago, IL, 60660
Phone: 312-506-1759
Fax: Same

URGE OVERKILL

Secret Society Internationale
Attention: Christine Vogel
P.O. Box 354
Kulpsville, PA 19443
Hotline: 610-489-8810

The Urge Overkill "U.S.S.I." is the official fan club offering a yearly membership. Membership includes "Confidential Files," 7" single, photos etc.

V

Velvet Underground

The Velvet Underground Appreciation Society
5721 S.E. Laguna Ave.
Stuart, FL 34997

Open House
Maximilanstr. 35
Luwigshafen
W-6700 Germany

Also see Lou Reed

BOBBY VINTON

Bobby Vinton Fan Club
Attention: Julia Walker, President
153 Washington Street
Mount Vernon, NY 10550-3541
914-664-6948
Best time to call: Anytime

New members of the club will receive a membership card and button, pictures of Vinton, including an autographed 8x10, a fact sheet, biography and letter from Bobby expressing his appreciation and welcome, participation in contests and much more. Dues are $6 per year, plus seven current stamps, $11 for two years, plus 14 current stamps.

VOODOO MONKEY CHILD

V.M.C./1753
Attention: Laurie Stansbury and Amy E. Allen
P.O. Box 2546
Glenview, IL 60025-2546
Phone: 312-283-2038
Best time to call: 7-11:00 p.m.
E-mail address: voodoomc@musicwerks.com
Web address: www.musicwerks.comm /chvymet/vodoo.htm

This official fan club of the rock band, Voodoo Monkey Child, has been in existence approximately four years. It offers band promotional items, clothing, photos, stickers and even artwork. It also has exclusive interviews with band members and stage crew. A lifetime membership is $13.

W

JERRY JEFF WALKER

The Tried and True Warriors
Attention: Pam Stock
P.O. Box 39
Austin, TX 78767
Phone: 512-477-0036
Best time to call: 9-5:00 weekdays.

The Tried And True Warriors is a free fan club organized on behalf of singersongwriter Jerry Jeff Walker. Benefits include a quarterly newsletter and preferential ticket selection to many of Walker's shows. The fan club also attends a weekend of concerts and events in Walker's hometown of Austin, Texas around the time of his birthday, each March.

WALKER BROTHERS/ SCOTT WALKER

WalkerPeople
Attention: Lynne Goodall
71 Cheyne Court Glengall Road
Woodford Green
Essex IG8 ODN
England

ROGER WATERS

Reg: The International Roger Waters Fan Club
Attention: Michael Simone
214 Lake Court
Aptos, CA 95003
Phone: 408-685-3950
Best time to call: Evenings, PST

The International Roger Waters Fan Club has members in Italy, Germany, France, Belgium, England, Scotland, Austria, the Netherlands, Malta, Spain, Portugal, Denmark, Sweden, Norway, Russia, the Ukraine, Japan, Australia, New Zealand, Canada, Argentina and all across the U.S.
Member is $20 U.S. and Canada and $25 elsewhere.
Membership fees pay for initiation fees, yearly club dues, subscription to the REG newsletter/magazine and club card fee. Send U.S. funds international check or U.S. postal money order made payable to Michael Simone.

Paul Weller

Soul Museum
P.O. Box 1896
Clovis, NM 88101

Soul Museum is a fanzine devoted Paul Weller, The Style Council and The Jam. Issue #3 available now. Cost is $3 US ($4 overseas) per issue and back issues are available. Features, concert information, single and LP reviews, discographies, acid jazz reviews, fan letters, interviews, color and b&w pictures, free classified ads, free music searches, buy, sell and trade selected music and items, question and answer forum and prize giveaways in every issue, plus lots more.

HANK WILLIAMS, JR.

Hank Williams Jr., Fan Club
P.O. Box 850
Paris, TX 38242
Phone: 800-FOR-HANK
E-mail address: Hankjr@hankjr.com
Web address: www.hankjr.com

This club has been in existence for over 20 years. It offers T-shirts, a biography, newsletter, souvenir catalog, 8x10 photos and smaller souvenir items to all members. Membership costs $12 pr. year ($16 foreign).

DENNIS WILSON

Friends of Dennis Wilson
Attention: Chris Duffy
1381 Maria Way
San Jose, CA 95117

FODW is an official fan/friend club, it's been in existence for over 12 years and it publishes a seasonal fanzine, Dennymania. FODW encourages member involvement.

WISHBONE ASH

USASH
Attention: Dr. John
2428 McKinney
Boise, ID 83704
Phone: 208-377-8742
Best time to call: Before 12 a.m., EST
E-Mail address: AshFan@ix.netcom.com
Web address: http://onweb.com/argus/ index.html

The Wishbone Ash Fan Club establishes a dirct link between the fans and the band. USASH features a full color cover, 32 pgs of interviews, pictures and merchandise at a discount for sub-scribers. MasterCard and Visa accepted. Wishbone appreciates your support.

TAMMY WYNETTE

Tammy Wynette International Fan Club
Attention: Cynthia King
P.O. Box 121926
Nashville, TN 37212

Fan club membership includes an autographed color 8x10 photo, biography specially written for the club, a fact sheet that lists awards Wynette has received during her career, membership card, bumper sticker, and a quarterly newsletter including tour schedule. Dues are $12.

X

Y

DWIGHT YOAKAM

The Dwight Yoakam Express
Attention: Andy Comer
P.O. Box 3013
Zanesville, OH 43702-3013

The Express reports on past and present career moves of Yoakam. It offers a buy, sell and trade column in the fanzine that it pub-lishes six times a year. The organization is over four years old and is an official fanzine.

Neil Young

Neil Young Appreciation Society
2A Llynfi St.
Bridgend
Mid Glamorgan
CF31 1SY Wales
U.K.
Web address: http://ourworld.compuserve. com/homepages/nyas

Z

NORMA ZIMMER

Norma Zimmer National Fan Club
Attention: Frances L. Young, President
1604 E. Susquehanna St.
Allentown, PA 18103-4398

Norma Zimmer is, of course, the lovely Champagne Lady on The Lawrence Welk Show. This is her official fan club and has been in existence for 35 years. Dues are $6 a year and members get a membership card, three bulletins a year, pictures of Norma, an eyeglass cleaner and lots more.

FOUNDATIONS, SOCIETIES, SPECIAL INTEREST CLUBS AND OTHER THINGS WORTH KNOWING ABOUT

American Federation of Jazz Societies
2787 Del Monte Street
West Sacramento, CA 95691

AFJS recently announced the initiation of its jazz Education Assistance Team program. Funded in part by a grant from the National Endowment for the Arts, the team is now available to provide non-profit jazz societies with gratis on-site counseling and assistance in undertaking such initiatives as: student scholarship programs, concerts in schools, student clinics, radio/television programming, adult education, student ensemble sponsorship, library programs and jazz curriculum programs. The Federation also publishes a newsletter, Federation Jazz. A recent issue contained articles about recent cuts in federal funding for jazz projects and preservation, jazz on the Internet, the jazz society scene and the Jersey Jazzfest.

Ball Buster
Sinbad Productions
David LaDuke Publishing
P.O. Box 58368
Louisville, KY 40268-0368

Ball Buster-The "official international underground hard music report."

Control-Alt-Delete
Attention: ::The Cat::
P.O. Box 38553-1010
Houston, TX 77238-8553
Phone: 281-448-3815
Best time to call: After 10:30 a.m.
E-mail adress: CADINFO@AOL.COM
Web address: HTTP://CAD.IAG.NET

This group is endorsed by many electronic bands: Information Society, Anything Box, Cause & Effect, Seven Red Seven and many others. Contro-AltDelete has been in existence since 1992. It has an online forum on AOL and has released four compilation albums.

Delta Blues Museum
Attention: Ronald H. Gorsegner, Director
114 Delta Avenue
Clarksdale, MS 38614
Phone: 601-627-6820
Best time to call: Mornings during the week

The Delta Blues Museum is dedicated to the preservation and perpetuation of the Delta Blues in its birthplace, the Mississippi Delta. Established in 1979, the museum is located near the legendary crossroads of highways 49 and 61.

Doo-Wop Society of Southern California
Attention: Marvin Kaminsky
1158 26th St
Santa Monica, CA 90403
Phone: 310-493-9058
Best time to call: Anytime

New York Sheet Music Society
Attention: Sam Teicher
P.O. Box 354
Hewlett, NY 11557-15354
Phone: (516)-295-0719

This society attempts to preserve American poular music and recognize the personalities that have contributed to its success, i.e. songwriters, singers, authors, publishers and bandleaders. We publish a newsletter 10 times a year. Dues are $25 a year.

Record Research Associates
Attention: Arthur Zimmerman
P.O. Box 158
Jericho, NY 11753
Phone: 516-681-7102
Best time to call: 9 a.m. to 10:00 p.m.

This group's interest is in the technical and discographical history of phonograph records. Most emphasis is in the pre-1950s, but not exclusively so. Meetings and the clubs newsletter both occur approximately monthly, from September through June. The primary musical interest of the members is in jazz and blues.

Voices From the Shadows
Unit 2D, Hull Road
Withernsea HU19 2EG
England
Phone: (0964) 614873
Fax: (0964) 614896

A magazine run by soul fans, for soul fans, about soul music.

Most Valuable British Invasion Records

Compiled by Tim Neely for the Goldmine British Invasion Record Price Guide

When we compiled the "most valuable platters" listing for the Goldmine British Invasion Price Guide, we made a not-so-startling revelation. If we had listed them strictly, fully 80 percent would have been by the Beatles.

So we split the list into the top Beatles collectibles and the top collectibles by everyone else.

These lists mix albums, singles, EPs and picture sleeves; they also mix US and UK pressings. But all of the top 20 Beatles records are American; that reflects the worldwide interest in them, and also that most of the top U.S. Beatles dealers only deal in American product because it is well documented.

Remember, the values quoted aren't for any old version of the below records; they must match the description exactly. And these are for Near Mint (almost perfect) copies; lesser condition items will bring much less.

If an A and B side are mentioned, the record is a 45; if four songs are mentioned, the record is a 7-inch EP; if only one title is mentioned, the record is an LP (unless otherwise noted). Records are listed in descending order of value; records of the same value are listed alphabetically by label. For simplicity's sake, every record advertised as stereo, regardless of stereo content, has an "S."

Here are the 20 most valuable Beatles records:

Value	Label/Number		Title (A Side/B Side)
$25,000	Vee Jay SR 1062	S	Introducing the Beatles

Song titles cover; with "Love Me Do" and "P.S. I Love You"; oval Vee Jay logo with colorband only! Perhaps half a dozen authentic copies have been discovered, with hundreds of thousands of counterfeits. The record itself must say "Stereo " on the label, and the words "Introducing the Beatles" and "The Beatles" must both be above the center hole. No exceptions!

15,000	Vee Jay PRO 202	DJ	Hear the Beatles Tell All

White label promo with blue print; only three known copies, a NM copy sold for $16.500 on April 24, 1997.

12,000	United Artists UAS 6366	S	A Hard Day's Night

Pink vinyl; only one copy known, probably privately (and secretly) done by a pressing-plant employee

Value	Label/Number		Title (A Side/B Side)
10,000	Decca 3138245		My Bonnie/The Saints

By "Tony Sheridan and the Beat Brothers"; black label with color bars (all-black label with star under "Decca" is likely a counterfeit)

| 10,000 | Vee Jay Spec. DJ No. 8 | 45 DJ | Ask Me Why/Anna |

One of the more controversial items in Beatles collecting; most Beatles experts say this is authentic, but it's also rumored to have been done by Vee Jay pressing plant employees in the 1970s.

| 10,000 | Vee Jay SR 1062 | S | Introducing the Beatles |

"Ad back" cover; with "Love Me Do" and "P.S. I Love You" (both mono); oval Vee Jay logo with colorband only!

| 10,000 | Vee Jay SR 1085 | S | The Beatles and Frank Ifield on Stage |

Portrait of Beatles cover; "Stereo" on both cover and label

| 8,000 | Apple SO-385 | DJ | The Beatles Again |

Prototypes with "The Beatles Again" on cover; not released to the general public

| 8,000 | Capitol ST 2553 | S | Yesterday and Today |

"First state" butcher cover (never had other cover on top); cover will be the same size as other Capitol Beatles LPs

| 8,000 | Vee Jay 1-903 | PS | Misery/Taste of Honey//Ask Me Why/Anna |

"Ask Me Why/The Beatles" plugged on promo-only sleeve

| 4,000 | Capitol 5150 45 | | Can't Buy Me Love/You Can't Do That |

Yellow vinyl (unauthorized); value is conjecture

| 4,000 | Capitol ST 2553 | S | Yesterday and Today |

"Third state" butcher cover (trunk cover removed, leaving butcher cover intact); cover will be about 3/16-inch narrower than other Capitol Beatles LPs; value is highly negotiable depending upon the success of removing the paste-over

| 4,000 | Capitol T 2553 | M | Yesterday and Today |

"First state" butcher cover (never had other cover on top); cover will be the same size as other Capitol Beatles LPs

| 4,000 | Vee Jay LP 1085 | M | The Beatles and Frank Ifield on Stage |

Portrait of Beatles cover; counterfeits are poorly reproduced and have no spine print

| 4,000 | Vee Jay SR 1062 | S | Introducing the Beatles |

Blank back cover; with "Love Me Do" and "P.S. I Love You"; oval Vee Jay logo with colorband only!

| 3,000 | Decca 3138245 DJ | | My Bonnie/The Saints |

By "Tony Sheridan and the Beat Brothers"; ' pink label, star on label under "Decca"

| 3,000 | United Artists UA-Help-Show | 45 DJ | United Artists Presents Help! |

One-sided interview with script (blue label)

| 3,000 | United Artists UAL 3366 | M-DJ | A Hard Day's Night |

White label promo

| 3,000 | Vee Jay DXS-30 | (2) S | The Beatles vs. The Four Seasons |

Combines "Introducing the Beatles" with "Golden Hits of the Four Seasons" (Vee Jay 1065)

| 3,000 | Vee Jay LP 1062 | M | Introducing the Beatles |

"Ad back" cover; with "Love Me Do" and "P.S. I Love You"; oval Vee Jay logo with colorband only!

And here are the top 20 by artists who aren't the Beatles, though we certainly stretch the definition with our No. 1 most valuable. When there is a tie at a particular value, the records are listed first alphabetically by artist, then alphabetically by label.

Value	ARTIST:	Label/Number		Title (A Side/B Side)
$20,000	QUARRY MEN, THE:	Percy Philips, Kensington (no #) (UK)		That'll Be The Day/In Spite Of All The Danger

John Rowe and Colin Hanton joined three fellows named John Lennon, Paul McCartney and George Harrison for this 1958 recording at a small studio. After McCartney bought the original acetate from Rowe in 1981, he had 50 or so copies pressed for private distribution, 25 on 78 and 25 on 45. No sales are known, so the value is conjecture. It is equally valid for either 45 or 78.

10,000	ROLLING STONES, THE:	London LL 3402 M 12 x 5		

Maroon label with "London" unboxed at top; possibly unique blue vinyl pressing

8,000	ROLLING STONES, THE:	London 909	PS	Street Fighting Man/No Expectations

Ultra-rare picture sleeve; only about a dozen copies are known to exist

 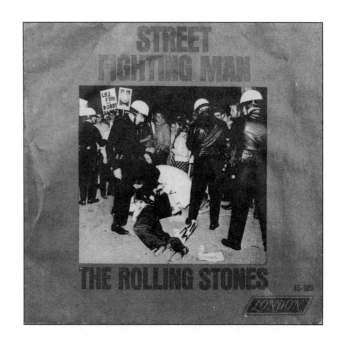

6,000	ROLLING STONES, THE:	London NP 1	M	Big Hits (High Tide and Green Grass)

With two lines of type on the front cover, all in small letters

6,000	ROLLING STONES, THE:	London NPS 3	PD	Through the Past, Darkly (Big Hits Vol. 2)

Prototype picture discs that used the cover art from "Big Hits (High Tide and Green Grass)" either on one or both sides.

4,000	ROLLING STONES, THE:	London 9641		I Wanna Be Your Man/Stoned

Stock copy of their first US record, which was quickly pulled from the market.

3,000	JOHN'S CHILDREN:	Track 604 005 (UK)		Midsummer Night's Scene/Sara Crazy Child

Considered to be the rarest UK stock copy 45 of all time; only 50 copies are believe to have been pressed. "Midsummer Night's Scene" was replaced by "Come and Play With Me in the Garden." Marc Bolan (later of T. Rex) is on this record.

3,000	ROLLING STONES, THE:	London LL 3375	DJ	England's Newest Hit Makers -- The Rolling Stones

White label promo; "London/ffrr" pressing, manufactured in UK for export to the US

3,000	ROLLING STONES, THE:	London RSD-1	DJ	The Rolling Stones -- The Promotional Album

Counterfeits exist of this rare promo (US version)

2,000	MARTIN, GEORGE:	United Artists 750	PS	A Hard Day's Night/I Should Have Known Better

Very rare sleeve desirable for its Beatles pictures.

Value	ARTIST:	Label/Number		Title (A Side/B Side)
1,200	ROLLING STONES, THE:	Rolling Stones 19309 PS		Beast of Burden/Before They Make Me Run

One of the rarest picture sleeves of the 1970s, and certainly the most valuable.

| 1,000 | BLUE MEN, THE: | Triumph TRX ST 9000 (UK) | | I Hear A New World |

The most sought-after Joe Meek production, this LP was planned on Meek's own label but never officially released. Demo copies are known to exist; the price is for the demo.

| 1,000 | KINKS, THE: | Pye NPL 18233 (UK) M | | The Kinks Are The Village Green Preservation Society |
| 1,000 | KINKS, THE: | Pye NSPL 18233 (UK) S | | The Kinks Are The Village Green Preservation Society |

Test pressings of the album with 12 tracks (the released version has 15). Both mono and stereo copies exist.

| 1,000 | ROLLING STONES, THE: | Decca RSM 1 (UK) | DJ | The Promotional Album |

UK version of the rare US promo with a similar number.

| 1,000 | ROLLING STONES, THE: | London 2PS 606/7 | S (2) | Hot Rocks 1964-1971 |

With alternate mixes of "Brown Sugar" and "Wild Horses" unavailable elsewhere. The date "11-5-71" is in the Side 4 trail-off area.

| 1,000 | ROLLING STONES, THE: | London PS 539 | | Beggars Banquet |

Manufactured in UK with US labels for export to Japan; with interview flexidisc in picture sleeve

| 800 | HIGH NUMBERS, THE: | Fontana TF 480 (UK) | | I'm The Face/Zoot Suit |

The first record by the band later known as The Who, with "I'm the Face" listed as the A-side.

| 800 | JONES, DAVIE, AND THE KING BEES: | Vocalion Pop V 9221 (UK) | | Liza Jane/Louie Louie Go Home |

Davie Jones was later known as David Bowie; this was his very first record anywhere. Counterfeits exist, but those are easily identifiable. Original UK pressings have a triangular center that can be punched out; even if it is gone, the indentations will be visible. Phonies never had a punch-out center, thus there will be no indentations in the center hole.

| 800 | YARDBIRDS, THE: | Epic 9709 | PS | I Wish You Could |

This picture sleeve was contained only on some promo copies. It had the title incorrect, as the song is really "I Wish You Would."

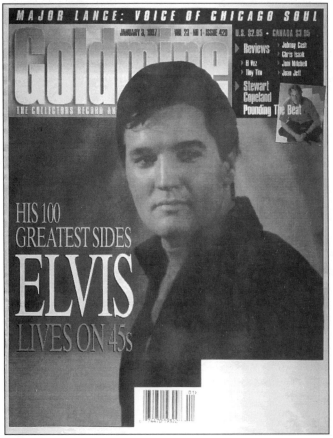

Grab the original!
Goldmine
The magazine that was there at the beginning.

In 1974, the first issue of **Goldmine** rolled off the presses as a small advertising-only publication aimed at avid record collectors. From that humble beginning **Goldmine** has grown to become internationally renowned for its in-depth looks at famous and obscure recording acts past and present. From early blues legends and rock 'n roll stars to recent alternative acts and jazz legends, **Goldmine** provides you with a wide variety of music coverage designed to enlighten and entertain even the most discriminating music lovers!

Each issue of **Goldmine** contains reviews of new releases and reissues, complete discographies, and insightful commentary on the latest news from the music and collecting industries from our experienced staff of writers and music insiders.

Goldmine has served collectors and music lovers by providing the largest marketplace for collectible recordings and memorabilia. Over the years, hundreds of thousands of rare, hard-to-find recordings worth thousands of dollars have exchanged hands as a result of ads in **Goldmine**.

If you can't find a recording in **Goldmine**, it either doesn't exist or it's not for sale!

If you are into collecting music join our 40,000 readers and grab this opportunity to subscribe at the money-saving rates below. Grab the original record and CD collecting publication—**Goldmine!**

Most Valuable Christmas Records

Compiled by Tim Neely; Exclusive for the 1998 Goldmine Annual

Let's face it: One of the appeals of collecting Christmas 45s and LPs is that most of them are undervalued in relation to their rarity, as is documented throughout the new Goldmine Christmas Record Price Guide.

But some of them do have significant value, primarily for reasons other than their holiday nature. In keeping with the relative values of Christmas records, the least valuable on this list is $400. Compare that to other lists in this Annual.

The LPs on this list are only those that are entirely or almost entirely holiday-related. We have not listed any that have, say, only one or two holiday tracks. The 45s, though, can have only one side fitting the holiday theme.

Again, as always, the values are for near-mint (almost perfect) copies. Records in lesser condition will bring much less.

Value	ARTIST:	Label/Number		Title (A Side/B Side)
$15,000	PRESLEY, ELVIS:	RCA Victor LOC-1035	LP/M	Elvis' Christmas Album

A unique red-vinyl pressing done by an RCA employee after hours in 1957. The known copy has small black flecks mixed with the red vinyl, indicating there was still some residue of the regular stuff on the stampers. Discovered in 1994 in the employee's collection. A blue-vinyl copy has also been disocvered, but more details on that were unknown at press time.

1,500	MOONGLOWS, THE:	Chance 1150	45	Just a Lonely Christmas/Hey, Santa Claus

Red vinyl version of this vocal-group classic. It may not legitimately exist on black vinyl.

1,000	ORIOLES, THE:	Jubilee 5017	45	What Are You Doing New Year's Eve/Lonely Christmas

The 1950s pressing of this record with a blue label.

1,000	ORIOLES, THE:	Jubilee 5017	PS	What Are You Doing New Year's Eve/Lonely Christmas

The sleeve wasn't released until 1954, so it's actually on later pressings, but it is excruciatingly rare.

1,000	VARIOUS ARTISTS:	RCA Victor SP-33-66	LP/DJ	Christmas Programming from RCA Victor

A promotional album for radio use, its value is because it has an Elvis Presley track on it. This has been counterfeited, but original copies have color covers while the counterfeits have black and white covers.

800	FIVE KEYS, THE:	Aladdin 3113	45	It's Christmas Time/Old Mac Donald

The 1951 original on the blue Aladdin label.

800	ORIOLES, THE:	Jubilee 5045	PS	Oh Holy Night/The Lord's Prayer

As with Jubilee 5017, the sleeve wasn't released until 1954, but is very rare.

800	PRESLEY, ELVIS:	RCA Victor UNRM-5697/8	LP/DJ	Special Christmas Programming

A radio show put together in 1967 on a white label for radio use. It came with a script; add another $200 if it is there.

750	LENNON, JOHN:	Apple S45X-47663/4	DJ	Happy Xmas (War Is Over)/Listen, the Snow Is Falling

As "John & Yoko/Plastic Ono Band with the Harlem Community Choir"; white label on styrene; "APPLE" in block capital letters at the top of the label. Other versions of this record are worth much less.

700	PRESLEY, ELVIS:	RCA Victor LOC-1035	LP/M	Elvis' Christmas Album

Gatefold cover, title printed in silver on LP spine; includes bound-in booklet but not "To" and "From" sticker.

Value	ARTIST:	Label/Number		Title (A Side/B Side)
600	ORIOLES, THE:	Jubilee 5045	45	Oh Holy Night/The Lord's Prayer

The 1950s pressing of this record with a blue label.

| 600 | PRESLEY, ELVIS: | RCA Victor LOC-1035 | LP/M | Elvis' Christmas Album |

Gatefold cover, title printed in gold on LP spine; includes bound-in booklet but not "To" and "From" sticker. This album actually reached No. 1 on the Billboard charts in 1957, but was only available for two years, a far shorter time than most Elvis LPs. In 1959 it was reissued with a new cover and catalog number.

| 600 | SWANS, THE: | Ballad 1007 | 45 | Happy/The Santa Claus Boogie |

Another group Christmas record.

| 600 | VARIOUS ARTISTS: | RCA Victor SPS-33-54 | LP/DJ | October Christmas Sampler 59-40-41 |

Radio station promo in stereo, although the Elvis track it contains is mono.

| 500 | DEL-VUES, THE: | U-Town 8008 | 45 | After New Year's/My Confession |

| 500 | HARRIS, GEORGIA, AND THE LYRICS: | Hy-Tone 111 | 45 | Let's Exchange Hearts for Christmas/It's Time to Rock |

| 500 | HARRIS, GEORGIA, AND THE LYRICS: | Hy-Tone 117 | 45 | Let's Exchange Hearts for Christmas/Kiss, Kiss, Kiss |

Two different releases of this song.

| 500 | MARSHALL BROTHERS, THE: | Savoy 825 | 45 | Mr. Santa's Boogie/Who'll Be the Fool from Now On |

A 1951 45 on a sought-after label.

| 400 | BEATLES, THE: | Apple SBC-100 | LP | The Beatles' Christmas Album |

Fan-club issue of the seven special Christmas messages the Fab Four did annually. This is much rarer than this value indicates; there are so many good counterfeits that telling a legitimate copy is often best left to an expert.

| 400 | BOOKER T. AND THE MC'S: | Stax ST-713 | M | In the Christmas Spirit |
| | | Stax STS-713 | S | In the Christmas Spirit |

Original copies of this album, available only during the 1966 Christmas season, have what is known as the "fingers and piano keys" cover.

The value is good for either mono or stereo copies.

| 400 | BROWN, CHARLES: | King KS-775 | S | Charles Brown Sings |
| | | | | Christmas Songs |

Stereo copies (whether true stereo or rechanneled, we don't know) exist on blue labels with ":King" in block letters (no crown).

| 400 | HEPSTERS, THE: | Ronel 107 | 45 | Rockin' N' Rollin' with Santa Claus/I |
| | | | | Had to Let You Go |

One of the earliest "true" rock and roll Christmas songs, this came out in 1955.

| 400 | LOVE, DARLENE: | Philles 125 | 45 | Christmas (Baby Please Come |
| | | | | Home)/X-Mas Blues |

Rare version with a rare B-side. Versions with other B-sides are valued less.

| 400 | VARIOUS ARTISTS: | Philles X-EP | PS | Christmas EP |

This is for the cover alone of this radio EP sampler from A Christmas Gift For You From Phil Spector. Add another $100 for the record.

| 400 | VALENTINES, THE: | Rama 186 | 45 | Christmas Prayer/K-I-S-S Me |

Original pressing on blue label (red label is not as valuable)

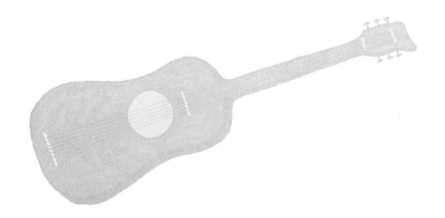

Most Valuable 45 RPM Records and Sleeves

Compiled by Tim Neely for the Goldmine Price Guide to 45 RPM Records

When compiling the Goldmine Price Guide to 45 RPM Rec-ords, we couldn't help but notice that the number of truly valu-able records has increased significantly over the years.

Twenty years ago, no more than about five 45s could have brought $1,000 in near-mint condition from a knowledgeable collector. And one of those was mythical — the legendary "Stormy Weather" by the Five Sharps on Jubilee 5104, which is only known to exist legitimately on 78s.

Now, nearly 300 45s, and perhaps more, could bring that figure in near-mint condition! Below are the 20 or so that are the most valuable of that group.

Most of these have never been seen in near-mint condi-tion. In fact, most, if not all, of these have been counter-feited or reproduced. Some collectors, therefore, might be suspicious of a copy that looks too good to be true. When no near-mint copy is known to exist, the value was determined based on what lesser-condition copies have brought.

Remember again, these values are for near-mint stock copies (unless otherwise noted). Records in lesser conditions will bring less.

Value	ARTIST:	Label/Number	Title (A Side/B Side)
$15,000	Hornets	States 127	I Can't Believe/Lonesome Baby

Red vinyl pressing of outrageously rare group record

| 12,000 | Wilson, Frank | Soul 35019 | Sweeter As the Days Go By/Do I Love You |

Only two copies are known of this, the rarest of all Motown-related 45s.

| 10,000 | Barrix, Billy | Chess 1662 | Cool Off Baby/Almost |

An outrageously rare rockabilly record

| 10,000 | Beatles | Decca 31382 | My Bonnie/The Saints |

The very first American Beatles record, released under the name "Tony Sheridan and the Beat Brothers"; black label with color bars (all-black label with star under "Decca" should be a counterfeit, although it may not be)

| 10,000 | Beatles | Vee Jay Spec. DJ No. 8 | Ask Me Why/Anna |

Most Beatles experts consider this an authentic, aborted promo attempt for Vee Jay's Beatles EP.

| 10,000 | Brenston, Jackie | Chess 1458 | Rocket "88"/Come Back Where You Belong |

This 1951 release is sometimes considered the first rock 'n' roll record; ob-scenely rare, even though the 45s weren't pressed until 1954

| 10,000 | Dells Vee Jay | 134 | Tell the World/Blues at Three |

Red vinyl pressing of this seminal Chicago group's first record.

| 10,000 | Impressions | Vee Jay 280 | For Your Precious Love/Sweet Was the Wine |

As "Jerry Butler and the Impressions"; this record also exists on far, far less valuable versions on the Falcon and Abner labels.

| 10,000 | Prisonaires | Sun 207 | There Is Love in You/What'll You Do Next |

One of record collecting's legendary rarities, this could bring much more at open auction.

8,000   Beatles   Vee Jay 1-903 PS   Misery/Taste of Honey//Ask Me Why/Anna
"Ask Me Why/The Beatles" plugged on promo-only sleeve

8,000   Flamingos   Parrot 811   I Really Don't Want to Know/Get With It
Red vinyl pressing; the Flamingos are considered to be among the best vocal groups of all time, and this is their rarest.

8,000   Hornets   States 127   I Can't Believe/Lonesome Baby
Black vinyl version of the No. 1 record above.

8,000   Presley, Elvis   RCA Victor 4-834-115 DJ I'll Be Back
One-sided promo with designation "For Special Academy Consideration Only"

8,000   Rolling Stones   London 909 PS   Street Fighting Man/No Expectations
Value is for the sleeve alone, of which about a dozen are known to exist.

8,000   Sof-Tones   Cee Bee1062   Oh Why//(B-side unknown)

8,000   Windsors   Back Beat 506   My Gloria/Cool Seabreeze

6,000   Crystals   Philles111 DJ   (Let's Dance) The Screw -- Part 1/
                                                              (Let's Dance) The Screw -- Part 2
Light blue label. Matrix numbers are stamped in dead wax. Counterfeits have numbers hand-etched. This record was Phil
Spector's kiss-off to his original business part-ner, Les Sill.

6,000   Hide-A-Ways   Ronni 1000   Can't Help Lovin' That Girl of Mine/
                                                              I'm Coming Home

5,000   Larks   Apollo 1190   Stolen Love/In My Lonely Room
Red vinyl version

5,000   Presley, Elvis   RCA Victor 47-8400 DJ Such a Night/Never Ending
An inexplicably rare regular white label promo

5,000   Presley, Elvis   RCA Victor 37-7992 PS Good Luck Charm/Anything That's Part of You
Special picture sleeve for Compact 33 Single record (the record itself adds another $2,500)

5,000   Velvet Underground   Verve10427 PS   All Tomorrow's Parties/I'll Be Your Mirror
Only one copy is known to exist of the sleeve for this proto-punk band's first 45.